THE SHORTER

MRS.

BEETON

THE SHORTER

MRS.

BEETON

WARD LOCK
LONDON

First published in Great Britain in 1987 by
Ward Lock Limited, 8 Clifford Street, London W1X 1RB,
an Egmont Company.

Designed and produced by Sheldrake Press Limited,
188 Cavendish Road, London SW12 0DA.

ANNE COPE, the compiler of this concise edition of
Beeton's Book of Household Management, has written two
craft books, edited many cookery books and reference
works on psychology, medicine and natural history, and
has run her own catering business.

EDITOR: SIMON RIGGE
Managing Editor: Eleanor Lines
Art Direction, Book Design and Jacket:
Ivor Claydon, Bob Hook
Photographers: Nic Barlow, Bob Komar
Editorial Assistants: Kathryn Cureton, Joan Lee

British Library Cataloguing in Publication Data
  Beeton, *Mrs.*
  The shorter Mrs. Beeton
  1. Cookery, International
  I. Title II. Cope, Anne III. Beeton,
  Mrs. Book of household management
  641.5   TX725.A1

ISBN 0-7063-6563-1

Printed in Hong Kong by
Imago Publishing Limited.

THE PHOTOGRAPHS

The colour photographs in this book were taken on
location in London and other cities and at some of the
great country houses of England. For their invaluable
assistance in buying, preparing and presenting the food
the editors are especially grateful to:

Lorna Levis, Chief Cook, At The Sign of the Angel,
Lacock, Wiltshire;

John Baily & Son, Poulterers and Game Dealers,
London;

John Webber, Head Chef, Cliveden, Buckinghamshire;

Anton Mosimann, Executive Chef, Dorchester Hotel,
London;

Joe Silk, Head Chef, The English House, London;

Geoffrey Welch, Head Chef, and Mandy Avern, Pastry
Chef, Flitwick Manor, Bedfordshire;

Mr. D.S. Linscott, Buyer, Fish Department, Harrods,
London;

Jacqueline Clarke, Head Chef, Hobbs & Co. (Mayfair)
Ltd.;

C. Lidgate, Butcher, London;

Michael Hasler, Head Chef, Mark's Club, London;

Neals Yard Dairy, Covent Garden, London;

Domingo Chinaro, Head Chef, Overton's Restaurant and
Oyster Bar, London;

Michael Croft, Head Chef, Royal Crescent Hotel, Bath;

Nick Steiger, Head Chef, Rules Restaurant, London;

Paul Pascoe, Head Chef, Sheekey's Restaurant, London;

Adam Sherif, Head Chef, Simpson's-in-the-Strand,
London;

Mark Harrington, Head Chef, Ston Easton Park,
near Bath.

THE PROPERTIES

The tableware and kitchen equipment
seen in the photographs was kindly
loaned by Kate Dyson of the Dining
Room Shop, by Angel of Tobias
and the Angel, Diana Frost of
Country Antiques and by Mrs. P.N.
O'Mahony, all of London, and by the
establishments listed above. Additional
properties were provided by Sheldrake Press Limited.

For a full list of locations, credits and acknowledgements
with addresses and telephone numbers see page 235.

THE RECIPES

All the recipes in this book were tested by Mrs. Beeton
herself, and many were re-tested during photography.
Occasionally, to make a recipe easier to follow, a
quantity or an ingredient has been slightly changed, but
in most recipes the original quantities and ingredients
are given.

Contents

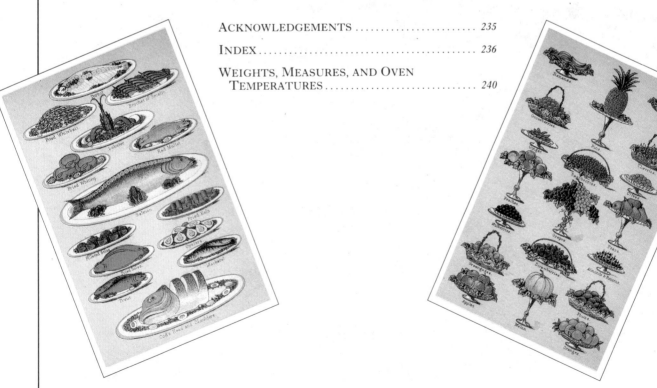

Introduction

The bare facts of Isabella Beeton's life are that she was born in London in 1836, the first of four children of Benjamin and Elizabeth Mayson. Her father died when she was four, and three years later her mother remarried. Henry Dorling, her stepfather, had four children by his first marriage, and with Elizabeth had thirteen more. At the age of 19 Isabella became engaged to Samuel Orchart Beeton, a young publisher who had made a small fortune by introducing Harriet Beecher Stowe's *Uncle Tom's Cabin* to the British public. They married a year later. Their first child, born in April 1857, died at the age of six months. Their second child, born in 1859, also died in infancy. Their third and fourth children, born in 1863 and 1865, survived. Isabella herself died of puerperal fever a week after giving birth to her fourth child. She was only 28. Sam lived until 1877, and was buried beside her in Norwood Cemetery. *The Book of Household Management*, published in 1861, is their joint monument.

Only three photographs of Isabella are known to exist, two studio portraits taken when she was 21 and 26, and a family snapshot taken when she was 27. She was of medium height, had blue eyes and heavy brown hair, and at least by today's standards was a little plump. She held herself very erect, and gave the impression of having great energy and go. She never used make-up, always took a hot bath in the morning, and thought nothing of going for long muddy walks.

Sam, who was five years her senior, was very thin, with fair hair and brilliant grey eyes. He was addicted to cigars, took cold baths in the morning, needed only five or six hours' sleep, did the work of two or three normal mortals, and refused to be inhibited by the chronic tuberculosis and bronchitis which finally killed him. On several occasions, having missed the last train back from London, he walked the 13 miles home to Pinner. But he was very solicitous of Isabella's health, as she was of his.

As the letters of their courtship make clear, Isabella did not realise that in marrying Sam she was marrying publishing. She complained of his rare appearances at her home in Epsom: "Anyone would think our house was some Ogre's Castle, you want so much pressing to come" or "Anyone would think you lived in Londonderry instead of London, you are so very sparing of your company." Sam was a shirt-sleeves publisher, pinioned to his desk by manuscripts, proofs, contracts, invoices, letters from readers, and correspondence with printers, paper merchants, and booksellers. He ran three magazines, the *Englishwoman's Domestic Magazine*, the *Boy's Own Magazine* and the *Boy's Own Journal*. Besides, he found the Dorlings, and Papa and Mama Dorling, hard to take.

In marrying Isabella, Sam also got more than he bargained for. He was clearly captivated by her looks, her lively intelligence, and good sense, but he could not have known the stamina and the capacity for intellectual discipline which lurked beneath.

Sam was, in many senses, a liberated man, and he made of Isabella–who needed very little encouragement–a liberated woman. He made it clear to her before their marriage that he did not want to "manage" her: she was to do precisely and exactly as she wished. He was also good about the house. Very few Victorian husbands would have attended personally to all the details of setting up home, let alone fulfilled Isabella's minute instructions about furnishing and decorating. He even saw to it that honeysuckle, mignonette, and runner beans were planted in the garden.

In temperament he and Isabella were opposites. He was ardent and impulsive, she was cool and steady. In a letter to Sam shortly before their marriage, Isabella says: "What a contrast is my frigid disposition to your generous, warm-hearted dear self; it often strikes me, but you know I cannot help it, it is my nature." "Frigid" is going too far, but it seems that the young Isabella was not entirely comfortable with her coolness.

The geography of Isabella's life, both before and after her marriage, was extremely varied. Her family moved house frequently and sent her to school on the Continent, and she travelled abroad with Sam on his business trips and on holiday. More than most women of her day, she was thrown into contact with a tremendous number of different people and situations quite early in life. This, combined with a natural shrewdness, probably explains why she so quickly matured into a woman of decided opinions and great self-assurance.

As a young girl she lived in Milk Street in the City of London, only yards from the trundling waggons and shouting barrow boys of Honey Lane Market. At the age of seven she moved to Epsom, a quiet town which erupted into a frenzy on race days. In the basement of the Dorlings' Georgian house in the High Street was the organised disorder of her stepfather's printing business. Henry was a printer of race cards and postcards before he became Clerk of the Course at Epsom, and he was a man of some wealth and influence. As more half-brothers and sisters were born, the house began to burst at the seams, so Isabella, the three other Mayson children, and the older

This daguerrotype portrait of Isabella, taken when she was 21, was presented to the National Gallery by her youngest son Mayson, knighted for his work in the Ministry of Munitions during the First World War. The dress she is wearing was made from a bolt of red striped silk given to her by a racehorse owner in Epsom.

Though the date of this study of Sam Beeton is uncertain, it has a romantic quality which suggests marriage rather than commerce. Sam was probably about 25 when he sat for it.

This view of Epsom racecourse on Derby Day clearly shows the Grandstand, where Isabella spent large portions of her childhood, in the background. The Stand was also the setting, on 10 July 1856, for Isabella and Sam's wedding breakfast.

Dorlings were sent to live in the draughty splendour of the newly built Grandstand on Epsom racecourse. This subsidiary ménage was headed by Granny Jerram, Isabella's maternal grandmother, and Isabella, as the eldest, was expected to help her. At the approach of race meetings, Granny Jerram and her charges vacated the refreshment room and the smaller offices and committee rooms where they lived and went back to Epsom High Street or down to Brighton, where Henry Dorling held a second office as Clerk of the Course.

For a short while, probably at the age of 16, Isabella went to a girls' boarding school in Colebrook Row, Islington, where the main subject of instruction was how to be a lady. Infinitely more to her taste was the German boarding school to which her stepfather then sent her. It was in Heidelberg, the curriculum was academic, and she enjoyed the challenge. She emerged from it with more or less fluent French and German, above average expertise on the piano, and an interest in pastry making.

Returning to Epsom in 1854, Isabella found herself missing the order and purpose of Heidelberg. She read a lot and practised the piano and played the part of the dutiful eldest daughter. Then she

began to go up to London for piano lessons with the famous composer Sir Julius Benedict. Propriety required a chaperone, and on at least a few occasions this seems to have been her mother, who took the opportunity of visiting Eliza Beeton, a good friend from her Milk Street days. The widowed Eliza was then landlady of the Dolphin Tavern in Milk Street, and it was here that Isabella and Sam first met, and fell in love. Their courtship was short by contemporary standards, with a mere thirteen months between their engagement and their marriage.

For their honeymoon they chose France, which they toured at speed, taking in Paris, Tours, Bordeaux, Bayonne and Biarritz. Even Sam, not noted for his lethargy, referred to it as "the race on the Continent". The race included a flying visit to Heidelberg to see Isabella's younger sisters, also receiving the benefit of a purposeful German education.

For the first years of their marriage Sam and Isabella lived at Chandos Villas, Pinner, Middlesex, about 13 miles from London. Every day Sam commuted up to the offices of S.O. Beeton in Bouverie Street, and later in the Strand. Their first holiday together in the autumn of 1857, with a family called English in Suffolk, was marked by tragedy; after a day or two in Suffolk, Samuel Orchart Beeton Jnr., born in April of that year, went down with croup and died. Isabella's feelings can be imagined, but there is no record of them; by this time she had already started work on *The Book of Household Management*.

No. 2 Chandos Villas, Pinner, Sam and Isabella's first home, was a red brick, semi-detached house two minutes walk from the station. The rent was £50 a year, with free commuter travel thrown in.

In March 1860 she and Sam went to Paris to arrange for fashion plates and dress patterns for the *Englishwoman's Domestic Magazine*, and in July the same year they took a holiday in Ireland; Isabella apparently enjoyed herself, but Sam worried about being away from his desk and went into every bookshop he saw.

In 1862 the Pinner lease expired, so for a short while the Strand offices became Isabella's home—as a veteran of Epsom Grandstand, she must have found the experience familiar. Not wanting to spend Christmas in such makeshift surroundings, she and Sam, and their second son, also called Samuel Orchart, travelled down to Brighton to spend it in style in a fashionable hotel. Once again, tragedy struck. The boy caught a virulent strain of scarlet fever and died on New Year's Eve. The homeless, childless months of early 1863 must have been very grim.

Some time in the spring Isabella found a house she liked, a rambling, creepered farmhouse at Greenhithe, 20 miles down the Thames from London. It was called Mount Pleasant, and had an unruly two acres of garden, and a field next door. The garden was soon made very pretty, and a horse called Gerty was bought to go in the field. Here Sam and Isabella spent their most prosperous and happy years together. There were two more business trips, in 1863 and 1864, both to Paris, one of them extended to take in Berlin, Dresden and Leipzig. And there the geography of Isabella's life ends.

Sam lived on at Greenhithe with his two boys, and his good friends, Mr. and Mrs. Browne, an editor and her husband who shared the house, until shortly before his death in 1877. The younger son, Mayson Beeton, later had a successful career in journalism and was knighted.

It is not absolutely clear when Isabella began writing, but within eight months of her marriage she was editing both the cookery and the household columns of Sam's *Englishwoman's Domestic Magazine*. The idea of compiling a cookery book—the inclusion of household management came later—seems to have surfaced some time during the summer of 1857. At all events, we find a friend of the Dorlings, a Mrs. English, the same Mrs. English with whom Sam and Isabella went to stay in Suffolk, writing to Isabella: "I see difficulties in your way as regards publishing a book on cookery. Cookery is a science that is only learnt by long experience and years of study which of course you have not had. Therefore my advice would be to compile a book from receipts from a variety of the best books published on cookery, and Heaven knows there is a great variety for you to choose from... Is your intended book meant for the Larger or the Higher Classes or the Middle Class? The latter is one I should recommend you..." These were Sam's sentiments exactly. The new middle classes of the day were long on money and aspirations but short on social and culinary know-how and keen for self-improvement.

The four years that followed were the most productive of Isabella's life. In between her articles for the *Englishwoman's Domestic Magazine*, she researched and wrote entries for *The Book of Household Management*. Sam, meanwhile, was engaged on a marathon of his own, his *Dictionary of Universal Information*.

Isabella never claimed authorship of *The Book of Household Management*. The title page of the first edition clearly states "Edited by Mrs. Beeton". Nevertheless she wrote every word of it, with the exception of the last three chapters on medicine and law. Although Sam solicited recipes from readers of the *Englishwoman's Domestic*

Magazine, and some 2,000 were received, most of them proved unsatisfactory when tested by Isabella. By far the greater number came–as Mrs. English had predicted–from works by Hannah Glasse, Mrs. Rundell, Dr. William Kitchener, Eustache Ude, Eliza Acton, and Alexis Soyer, and from friends. All but a few of them were changed and completely rewritten. Only occasionally is the debt acknowledged, copyright law being flimsier then than it is today.

    The only recipes to which Isabella lays claim herself are "Sausages (Author's Oxford Recipe)" and "Useful Soup for Benevolent Purposes". She tells us, in a conscientious note, that she distributed eight or nine gallons a week of this soup to a dozen poor families in

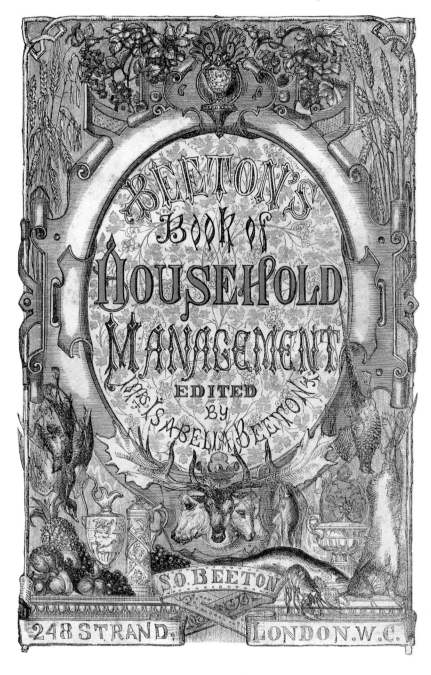

The title page of the first edition of Beeton's Book of Household Management.

Pinner in the winter of 1858. After Alexis Soyer's prodigious efforts
to feed the victims of the potato famine in Ireland a decade earlier,
soup-giving had become almost fashionable.

For miscellaneous, fascinating facts about food Isabella relied
heavily on Soyer's *Pantropheon* and on Brillat-Savarin's *Physiologie du
Goût*; other interesting facts were culled from Sam's *Dictionary of
Universal Information*, an encyclopaedia of agriculture edited by John
C. Morton, various contemporary natural histories, and Florence
Nightingale's *Notes on Nursing*. For household information, her
sources were ladies' magazines, including the *Englishwoman's Domestic
Magazine*, acquaintances, and probably interviews. She may well
have consulted, for example, Mr. Orpwood, cook to the Duke of
Rutland at Belvoir Castle.

The Book of Household Management appeared first in instalments,
or rather as supplements to the *Englishwoman's Domestic Magazine*.
The first instalment was published in December 1859, and the rest
followed at monthly intervals. Each instalment contained 48 pages,
with illustrations, and cost 3d. The final parts, in fact, were overtaken
by publication of the single volume in October 1861, brought forward
no doubt to catch the Christmas market. It was priced at 7/6d.

By that time, however, the chief concern in the Beetons' life was
Sam's newly launched magazine, *The Queen*. Isabella, who had taken
over the fashion pages of the *Englishwoman's Domestic Magazine* the
year before, became *The Queen*'s first fashion editor. She was, by this
time, an accomplished journalist, confident of her administrative
abilities, no longer Sam's pupil, but his creative equal. She no longer
worked from home, as Sam's other female contributors did, but
commuted up to the Strand each morning, breaking the male
monopoly of the railway carriages at that time of day. Sam's all-male
staff accepted her without fuss.

*Colour fashion
plates from
Paris, and paper
patterns for
making the
garments shown
in them,
transformed the
appearance of
The English-
woman's
Domestic
Magazine when
Isabella began to
edit its fashion
pages in 1860.*

In its first year of publication *The Book of Household Management* sold 60,000 copies. It reprinted in 1863, and again in 1868 and 1879. In 1865 the first of many reworkings of the great original was published, at the more approachable price of 3/6d.–whether this was Isabella's idea or Sam's we do not know. Unlike all later reworkings, however, this one was supervised by Isabella. It was called *Beeton's Every-Day Cookery and Housekeeping Book,* and contained all the practical culinary information of the original in strict alphabetical order: Game, Hashed; German Puffs; Gherkins, Pickled; Giblet Pie; Giblet Soup; Ginger, Apple (A Dessert Dish); Ginger Beer; and so on. Isabella was apparently correcting the proofs when she went into labour with her fourth child. A week later she was dead.

After her death, Sam tried to numb himself with work. He had financial problems, which he tried to solve by bringing out a series of boys' books and his 1865 *Beeton's Christmas Annual.* In May 1866, however, he and many others were ruined by the crash of the finance house Overend, Gurney, and Co. Ltd. Hearing of his situation, the rival publishing firm of Ward, Lock and Tyler offered to take over his business and all his titles, including *The Book of Household Management,* the *Englishwoman's Domestic Magazine,* and the two boys' magazines, in return for the exclusive use of the Beeton name. Sam was retained as an editor, at a salary of £400 a year.

This arrangement lasted for eight years, during which Sam commissioned, compiled or wrote nearly 50 titles. It ended when Ward and Lock (Tyler had left the partnership) decided they could no longer associate themselves with the ferociously radical opinions Sam expressed in his Christmas annuals. Two court cases followed, which resulted in Sam recovering the right to publish under his own name, and Ward Lock agreeing not to use the Beeton name except on books already published by him or originated by him during his employment with them. By this time Sam was extremely ill, strikingly emaciated and weak, but intellectually as vigorous as ever. Had he lived, he would probably have remade his fortunes as a publisher, with politics rather than education as his passion. Mr. Beeton was a great deal more than Mrs. Beeton's husband.

It is often assumed that the success of *The Book of Household Management* had much to do with its novelty. It was certainly the first cookery book to be published in cheap instalments, and as a single volume it had no rivals that dealt so comprehensively with cookery and household matters. It was also the first cookery book whose recipes were rigorously tested and adjusted. The full-page colour plates were also novel. So were the costs which Isabella appended to each recipe, and her notes on seasonability. The separation of ingredients from recipe instructions was not new–the credit for that belongs to Dr. William Kitchener, author of *The Cook's Oracle,* published in 1818–nor was the habit of giving precise weights and measures and summarising cooking times at the end of recipes–that was the invention of Eliza Acton, author of *Modern Cookery for Private Families,* published in 1845.

The magnificence of Isabella's choice of recipes is the profounder reason for its success. She set out to appeal to as wide an audience as possible. Most of her recipes are for four to six people, not for grand gatherings and balls, as many people today suppose. And most of them are still appealing because, *mutatis mutandis,* people who care about food today are buying ingredients as wholesome and as unprocessed as they can get them, as Isabella did. There were plain and thrifty recipes for the hard up, rich and complicated recipes for cooks eager to improve their reputations, and French, German and Italian recipes for hostesses aspiring to cosmopolitan chic. And at every opportunity her readers were told what to serve with what, cucumber with salmon, sage and onion with pork, peas with lamb, and so on. In a manner of speaking *The Book of Household Management* is a glorious mould in which English eating habits of the late 1850s remained frozen, or at least substantially unchanged, until the Second World War.

Her book represents the triumph of the amateur, who nicely judges what other amateurs want to know, over professionals such as Eustache Ude and Alexis Soyer, both contemporaries, both brilliant chefs, both prolific writers of cookery books. Where are their books now?

Isabella was not obsessed by food, nor apparently was she more than an average cook. In fact, on one occasion, we are told, she served up an atrocious meal as a lesson to the husbands present not to expect too much from their wives. In her letters and diaries of visits abroad one finds only the tersest descriptions of food, no sensual adjectives, no extravagant appreciation. She ate to live. "Dine we must," she says, "and we may as well dine elegantly as well as wholesomely." She liked a substantial breakfast, because it set her up for the day, and persuaded Sam to breakfast properly too.

Although she liked entertaining, she disliked formal dinner parties, "formal feeds" she called them; no doubt they reminded her of the tedium of many duty dinners at home in Epsom, but they touched something deeper than that, a fear of letting slip the pleasing mask of Victorian womanhood and allowing sharp words to escape. Far more to her taste were dances and suppers, at which she could, metaphorically at least, let her hair down. She clearly had a penchant for pretty salads and desserts, fancy pastry, and elegant bowls of fruit and flowers, all of which occurred in great profusion at ball suppers.

A most interesting conflict is at work throughout *The Book of Household Management*: one voice is that of the young Isabella, gravely telling her readers to be amiable, considerate, and even-tempered; the other voice is critical, forthright, possessed of strong opinions, and inclined to lay down the law. The one is not stronger than the other, but posterity has unerringly given its allegiance to the "hard" Isabella.

Although *The Book of Household Management* contributed vastly to the thesis "a woman's place is in the home", Isabella's place was certainly not in the home. She exemplified, without knowing it, the New Woman, although to describe her as such is anachronistic since the Woman Question, as it was called, did not really become a public issue until the late 1860s. On the whole her book can be said to have given women honour in their own eyes and, in many cases, if they read it carefully, a more thorough education than they would have received elsewhere.

The first edition of *The Book of Household Management*, on which this edition is based, has the dimensions of a stout brick, being approximately 7 inches by 4¼ inches, and 3 inches thick, no doubt the most profitable format for a book intended to relieve the purchaser of 7/6d. It has 1,112 pages, set in small and very small type, and is sprinkled with instructive little engravings. There are also 12 full-page colour engravings, which Isabella quietly refers to in her Introduction as "a novelty not without value". The index is at the front, a sensible habit unusual today.

The idea and feel of the book were Sam's. He saw, and to a large extent created, the market for it; he saw how it might be structured in monthly instalments and then presented as a single volume; he saw how the work of compiling it was to be done; he also decided that the formula for success was to lace practical instruction with improving, entertaining, and even poetic asides.

In structure the book is like a many-layered sandwich. At the top is a thick slice of preamble, concerning the mistress, the housekeeper, the kitchen, and the kitchen staff; at the bottom are five substantial chapters concerning dinners and dining, domestic servants, the rearing of children, the doctor, and legal memoranda. In between come all the cookery chapters, with chapters of recipes and chapters of general information alternating. Thus, the soup recipes are

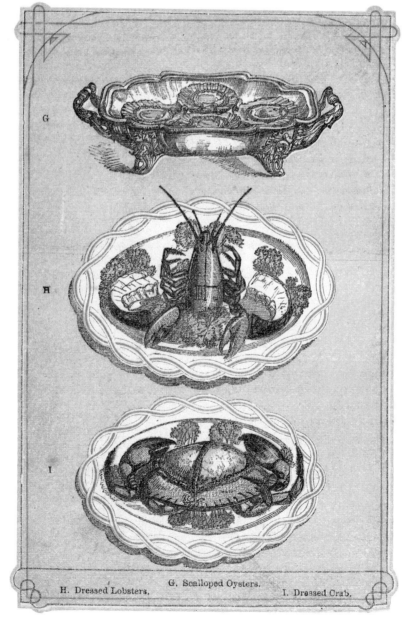

H. Dressed Lobsters.   G. Scalloped Oysters.   I. Dressed Crab.

Twelve colour plates were included in the first edition of Beeton's Book of Household Management, *an almost unheard-of bonus in a book priced at 7/6d. They were not coloured by hand but printed by a new process, which is perhaps why Isabella commissioned them more than a year before publication. Many of the dishes illustrated were, it must be said, shamelessly copied from Eliza Acton's* Modern Cookery for Private Families. *The plate shown here appears in the Fish section.*

prefaced by a chapter entitled "General Directions for Making Soups", the fish recipes by "The Natural History of Fishes", the meat recipes by "General Observations on Quadrupeds", and so on.

This structure reflects three things: the domestic hierarchy to which many mid-Victorian middle-class families aspired; the order of importance which Isabella and Sam attached to various topics; and the way in which formal menus of the period were constructed. In a general way, this shorter edition follows the same structure.

The mistress, at least in the practical running of her home, reigned over husband, children, servants and tradesmen, and so she appears first. The fitting out and staffing of the kitchen, "the great laboratory" of every household, are also dealt with early in the book. These are the necessary preliminaries to the grand, the central, topic of the book: cookery. Isabella firmly believed that wholesome, appetising cooking was the lynchpin of family health and contentment.

Three-quarters of the book, and a similar proportion of this shorter edition, are devoted to recipes. First come the Soups and Fish dishes of the First Course; then the Meats, Poultry, and Game of the Entrée Course, the Second Course, and the Third Course; then the Vegetables, which seldom made their appearance until the Second or Third Course; then the Puddings, Pastries, Creams, Jellies, Soufflés and Omelettes which "removed" the Third Course or appeared as "entremets" between the Third Course and the Dessert; then the sweet excitements of the Dessert proper, Ices, Preserves, Confectionery, and Fruit; then the tempting egg and cheese savouries most commonly consumed at breakfast and supper; then tea-time Breads, Cakes, and Biscuits; and lastly Beverages, the innocent and the alcoholic, and Invalid Cookery. In this edition invalid cookery is omitted, with the exception of such comforting recipes as Beef Tea and Chicken Broth.

After this *tour de force*, Isabella turns to the subject of entertaining. In many ways the chapter entitled Dinners and Dining contains the most seductive pages of the great original, being filled with bills of fare which show how the formal feeds which made Isabella so nervous were constructed and presented. It is a mark of Isabella's great conscientiousness that she composed, for each month of the year, five dinner party menus for numbers of guests ranging from 6 to 18, and 14 menus for "plain family dinners". Some of her more elaborate table plans are reproduced in this book.

To gourmets of today it may seem puzzling that so many dishes appear on the table at once, but in Isabella's day *service à la française*, as it was called, was the fashion at formal dinners. All the dishes for each course were placed on the table together. Thus at the First Course, where both soup and fish were served, either the fish got cold while you drank your soup, or you had the fish and gave the soup a miss—usually the soup was served by the host and the fish by the hostess, and the plates were handed round by a footman or a maid depending on the opulence of the establishment.

A similar choice between lesser evils attended the Entrée Course, the Second Course, and the Third Course, unless heated serving dishes were used. All the carving was done at table by the master of the house. After the Third Course the table was cleared for the Dessert, the most ornamental and relaxed part of the meal. In *service à la russe*, on the other hand, daringly new when Isabella was writing, each dish was brought up from the kitchen separately. Food presented in this way did not please the greedy eye as well as *service à la française*, but it was more likely to be served hot. Dinners and Dining ends with suggestions for a Pickwickian picnic for 40 persons.

The less lucky individuals who made possible these *grandes bouffes*, and who scrubbed and cleaned and fetched and carried, appear towards the end of the book. Like most ambitious architects, Isabella "sells" the concept first, and solves the industrial relations afterwards! Here, in order of rank, men first, come the domestic staff, with all their duties and arts and crafts spelled out. The medical and legal chapters which follow, and bring the book to a close, were considered very good in their day–they were written by a doctor and a lawyer–but today they are of narrower interest than the rest of the book, and so form no part of this edition.

The challenge in a shorter edition is to reflect accurately the best of the original while keeping all its themes in play. The original is far from perfect. It bears the marks, in its inconsistencies of spelling and punctuation, of having been produced in some haste. The engravings, by Harrison Weir, are not those of a first-rate artist, but they have their charm (the fuzzy and fuming Westphalian boar which appears on page 370 of the original is irresistible). As many as will reproduce respectably have been used, on the grounds that at least they were passed, if not commissioned, by Isabella herself.

Here and there the writing loses itself in subordinate clauses or says not very much in long latinate words. For the modern reader, and probably for the middle-class housewife of 1861 too, the constant references to the Greeks and Romans are tiresome. One also suspects that the large chunks of natural history and biology cemented into the opening chapters on Fish, Poultry, and Vegetables went over the heads of many of her readers, the more discerning of whom would have found the introduction to Creams, Jellies, Soufflés, Omelettes, and Sweet Dishes, with its meandering course down the byways of cream, gelatine and calves' foot jelly, the most irrelevant in the book.

Such flaws as these are partly explained by the inexorable pressure of producing a book in monthly instalments. Dickens managed it, but he was an experienced journalist and had the luxury of inventing things as he went along. Isabella was not experienced, and was obliged to import a lot of information from encyclopaedias and other contemporary works of reference. That she achieved what she did,

From a chance remark of Isabella's it seems that Harrison Weir took his sketchbook into fields and farmyards to draw some of his animals. Many more breeds of cattle, pigs, chickens, pigeons, and rabbits grace the meat section of the first edition than are strictly necessary, but this is because Isabella liked them and was very concerned for their welfare. Some of her descriptions of animals display great feeling. On the right is the Westphalian boar which ornaments her discourse on "The Hog"

Alderney cow

Alderney bull

virtually unaided, except by Sam's encouragement, without typewriters, photocopiers, word processors, telephones, or cars, and while running a home and producing two children, is extraordinary. It cost her an immense effort. In her Preface to the first edition she confesses as much, but there is no hint of triumph or self-congratulation; she matter-of-factly states the why, what, and how of her book, thanks the medical and legal contributors, and signs off.

For Isabella at her factual best one must look to the recipes; in writing these she took great pains not to standardise her descriptions, and not to write always in the imperative. For Isabella at her most magisterial and provocative, one must look to her general remarks on the duties of the mistress and on various points of etiquette: for example, "Hospitality is a most excellent virtue; but care must be taken that the love of company, for its own sake, does not become a prevailing passion; for then the habit is no longer hospitality, but dissipation." It is unlikely that Isabella intended such remarks to be amusing, although their epigrammatic style may make them sound so to modern ears.

For Isabella at her most amusing one must look to sly little observations such as "Guests invited for the evening...are generally considered at liberty to arrive whenever it will best suit themselves. ... By this arrangement, many fashionable people and others, who have numerous engagements to fulfil, often contrive to make their appearance at two or three parties in the course of one evening", or "As the visitors are announced by the servant, it is not necessary for the lady of the house to advance each time towards the door", or "... when a lady of fashion chooses her footman without any other consideration than his height, shape, and *tournure* of his calf, it is not surprising that she should find a domestic who has no attachment for the family". Isabella derived a lot of quiet amusement from the social conventions of the day.

In compressing the many excellent facets of the first edition into the scope of 240 pages, a number of liberties have been taken, some to suit the standard principles of modern cookery editing, and some for the greater ease and convenience of modern readers. It can be argued of course that abridging and reconstituting 25 per cent of anything is an essentially distorting operation. Equally it can be argued that few people nowadays are likely to wade through the whole of Mrs. Beeton and that a slice of cake is frequently a fair sample of the whole. If there were such an instrument as a literary spectrometer, and if it were applied to this shortened version, it would detect almost the entire range of frequencies emitted by the original.

With the exception of this introduction, and the single instance mentioned below, the text is Mrs. Beeton's. Punctuation and spellings have been tidied up or modernised here and there–for example, shalot is now shallot, cocoa-nut now coconut, brocoli now broccoli. Archaic words have been replaced by modern equivalents–standish by inkstand, clouted by clotted, salamander by grill, and so on. Old measures such as drams and pecks and gills have been converted to modern measures.

Because they are mere curiosities today, the costs attached to the end of all the recipes in the original have been omitted, as have notes about seasonability, except in the Game chapter. Readers will be enchanted to know that in 1861 rump steak was a shilling a pound, lettuces and eggs, when most plentiful, were a penny each, and cream

PREFACE.

—◦✕◦—

A facsimile of the Preface to the 1861 edition of Beeton's Book of Household Management.

I MUST frankly own, that if I had known, beforehand, that this book would have cost me the labour which it has, I should never have been courageous enough to commence it. What moved me, in the first instance, to attempt a work like this, was the discomfort and suffering which I had seen brought upon men and women by household mismanagement. I have always thought that there is no more fruitful source of family discontent than a housewife's badly-cooked dinners and untidy ways. Men are now so well served out of doors,—at their clubs, well-ordered taverns, and dining-houses, that in order to compete with the attractions of these places, a mistress must be thoroughly acquainted with the theory and practice of cookery, as well as be perfectly conversant with all the other arts of making and keeping a comfortable home.

In this book I have attempted to give, under the chapters devoted to cookery, an intelligible arrangement to every recipe, a list of the *ingredients*, a plain statement of the *mode* of preparing each dish, and a careful estimate of its *cost*, the *number of people* for whom it is *sufficient*, and the time when it is *seasonable*. For the matter of the recipes, I am indebted, in some measure, to many correspondents of the " Englishwoman's Domestic Magazine," who have obligingly placed at my disposal their formulæ for many original preparations. A large private circle has also rendered me considerable service. A diligent study of the works of the best modern writers on cookery was also necessary to the faithful fulfilment of my task. Friends in England, Scotland, Ireland, France, and Germany, have also very materially aided me. I have paid great attention to those recipes which come under the head of " COLD MEAT COOKERY." But in the department belonging to the Cook I have striven, too, to make my work something more than a Cookery Book, and have, therefore, on the best authority that I could obtain, given an account of the natural history of the animals and vegetables which we use as food. I have followed the animal from his birth to his appearance on the table ; have described the manner of feeding him, and of slaying him, the position of his various joints, and, after giving the recipes, have described the modes of carving Meat, Poultry, and Game. Skilful artists have designed the numerous drawings which appear in this work, and which illustrate, better than any description, many important and interesting items. The coloured plates are a novelty not without value.

Besides the great portion of the book which has especial reference to the cook's department, there are chapters devoted to those of the other servants of the household, who have all, I trust, their duties clearly assigned to them.

Towards the end of the work will be found valuable chapters on the " Management of Children "—" The Doctor," the latter principally referring to accidents and emergencies, some of which are certain to occur in the experience of every one of us ; and the last chapter contains " Legal Memoranda," which will be serviceable in cases of doubt as to the proper course to be adopted in the relations between Landlord and Tenant, Tax-gatherer and Tax-payer, and Tradesman and Customer.

These chapters have been contributed by gentlemen fully entitled to confidence ; those on medical subjects by an experienced surgeon, and the legal matter by a solicitor.

I wish here to acknowledge the kind letters and congratulations I have received during the progress of this work, and have only further to add, that I trust the result of the four years' incessant labour which I have expended will not be altogether unacceptable to some of my countrymen and countrywomen.

ISABELLA BEETON.

A colour plate from the 1898 edition of Beeton's Book of Household Management. By this time hundreds of new recipes – English, French German, Italian, American, Australian, and Indian – had been added, with new sections on breakfasts, luncheons, teas, tableware, and table decorations.

DINNER AND DESSERT CHINA.

4 Dinner Plates _ 4 Dessert Plates _ 2 Vegetable Dishes _ 1 Soup Tureen _ 1 Jug _ 1 Cheese Dish.
1 Ice Pail _ 2 Salts _ 1 Strawberry Dish _ 1 Fruit Dish _ 1 Spoon Warmer _

was a shilling a pint! Even with the costs omitted, the prime importance Isabella attached to economy is still apparent in such remarks as "This dish may be made less expensively by...", of which there are many.

In Isabella's mind the rock upon which a happy home is built is Economy: without economy, it must crumble to pieces. Buying things in their due season is an aspect of economy; bottling and preserving are aspects of economy, regular maintenance of all kitchen equipment, linen, furnishings and fittings is an aspect of economy. Economy in fact was Isabella's grand, underlying theme.

The 400 or so recipes in this edition are, for the most part, in their original alphabetical order, but a few have migrated from their original positions: for example, Beef Tea and Chicken Broth, originally in Invalid Cookery, now appear under Beverages and Soups respectively; for convenience, all the shellfish are now together at the end of the Fish section, rather than dispersed throughout it; exercising similar logic, all the sauces, pickles, forcemeats, puddings, pastries, and so on have their own groupings rather than forming part of alphabetical job lots. Where Mrs. Beeton had a chapter each on beef, mutton and lamb, pork, and veal, *and* an introductory chapter for each, *and* an overall introduction entitled "Observations on Quadrupeds", there is now a single chapter on Meat.

All the non-recipe sections have been carefully shortened, erring where possible on the side of practical advice which holds good today rather than natural history, biology, or food chemistry. Items of historical curiosity have been relegated to the margins. In only one instance was anything more than excerpting and neatly arranging the excerpts necessary, and that was in the preface to the Creams, Jellies, Soufflés, Omelettes, and Sweet Dishes, already referred to; snippets of it have been woven into four short paragraphs written in the Beeton style. The only substantial re-ordering of the non-recipe sections concerns the giving of dinner parties and evening parties; originally part of the daily routines of the mistress, these now sit more comfortably at the front of Dinners and Dining.

Mrs. Beeton is a curious and unique phenomenon. The name has a power which far exceeds the very real merits of the original, which began to display, as early as 1888, some of the properties of a black hole, if one may be so indelicate. Its compact energy was great enough to suck in all sorts of additions and updatings; and every time it ingested more material, it was renewed and became more potent. Very few works of reference have remained in a state of continuous creation for a century and a quarter.

The evergreen appeal of a really good cookbook, especially one that is kept carefully up to date, is obvious. But why a book by Mrs. Beeton, of whom the general public knew, and still knows, very little, despite the biographies by Nancy Spain, H. Montgomery Hyde and Sarah Freeman? Why does the name Mrs. Beeton still command attention? Careful publishing husbandry is certainly one of the answers, but it is difficult to create a powerful name out of a nonentity. The triumphant scope of her work is certainly one of the answers. But another answer is that generations of cooks and housewives have responded, instinctively, to the dowager side of Isabella's personality. It takes little effort, reading her admonitions and recommendations, to picture her as a culinary Queen Victoria, all black bombazine and pursed lips. Inaccurate as that picture is, it has endowed *The Book of Household Management* with tremendous authority. That is the spark which flashed from Isabella herself, and which no other writer could have brought to the enterprise, and that is the spark which still fuels the Beeton phenomenon.

Anne Cope
Bath, March 1987

CHAPTER 1

Management and Economy of the Kitchen

AS WITH THE COMMANDER OF AN ARMY, or the leader of any enterprise, so is it with the mistress of a house. Her spirit will be seen through the whole establishment, and just in proportion as she performs her duties intelligently and thoroughly, so will her domestics follow in her path.

FRUGALITY AND ECONOMY ARE HOME VIRTUES, without which no household can prosper. The necessity of practising economy should be evident to everyone, whether in the possession of an income no more than sufficient for a family's requirements, or of a large fortune which puts financial adversity out of the question. We must always remember that it is a great merit in housekeeping to manage a little well. Economy and frugality must never, however, be allowed to degenerate into parsimony and meanness.

In marketing, that the best articles are the cheapest may be laid down as a rule; also that one of the most essential pieces of knowledge which enter into the economy of the kitchen is to be acquainted with the periods when things are in season. It is desirable, unless an experienced and confidential housekeeper be kept, that the mistress should herself purchase all provisions and stores needed for the house. A housekeeping account book should invariably be kept, and kept punctually and precisely. The plan for keeping household accounts, which we should recommend, would be to write down into a daily diary every amount paid on a particular day, be it ever so small; then, at the end of the month, let these various payments be ranged under their specific heads of Butcher, Baker, etc. Thus will be seen the proportions paid to each tradesman, and any one month's expenses may be contrasted with another.

AFTER BREAKFAST IS OVER, it will be well for the mistress to make a round of the kitchen and other offices, to see that all are in order, and that the morning's work has been properly performed by the various domestics. The orders for the day should then be given, after which the mistress, if a mother of a young family, may devote herself to the instruction of some of its younger members, or to the examination of the state of their wardrobe, leaving the later portion of the morning for reading, or for some amusing recreation.

These duties and pleasures being performed and enjoyed, the hour of luncheon will have arrived. This is a very necessary meal between an early breakfast and a late dinner, as a healthy person, with good exercise, should have a fresh supply of food once in four hours. It should be a light meal, but its solidity must be, in some degree, proportionate to the time it is intended to wait for dinner, and the amount of exercise taken in the meantime. At this time, also, the servants' dinner will be served.

THE DINNER is, in most establishments, the next great event of the day. It is in serving up food that is at once appetising and wholesome that the skill of the modern housewife is severely tasked, and she has scarcely a more important duty to fulfil. It is, in fact, her particular vocation, in virtue of which she may be said to hold the health of the family, and of the friends of the family, in her hands from day to day.

Coffee and tea canisters

THE KITCHEN, it must be remembered, is the great laboratory of every household. A good kitchen, therefore, should be erected with a view to the following particulars. 1. Convenience of distribution in its parts, with largeness of dimension. 2. Excellence of light, height of ceiling, and good ventilation. 3. Easiness of access, without passing through the house. 4. Sufficient remoteness from the principal apartments of the house, that the members, visitors, or guests of the family may not perceive the odour incident to cooking, or hear the noise of culinary operations. 5. Plenty of fuel and water which, with the scullery, pantry, and storeroom, should be near it so as to offer the smallest possible trouble in reaching them.

Boiling pot

AMONGST THE MOST ESSENTIAL IMPLEMENTS of the kitchen, without which no cook can be expected to perform her office, are scales or weighing machines. Accompanying these, there should be spice boxes, and sugar and biscuit canisters of either white or japanned tin; the covers of these should fit tightly.

As not only health but life may be said to depend on the cleanliness of culinary utensils, great attention must be paid to their condition generally, but more especially to that of saucepans, stewpans, and boilers. Inside they should be kept perfectly clean, and the outside as clean as possible. Care should be taken that the lids fit tight and close, so that soups or gravies may not be suffered to waste by evaporation. Soup pots and kettles should be washed immediately after being used, and dried in a warm place. Copper utensils should never be used in the kitchen unless tinned, and the utmost care should be taken not to let the tin be rubbed off, lest the copper impregnate with poison what is intended to be eaten. Stone and earthenware vessels should be provided for soups and gravies not intended for immediate use, and also plenty of common dishes for the larder. Great care should also be taken that all sieves, jelly bags, tapes, and pudding cloths be well washed and scalded, and kept dry, or they will impart an unpleasant flavour when next used.

Iron saucepan, with steamer

THE MODERN ENGLISH WEIGHTS were adjusted by the 27th chapter of Magna Carta, the great charter forced by the barons from King John at Runnymede, in Surrey. Therein it is declared that the weights, all over England, shall be the same, although for different commodities there were two different kinds, Troy and Avoirdupois. The origin of both is taken from a grain of wheat gathered in the middle of an ear.

FOR KEEPING PROVISIONS, in the absence of proper places, a hanging safe, suspended in an airy situation, is the best substitute. A well ventilated larder, dry and shady, is better for meat and poultry,

Jelly bag and stand

which require to be kept for some time; vegetables keep best on a stone floor, if the air be excluded; meat, in a cold dry place; as also salt, sugar, sweetmeats, candles, dried meats, and hams. Rice, and all sorts of cereal grains for puddings, should be closely covered to preserve them from insects, but even this will not prevent them from being affected by these destroyers if they are long and carelessly kept.

KITCHEN UTENSILS.– The list displayed here, supplied by Messrs. Richard & John Slack, 336, Strand, will show the articles required for the kitchen of a family in the middle class of life, although it does not contain all the things that may be deemed necessary for some families, and may contain more than are required for others.

	s.	d.		s.	d.
1 Tea-kettle	6	6	1 Dripping-pan and Stand	6	6
1 Toasting-fork	1	0	1 Dustpan	1	0
1 Bread-grater	1	0	1 Fish and Egg-slice	1	9
1 Pair of Brass Candlesticks	3	6	2 Fish-kettles	10	0
1 Teapot and Tray	6	6	1 Flour-box	1	0
1 Bottle-jack	9	6	3 Flat-irons	3	6
6 Spoons	1	6	2 Frying-pans	4	0
2 Candlesticks	2	6	1 Gridiron	2	0
1 Candle-box	1	4	1 Mustard-pot	1	0
6 Knives and Forks	5	3	1 Salt-cellar	0	8
2 Sets of Skewers	1	0	1 Pepper-box	0	6
1 Meat-chopper	1	9	1 Pair of Bellows	2	0
1 Cinder-sifter	1	3	3 Jelly-moulds	8	0
1 Coffee-pot	2	3	1 Plate-basket	5	6
1 Colander	1	6	1 Cheese-toaster	1	10
3 Block-tin Saucepans	5	9	1 Coal-shovel	2	6
5 Iron Saucepans	12	0	1 Wood Meat-screen	30	0
1 Ditto and Steamer	6	6			
1 Large Boiling-pot	10	0	The Set	£8 11	1
4 Iron Stewpans	8	9			

THE COOK, KITCHEN MAID, AND SCULLERY MAID

THE DUTIES OF THE COOK, THE KITCHEN MAIDS, AND THE SCULLERY MAIDS are so intimately associated that they can hardly be treated of separately. The cook, however, is at the head of the kitchen, and in proportion to her possession of the qualities of cleanliness, neatness, order, regularity, and celerity of action, so will her influence appear in the conduct of those who are under her.

Her first duty should be to set her dough for the breakfast rolls, and then to engage herself with those numerous little preliminary occupations which may not inappropriately be termed laying out her duties for the day. This will bring in the breakfast hour of eight, after which directions must be given, and preparations made, for the different dinners of the household and family. It is the cook's department, generally, in smaller establishments, to wait at breakfast, as the housemaid, by this time, has gone upstairs into the bedrooms. The cook usually answers the bells and single knocks at the door in the early part of the morning, as the tradesmen, with whom it is her more special business to speak, call at these hours.

In those numerous households where a cook and housemaid only are kept, the general custom is that the cook should have the charge of the dining room. The hall, the lamps, and the doorstep are also committed to her care, and any other work there may be on the outside of the house. The cleaning of the kitchen, pantry, passages, and kitchen stairs must always be over before breakfast.

It is in her preparation of the dinner that the cook begins to feel

IT IS IN THE LARGE ESTABLISHMENTS of princes, noblemen, and very affluent families alone that the man cook is found in this country. He holds a high position in such households, being inferior in rank only to the house steward, the valet, and the butler.

IN ANTIQUITY, no cooks were kept, and we know from Homer that his ancient heroes prepared and dressed their victuals with their own hands. Ulysses, we are told, like a modern charwoman, excelled at lighting a fire, whilst Achilles was an adept at turning a spit.

THE POSITION OF SCULLERY MAID is not, of course, one of high rank, nor is the payment for her services large. But we are acquainted with the case of a young girl who so strongly wished to become connected with the kitchen and cookery that she absolutely left her parents and engaged herself as a scullery maid in a gentleman's house. Here she showed herself so active and intelligent that she very quickly rose to the rank of kitchen maid; and from this, so great was her gastronomical genius, she became, in a short space of time, one of the best women cooks in England.

the weight and responsibility of her situation, as she must take upon herself all the dressing and the serving of the principal dishes, which her skill and ingenuity have mostly prepared. Whilst these, however, are cooking, she must be busy with her pastry, soups, gravies, ragoûts, etc. Stock, being the basis of most made dishes, must be always at hand, in conjunction with her sweet herbs and spices for seasoning. "A place for everything, and everything in its place" must be her rule. In dishing up to send to table, the cook takes charge of the fish, soups, and poultry, and the kitchen maid of the vegetables, sauces, and gravies.

When the dinner has been served, the most important feature in the daily life of the cook is at an end. She must, however, now begin to look to the contents of her larder, taking care to keep everything sweet and clean, so that no disagreeable smells may arise.

Whilst the cook is engaged with her morning duties, the kitchen maid is also occupied with hers. Her first duty, after the fire is lighted, is to sweep and clean the kitchen, and the various offices belonging to it. This she does every morning, besides cleaning the stone steps at the entrance of the house, the halls, the passages, and the stairs which lead to the kitchen. Her general duties, besides these, are to wash and scour all these places twice a week, with the tables, shelves, and cupboards. She has also to cook the nursery and servants' hall dinners, to prepare all fish, poultry, and vegetables, trim meat joints and cutlets, and do all such duties as may be considered to enter into the cook's department in a subordinate degree.

Banister brush

AMONG THE STOVES IN USE TODAY are the simple open range and the kitchener; the former is completely fitted up with oven, boiler, sliding cheek, wrought-iron bars, revolving shelves, and brass tap; of the latter we take as our specimen the Improved Leamington Kitchener, which is said to surpass any other range in use for easy cooking by one fire.

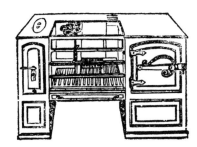

Simple open range

Improved Leamington Kitchener

CHAPTER 2

Soups

IT HAS BEEN ASSERTED that English cookery is, nationally speaking, far from being the best in the world. More than this, we have been frequently told by brilliant foreign writers, half philosophers, half *chefs*, that we are the *worst* cooks on the face of the earth, and that the proverb which alludes to the divine origin of food and the precisely opposite origin of its preparers, is peculiarly applicable to us islanders. Not, however, to the inhabitants of the whole island; for it is stated in a work which treats of culinary operations north of the Tweed that the "broth" of Scotland claims, for excellence and wholesomeness, a very close second place to the *bouillon* or common soup of France. We are glad to note, however, that soups of vegetables, fish, meat, and game are now very frequently found in the homes of the English middle classes, as well as in the mansions of the wealthier and more aristocratic; and we take this to be one evidence that we are on the right road to an improvement in our system of cookery.

LEAN, JUICY BEEF, MUTTON, AND VEAL form the basis of all good soups. The principal art in composing good rich soup is so to proportion the several ingredients that the flavour of one shall not predominate over another, and that all the articles of which it is composed shall form an agreeable whole. To accomplish this, care must be taken that the roots and herbs are perfectly well cleaned, and that the water is proportioned to the quantity of meat and other ingredients. Generally a pint of water may be allowed to half a pound of meat for soups. In making soups, gentle stewing or simmering is incomparably the best. It may be remarked, however, that a really good soup can never be made but in a well-closed vessel, although perhaps greater wholesomeness is obtained by an occasional exposure to the air.

FOR THE SEASONING OF SOUPS, bayleaves, tomato, tarragon, chervil, parsley, common thyme, lemon thyme, orange thyme, marjoram, sage, mint, winter savory, basil, burnet, allspice, cinnamon, ginger, nutmeg, clove, mace, black and white pepper, essence of anchovy, lemon peel and juice, and Seville orange juice, are all taken. The latter imparts a finer flavour than the lemon, and

I T IS ON A GOOD STOCK, or first good broth and sauce, that excellence in cookery depends. If the preparation of this basis of the culinary art is entrusted to negligent or ignorant persons, and the stock is not well skimmed, it will never be clear. In the proper management of the stock pot an immense deal of trouble is saved, inasmuch as one stock serves for many purposes.

the acid is much milder. These materials, with wine, mushroom ketchup, Harvey's sauce, and tomato sauce, combined in various proportions, are, with other ingredients, manipulated into an almost endless variety of excellent soups. Sliced onions, fried with butter and flour till they are browned, and then rubbed through a sieve, are excellent to heighten the colour and flavour of brown soups. The older and drier the onion, the stronger will be its flavour.

BEEF MAKES THE BEST STOCK; veal stock has less colour and taste; whilst mutton sometimes gives it a tallowy smell, far from agreeable, unless the meat has been previously roasted or broiled. Fowls add very little to the flavour of stock, unless they be old and fat. Pigeons, when they are old, add the most flavour to it; and a rabbit or partridge is also a great improvement.

Bones and any meat trimmings can now be added to the stock, tied up in a bag. Bones yield gelatine, which is the nutritious portion of stock. Where there is an abundance of gelatine, it causes the stock, when cold, to become a jelly. Cover the stock pot well to prevent evaporation. After six hours' slow and gentle simmering, the stock will be done.

— Medium Stock —

Ingredients.–4 lbs. of shin of beef, or 4 lbs. of knuckle of veal, or 2 lbs. of each; any bones, trimmings of poultry, or fresh meat, ½ lb. of lean bacon or ham, 2 oz. of butter, 2 large onions, each stuck with 3 cloves, 1 turnip, 3 carrots, ½ leek, 1 head of celery, 2 oz. of salt, ½ teaspoonful of whole pepper, 1 large blade of mace, 1 small bunch of savoury herbs, 8 pints and ½ pint of cold water.

Mode.–Cut up the meat and bacon or ham into cubes; rub the butter on the bottom of the stewpan; put in ½ pint of water, the meat, and all the other ingredients. Cover the stewpan, and place it on a moderate heat, occasionally stirring its contents. When the bottom of the pan becomes covered with a pale, jelly-like substance, add 8 pints of cold water, and simmer very gently for 5 hours. Skim off every particle of fat whilst it is doing, and strain it through a fine sieve. This is the basis of many soups, and will be found quite strong enough for ordinary purposes.

Time.–5½ hours.

— Consommé or White Stock —
(FOR THE PREPARATION OF WHITE SOUPS)

Ingredients.–4 lbs. of knuckle of veal, any poultry trimmings, 4 slices of lean ham, 1 carrot, 2 onions, 1 head of celery, 12 white peppercorns, 1 oz. of salt, 1 blade of mace, 1 oz. of butter, 8 pints and ½ pint of water.

Mode.–Cut up the veal, and put it with the bones and trimmings of poultry, and the ham, into the stewpan, which has been rubbed with the butter. Moisten with ½ pint of water, and simmer till the meat juices begin to flow. Then add the 8 pints of water and the remainder of the ingredients; simmer for 5 hours. After skimming and straining it carefully, it will be ready for use.

Time.–5½ hours.

T HE CALF.–The flesh of this animal is called veal, and when young, that is under two months old, yields a large quantity of soluble extract, and is, therefore, much employed for soups and broths.

Vegetable cutter

C UT VEGETABLES FOR SOUPS, etc.– The annexed engraving represents a cutter for shaping vegetables for soups, ragoûts, stews, etc., carrots and turnips being the usual vegetables for which this utensil is used. Cut the vegetables into slices about ¼ inch thick, stamp them out with the cutter, and boil them for a few minutes in salt and water, until tender. Turnips should be cut in rather thicker slices than carrots, on account of the former boiling more quickly to a pulp than the latter.

Ingredients for
Medium Stock

— C h i c k e n   B r o t h —

Ingredients.–½ fowl, or the inferior joints of a whole one, 2 pints of water, 1 blade of mace, ½ onion, a small bunch of sweet herbs, salt to taste, 10 peppercorns.

Mode.–An old fowl not suitable for eating may be converted into very good broth, or, if a young one be used, the inferior joints may be put in the broth. Put the fowl into a saucepan, with all the other ingredients, and simmer gently for 1½ hours, carefully skimming the broth well. When done, strain, and put by in a cool place until wanted; then take all the fat off the top, warm up as much as may be required, and serve.

Time.–1½ hours. **Sufficient** to make rather more than 1 pint.

— C o c k - a - L e e k i e   S o u p —

Ingredients.–A capon or large fowl (sometimes an old cock, from which the recipe takes its name, is used), 5 or 6 lbs. of fine leeks, 10 pints of MEDIUM STOCK, pepper and salt to taste.

Mode.–Well wash the leeks, taking off the roots and part of the heads, and cut them into lengths of about 1 inch. Truss the fowl as for boiling, put it into the stock with, at first, one half of the leeks, and allow it to simmer gently. In ½ hour add the remaining leeks, and then it may simmer for 3 or 4 hours longer. It should be carefully skimmed, and can be seasoned to taste. In serving, take out the fowl and carve it neatly, placing the pieces in a tureen and pouring over them the soup, which should be very thick.

Time.–4 hours.

THE LEEK is one of the alliaceous tribe, which consists of the onion, garlic, chive, shallot, and leek. It is the national badge of the Welsh, and tradition ascribes to St. David its introduction to that part of Britain. The wearing of the leek on St. David's day probably originated from the custom of *Cymhortha*, or the friendly aid, practised among farmers. In some districts of South Wales, all the neighbours of a small farmer were wont to appoint a day when they attended to plough his land, and the like; and, at such time, it was the custom for each to bring his portion of leeks with him for making the broth or soup. Others derive the origin of the custom from the Battle of Cressy.

Oxtail Soup

THE OX.–There are no animals of greater use to man than the tribe to which the ox belongs. There is hardly a part of them that does not enter into some of the arts and purposes of civilized life. Of their horns are made combs, knife handles, boxes, spoons, and drinking cups. Glue is made from their gristles, cartilages, and portions of their hides. Their bones often form a substitute for ivory; their skins, when calves, are manufactured into vellum; their blood is the basis of Prussian blue; their sinews furnish fine and strong threads, used by saddlers; their hair enters into various manufactures; and their tallow is made into candles.

— Oxtail Soup —

Ingredients.–2 oxtails cut into pieces, 2 slices of ham, 1 oz. of butter, 2 carrots, 2 turnips, 3 onions, 1 leek, 1 head of celery, 1 bunch of savoury herbs, 1 bayleaf, 12 whole peppercorns, 4 cloves, 1 tablespoonful of salt, 2 tablespoonfuls of TOMATO KETCHUP, ½ glass of port, 6 pints of water, a little flour and butter to thicken.

Mode.–Wash the tails and put them in a stewpan, with the butter. Cut the vegetables in slices, and add them, with the peppercorns and herbs. Put in ½ pint of water, and stir over a sharp heat till the juices are drawn. Fill up the stewpan with the water and, when boiling, add the salt. Skim well, and simmer very gently for 4 hours, or until the tails are tender. Take them out, skim and strain the soup, thicken with a little flour worked together with butter, and flavour with the ketchup and port. Put back the tails, simmer for 5 minutes, and serve.

Time.–4½ hours.

— F i s h S t o c k —

Ingredients.–2 lbs. of beef or veal (these can be omitted), any kind of white fish trimmings (of fish which are to be dressed for table), 2 onions, the rind of ½ lemon, a bunch of sweet herbs, 2 carrots, 4 pints of water.

Mode.–Cut up the fish and put it, with the other ingredients, into the water. Simmer for 2 hours, skim the liquor carefully, and strain it. When a richer stock is wanted, fry the vegetables and fish before adding the water.

Time.–2 hours.

Note.–Do not make fish stock too long before it is wanted as it soon turns sour.

— L o b s t e r S o u p —

Ingredients.–3 large cooked lobsters, or 6 small ones, 1 teacupful of white breadcrumbs, 2 fresh anchovies, 1 onion, 1 small bunch of sweet herbs, 1 strip of lemon peel, 4 pints of water, 2 oz. of butter, a little nutmeg, 1 teaspoonful of flour, 1 pint of cream, 1 pint of milk; forcemeat balls made of breadcrumbs, pounded mace, salt and pepper to taste, 1 egg, a little flour.

Mode.–Pick the meat from the tails and claws of the lobsters, and reserve the coral, previously discarding the intestines, gills, and the bag in the head. Put the tail and claw meat in a stewpan, with the cup of breadcrumbs, the anchovies, onion, herbs, lemon peel, and water; simmer gently till all the goodness is extracted, and strain off the liquor. Now pound the coral in a mortar, with the butter, nutmeg, and flour, and mix with it the cream and milk. Give one boil up, at the same time adding the tails cut in pieces. Mix together the ingredients for the forcemeat balls, adding to them the remainder of the lobster; heat them in the soup, and serve.

Time.–2 hours, or rather more.

— A s p a r a g u s S o u p —

Ingredients.–1½ lbs. of green split peas, 1 teacupful of MEDIUM STOCK, 4 mild onions, 1 lettuce cut small, ½ head of celery, ½ lb. of asparagus cut small, ½ pint of cream, 6 pints of water.

Mode.–Boil the peas until tender, and rub them through a sieve; add the stock, and then stew by themselves the celery, onions, lettuce, and asparagus, with the water. After this, stew together all the ingredients, add the cream, and serve.

Time.–Peas 2½ hours, vegetables 1 hour; altogether, 4 hours.

— B a r l e y S o u p —

Ingredients.–2 lbs. of shin of beef, ¼ lb. of pearl barley, a large bunch of parsley, 4 onions, 6 potatoes, salt and pepper, 8 pints of water.

Mode.–Cut the meat, onions, and potatoes into small pieces, and put them into the stewpan with the rest of the ingredients; simmer gently for 3 hours.

Time.–3 hours.

BARLEY is, in Britain, the next plant to wheat in point of value. It is less nutritive than wheat, and in 100 parts has of starch 79, gluten 6, saccharine matter 7, husk 8. It is, however, a lighter and less stimulating food than wheat, which renders a decoction of it well adapted for invalids whose digestion is weak.

ASPARAGUS is often vulgarly called, in London, sparrowgrass, and in its cultivated form hardly bears any resemblance to the original plant. Immense quantities of it are raised for the London market at Mortlake and Deptford, but it belongs rather to the class of luxurious than necessary food. It is light and easily digested, but is not very nutritious.

THE CARROT.– The garden carrot in general use was introduced in the reign of Queen Elizabeth, and was, at first, so highly esteemed that the ladies wore leaves of it in their head-dresses. It is of great value in the culinary art, especially for soups and stews. It can be used also for beer, instead of malt, and, in distillation, it yields a large quantity of spirit.

— Soupe à la Cantatrice —
(VERY BENEFICIAL FOR THE VOICE)

Ingredients.–3 oz. of sago, ½ pint of cream, the yolks of 3 eggs, ½ teaspoonful of sugar, seasoning to taste, 1 bayleaf if liked, 4 pints of MEDIUM STOCK.

Mode.–Having washed the sago in boiling water, let it be gradually added to the nearly boiling stock. Simmer with the sugar, seasoning and bayleaf for ½ hour, when it should be well dissolved. Beat up the yolks of the eggs, add to them the very hot cream; stir these quickly into the soup, and serve immediately. Do not let the soup boil, or the eggs will curdle.

Time.–40 minutes.

— Soupe à la Crécy —

Ingredients.–4 carrots, 2 sliced onions, 1 cut lettuce, a little chervil, 2 oz. of butter, 1 pint of lentils, the crumbs of 2 slices of white bread, ½ teacupful of rice, 4 pints of MEDIUM STOCK.

Mode.–Put the vegetables and butter in the stewpan, and let them simmer 5 minutes; then add the lentils and 1 pint of the stock, and stew gently for ½ hour. Now fill it up with the remainder of the stock, let it boil another hour, and put in the breadcrumbs. When well soaked, rub all through a sieve. Have ready the rice boiled; pour the soup over this, and serve.

Time.–1¾ hours.

Soupe à la Julienne and Soupe à la Crécy

— Cucumber Soup —
(FRENCH RECIPE)

Ingredients.–1 large cucumber, a piece of butter the size of a walnut, a little chervil and sorrel cut in large pieces, salt and pepper to taste, the yolks of 2 eggs, ¼ pint of cream, 2 pints of MEDIUM STOCK.

Mode.–Peel the cucumber, quarter it, and take out the seeds; cut it in thin slices, and put these on a plate with a little salt to draw the water from them; drain, and put them in your stewpan, with the butter. When they are warmed through, without being browned, pour the stock on them. Add the sorrel, chervil, and seasoning, and boil for 40 minutes. Mix the well-beaten yolks of the eggs with the cream, which add at the moment of serving.

Time.–1 hour.

— Soupe à la Flamande —
(FLEMISH)

Ingredients.–1 turnip, 1 small carrot, ¼ head of celery, 6 spring onions shredded very fine, 1 lettuce cut small, chervil, ½ teacupful of asparagus cut small, ½ teacupful of fresh peas, 2 oz. of butter, the yolks of 4 eggs, ¼ pint of cream, salt and sugar to taste, 4 pints of MEDIUM STOCK.

Mode.–Put the vegetables in the butter to stew gently for an hour with a teacupful of the stock; then add the remainder of the stock, and simmer for another hour. Now beat the yolks of the eggs well, mix with the cream (previously heated), and strain through a sieve. Take the soup off the heat, stir in the egg yolks, and keep stirring well. Bring it just to a boil, but do not leave off stirring, or the eggs will curdle. Season with salt, and add the sugar.

Time.–2½ hours.

Jerusalem Artichoke Soup

Ingredients.–3 slices of lean bacon or ham, ½ head of celery, 1 turnip, 1 onion, 3 oz. of butter, 4 lbs. of artichokes, 1 pint of boiling milk or ½ pint of very hot cream, salt and cayenne to taste, 1 teaspoonful of sugar, 5 pints of WHITE STOCK.

Mode.–Put the bacon and vegetables, which should be cut into thin slices, into the stewpan with the butter. Braise these for ¼ hour, keeping them well stirred. Wash and peel the artichokes, and after cutting them into thin slices, add them, with a pint of stock, to the other ingredients. When these have gently stewed down to a smooth pulp, put in the remainder of the stock. Stir it well, adding the seasoning, and when it has simmered for 5 minutes, pass it through a sieve. Now pour it back into the stewpan, let it again simmer 5 minutes, taking care to skim it well, and stir into it the boiling milk or hot cream. Serve with small sippets of bread fried in butter.

Time.–1 hour.

— S o u p e   à   l a   J u l i e n n e —

Ingredients.–4 large carrots, 2 large turnips, 1 large onion, 2 or 3 leeks, ½ head of celery, 1 lettuce, a little sorrel and chervil if liked, 2 oz. of butter, 4 pints of MEDIUM STOCK.

Mode.–Cut the vegetables into strips of about 1¼ inches long, and be particular they are all the same size, or some will be hard whilst the others will be done to a pulp. Cut the lettuce, sorrel, and chervil into larger pieces; fry the carrots in the butter, boil up the stock, and pour it on to them. When this is done, add all the other vegetables and herbs, and stew gently for at least 1 hour. Skim off all the fat, pour the soup over rounds of thin bread cut about the size of a shilling, and serve.

Time.–1½ hours.

Note.–In summer, green peas, asparagus tops, French beans, etc. can be added.

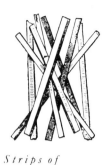

Strips of vegetable

SORREL is one of the spinaceous plants, which take their name from spinach, which is the chief among them. It is little used in English cookery, but a great deal in French, in which it is employed for soups, sauces, and salads. In English meadows it is usually left to grow wild, but in France, where it is cultivated, its flavour is greatly improved.

— O n i o n   S o u p —

Ingredients.–6 large onions, 2 oz. of butter, salt and pepper to taste, ¼ pint of cream, 2 pints of MEDIUM STOCK.

Mode.–Chop the onions and fry them in a pan with the butter; stir them occasionally, but do not let them brown. When tender, add the stock to them, and season; strain the soup, and add the cream, previously made very hot.

Time.–1½ hours.

Potage Printanier and Spanish Chestnut Soup

THE ONION.–Like the cabbage, this plant was erected into an object of worship by the idolatrous Egyptians 2,000 years before the Christian era, and it still forms a favourite food in the country of these people, as well as in other parts of Africa. In warmer climates it is much milder in its flavour. Although all the species have highly nutritive properties, they impart such a disagreeable odour to the breath that they are often rejected even where they are liked. Chewing a little raw parsley is said to remove this odour.

— *Green Pea Soup* —

Ingredients.–1 ½ lbs. of shelled green peas, ¼ lb. of butter, 2 or 3 thin slices of ham, 6 onions sliced, 4 shredded lettuces, 1 ½ teacupfuls of fresh breadcrumbs, ½ lb. of spinach, ½ teaspoonful of sugar, 2 pints of MEDIUM STOCK.

Mode.–Put the butter, ham, two-thirds of the shelled peas, the onions, and lettuces into a stewpan with 1 pint of the stock, and simmer for 1 hour; then add the remainder of the stock, with the breadcrumbs, and boil for another hour. Now boil the spinach, and squeeze it very dry. Rub the soup through a sieve, and the spinach with it, to colour it. Have ready the rest of the peas boiled; add them to the soup, put in the sugar, give one boil, and serve. If necessary, add salt.

Time.–2 ½ hours.

Note.–It will be well to add, if the peas are not quite young, a little sugar. Where economy is essential, water may be used instead of stock for this soup, boiling in it likewise the pea shucks, but use a double quantity of vegetables.

THE PEA was well known to the Romans and, probably, was introduced to Britain at an early period, for we find peas mentioned by Lydgate, a poet of the 15th century, as being hawked in London. They seem, however, for a considerable time, to have fallen out of use, for in the reign of Queen Elizabeth, Fuller tells us, they were brought from Holland and were accounted "fit dainties for ladies, they came so far and cost so dear". From the quantity of farinaceous and saccharine matter contained in the pea, it is highly nutritious as an article of food.

Potage Printanier, or — *Spring Soup* —

Ingredients.– ½ lb. of shelled green peas, a little chervil, 2 shredded lettuces, 2 onions, a very small bunch of parsley, 2 oz. of butter, the yolks of 3 eggs, 1 pint of water, seasoning to taste, 4 pints of MEDIUM STOCK.

Mode.–Put in a clean stewpan the peas, chervil, lettuces, onions, parsley and butter, with the water, and let them simmer till tender. Season with salt and pepper; when done, strain off the vegetables, and put two-thirds of the liquor they were boiled in to the stock. Beat up the yolks of the eggs with the other third, give it a toss over the heat, and at the moment of serving, add this, with the vegetables which you strained off, to the soup.

Time.– ¾ hour.

— *Spanish Chestnut Soup* —

Ingredients.– ¾ lb. of Spanish chestnuts, ¼ pint of cream, seasoning to taste of salt, cayenne, and mace, 2 pints of MEDIUM STOCK.

Mode.–Put the chestnuts into a large pan of warm water. As soon as this becomes too hot for the fingers to remain in it, take out the chestnuts, peel them quickly, immerse them in cold water, and wipe and weigh them. Now cover them with some of the stock, and stew them gently for rather more than ¾ hour, or until they break when touched with a fork; then drain, pound, and rub them through a fine sieve; add the rest of the stock, mace, cayenne, and salt, and stir it often until it boils. Take it off the heat and put in the cream.

Time.–Rather more than 1 hour.

THE CHESTNUT is said, by some, to have originally come from Sardis in Lydia, and by others from Castanea, a city of Thessaly, from which it takes its name. By the ancients it was much used as a food, and is still common in France and Italy, to which countries it is, by some, considered indigenous. The tree was introduced into Britain by the Romans, but it only flourishes in the warmer parts of the island, the fruit rarely arriving at maturity in Scotland. It attains a great age, as well as an immense size.

CHAPTER 3

Fish

IN NATURAL HISTORY, FISHES FORM THE FOURTH CLASS in the system of Linnaeus, and are described as having long under-jaws, eggs without white, organs of sense, fins for supporters, bodies covered with concave scales, gills to supply the place of lungs for respiration, and water for the natural element of their existence. Had mankind no other knowledge of animals than of such as inhabit the land and breathe their own atmosphere, they would listen with incredulous wonder if told that there were other kinds of beings which existed only in the waters, and which would die almost as soon as they were taken from them.

IN CHOOSING FISH, it is well to remember that it is possible it may be fresh, and yet not good. Nothing can be of greater consequence to a cook than to have fish good, as if this important course in a dinner does not give satisfaction, it is rarely that the repast goes off well.

In dressing fish of any kind, the first point to be attended to is to see that it be perfectly clean. It is a common error to wash it too much, as by doing so the flavour is diminished. If the fish is to be boiled, a little salt and vinegar should be put into the water, to give it firmness, after it is cleaned. Cod, whiting, and haddock are far better if a little salted, and kept a day.

Fish should be put into cold water if it is to be boiled or done in a fish kettle, and set on the heat to do very gently, or the outside will break before the inner part is done. Unless the fishes are small they should never be put into warm water; nor should water, either hot or cold, be poured on to the fish, as it is liable to break the skin. When the fish is ready it is easily separated from the bone. It should then be immediately taken out of the water, or it will become woolly.

If fish is to be fried, it must be dried after it is well cleaned and washed. Brush it over with egg, and sprinkle it with some fine crumbs of bread. If done a second time with the egg and bread, the fish will look so much the better. If required to be very nice, a sheet of absorbent paper must be placed to receive it, that it may be free from all grease. It must also be of a beautiful colour, and all the crumbs appear distinct. Butter gives a bad colour; lard and clarified dripping can be used, but oil is best. The fish should be put into the fat when boiling, and there should be a sufficiency of this to cover it.

When fish is broiled, or grilled, it must be seasoned, floured, and laid on a very clean gridiron which, when hot, should be rubbed with fat to prevent the fish from sticking.

In carving fish care should be taken to help it in perfect flakes, as if these are broken the beauty of the fish is lost. The carver should be acquainted, too, with the choicest parts and morsels, and to give each guest an equal share of these titbits should be his maxim.

We will conclude this portion of our subject with the following hints:

1. Fish shortly before they spawn are, in general, best in condition. When the spawning is just over, they are out of season, and less fit for human food.

2. When fish is out of season, it has a transparent, bluish tinge, however much it may be boiled; when it is in season, its muscles are firm, and boil white and curdy.

3. As food for invalids, white fish such as the ling, cod, haddock, coal-fish or coley, and whiting are the best; flat fish, such as soles, skate, turbot, and flounders are also good.

4. Salmon, mackerel, herrings, and trout soon spoil or decompose after they are killed; therefore, to be in perfection, they should be prepared for the table on the day they are caught. With flat fish, this is not of such consequence, as they will keep longer. The turbot, for example, is improved by being kept a day or two.

Fish carvers

Anchovy Butter and Fish Pie

THE AGE OF CARP.–This fish has been found to live 150 years. The pond in the garden of Emmanuel College, Cambridge, contained one that had lived there 70 years. Dr. Smith, in his *Tour on the Continent*, says, in reference to the Prince of Condé's seat at Chantilly: "The most pleasing things about it were the immense shoals of very large carp; when any passengers approached their watery habitation, they used to heave each other out of the water, begging for bread. They would even allow themselves to be handled."

— Anchovy Butter or Paste —

Ingredients.–2 dozen fresh anchovies, ½ lb. of butter.
Mode.–Wash the anchovies thoroughly; bone and wipe them dry, and pound them in a mortar to a paste. Mix the butter gradually with them, and rub the whole through a sieve. Put it by in small pots for use, carefully excluding the air with a layer of CLARIFIED BUTTER.

— Fried Anchovies —

Ingredients.–1 tablespoonful of olive oil, ½ glass of white wine, flour, 12 fresh anchovies.
Mode.–Mix the oil and wine together, with sufficient flour to make them into a thickish paste; cleanse the anchovies, wipe them, dip them in the paste, and fry a nice brown colour.
Time.– ½ hour. **Sufficient** for 3 persons.

— Anchovy Toast —

Mode.–Toast 2 or 3 slices of bread, or if wanted very savoury fry them in butter, and spread on them ANCHOVY BUTTER OR PASTE. Made mustard, or a few grains of cayenne, may be added to the paste before laying it on the toast.

— Cod à la Crème —

Ingredients.–1 large fillet of cod, 1 oz. of butter, 1 chopped shallot, a little minced parsley, ¼ teacupful of WHITE STOCK, ¼ pint of milk or cream, flour to thicken, cayenne and lemon juice to taste, ¼ teaspoonful of sugar.
Mode.–Boil the cod, and while hot, break it into flakes; put the butter, shallot, parsley, and stock into a stewpan, and let them boil for 5 minutes. Stir in sufficient flour to thicken, and add to it the milk or cream. Simmer for 10 minutes, add the cayenne and sugar, and, when liked, a little lemon juice. Put the fish in the sauce to warm gradually, but do not let it boil. Serve in a dish garnished with croûtons.
Time.–Rather more than ½ hour. **Sufficient** for 3 persons.

— Cod à l'Italienne —

Ingredients.–4 small fillets of cod, 1 shallot, 1 slice of ham minced very fine, ½ pint of WHITE STOCK, ½ teacupful of cream, salt to taste, a few drops of garlic vinegar, a little lemon juice, ½ teaspoonful of sugar.
Mode.–Chop the shallot, mince the ham very fine, pour on the stock, and simmer for 15 minutes. Add cream in the above proportion, and strain it through a fine sieve; season it, and put in the vinegar, lemon juice, and sugar. Now skin the cod fillets, which roll and tie round with string; boil them until just tender, remove the string, put them on the dish without breaking, and pour the sauce over them.
Time.–¾ hour. **Sufficient** for 4 persons.

THE ANCHOVY.– In his book of *British Fishes*, Mr. Yarrell states that "the anchovy is a common fish in the Mediterranean, from Greece to Gibraltar, and was well known to the Greeks and Romans, by whom the liquor prepared from it, called *garum*, was in great estimation. The fishing for them is carried on during the night, and lights are used with the nets. The anchovy has been taken on the Hampshire coast, and in the Bristol Channel."

BOILING COD.– Cod may be boiled whole, but a large head and shoulders are quite sufficient for a dish, and contain all that is usually helped, because, when the thick part is done, the tail is insipid and overdone. The latter, cut in slices, makes a very good dish for frying, or it may be salted down and served with an egg sauce and parsnips. Cod, when boiled quite fresh, is watery; salting it a little before cooking renders it firmer.

ANCHOVY PASTE.–This paste is usually eaten spread upon toast, and is said to form an excellent *bonne bouche*, which enables gentlemen at wine parties to enjoy their port with redoubled gusto. Unfortunately, in six cases out of ten, the only portion of these bought delicacies that contains anything indicative of anchovies is the paper label pasted on the bottle or pot, on which the word itself is printed.

THE HABITAT OF THE COD.–This fish is found only in the seas of the northern parts of the world, between the latitudes of 45° and 66°. Its great rendezvous are the sandbanks of Newfoundland, Nova Scotia, Cape Breton, and New England. These places are its favourite resorts, for there it is able to obtain great quantities of worms, a food peculiarly grateful to it. Another cause of its attachment to these places has been said to be on account of the vicinity to the polar seas, where it returns to spawn. Few are taken north of Iceland, and the shoals never reach so far south as the Straits of Gibraltar.

THE JOHN DORY OR DORU.–This fish is of a yellowish golden colour, and is, in general, rare, although it is sometimes taken in abundance on the Devon and Cornish coasts. It is highly esteemed for the table, and its flesh, when dressed, is of a beautiful clear white. Being a ground fish, it is not the worse for being kept two or even three days before it is cooked.

— S a l t   C o d —

Ingredients.–Sufficient water to cover the fish, ¼ pint of vinegar.

Mode.–Wash the fish, and lay it all night in water, with the vinegar. When thoroughly soaked, take it out, see that it is perfectly clean, and put it in the fish kettle with sufficient cold water to cover it. Heat it gradually, but do not let it boil much, or the fish will be hard. Skim well, and when done, drain the fish and put it on a napkin garnished with hard-boiled eggs cut in rings.

Time.–About 1 hour. **Sufficient** for 5 or 6 persons.

Note.–Serve with EGG SAUCE and parsnips.

— J o h n   D o r y —

Ingredients.–A large John Dory, ½ oz. of salt to each pint of water.

Mode.–This fish, which is esteemed by most people a great delicacy, is dressed in the same way as a turbot, which it resembles in firmness, but not in richness. Cleanse it thoroughly and cut off the fins; lay it in a fish kettle, cover with cold water, and add salt in the above proportion. Bring it gradually to a boil, and simmer gently for ¼ hour, or rather longer, should the fish be very large. Serve on a hot napkin, and garnish with lemon and parsley. LOBSTER, ANCHOVY, or SHRIMP SAUCE, and melted butter, should be sent to table with it.

Time.–After the water boils, ¼ to ½ hour, according to size.

— E e l   P i e —

Ingredients.–1 lb. of eels, a little chopped parsley, 1 shallot, grated nutmeg, pepper and salt to taste, the juice of ½ lemon, a small quantity of FORCEMEAT, ¼ pint of BECHAMEL, ½ lb. of PUFF PASTE.

Mode.–Skin and wash the eels, cut them into pieces 2 inches long, and line the bottom of the pie dish with FORCEMEAT. Put in the eels, and sprinkle them with the parsley, shallots, nutmeg, seasoning, and lemon juice, and cover with puff paste. Bake for 1 hour, or rather more; make the béchamel hot, and pour it into the pie.

Time.–Rather more than 1 hour. **Sufficient** for 3 or 4 persons.

THE COMMON EEL.–This fish is known frequently to quit its native element and to set off on a wandering expedition in the night, or just about the close of day, over the meadows in search of snails and other prey. It also, sometimes, betakes itself to isolated ponds, apparently for no other pleasure than that which may be supposed to be found in a change of habitation. This, of course, accounts for eels being found in waters which were never suspected to contain them.

— F i s h   C a k e —

Ingredients.–The remains of any cold fish, 1 onion, 1 bunch of sweet herbs, salt and pepper to taste, 1 pint of water, equal quantities of breadcrumbs and cold potatoes, ½ tablespoonful of chopped parsley, 1 egg, breadcrumbs.

Mode.–Pick the meat from the bones of the fish, which latter put, with the head and fins, into a stewpan with the water; add pepper and salt, the onion and herbs, and stew slowly for stock about 2 hours. Chop the fish fine, and mix it well with the breadcrumbs and cold potatoes, adding the parsley and seasoning; make the whole into a cake with the white of an egg, brush it over with egg, cover with breadcrumbs, and fry of a light brown; strain the stock, pour it over, and stew gently for ¼ hour, stirring it carefully once or twice. Serve hot, and garnish with slices of lemon and parsley.

Time.–½ hour, after the stock is made.

THE HADDOCK.– This fish migrates in immense shoals, and arrives on the Yorkshire coast about the middle of winter. It is an inhabitant of the northern seas of Europe, but does not enter the Baltic, and is not known in the Mediterranean. On each side of the body, just beyond the gills, it has a dark spot, which superstition asserts to be the impression of the finger and thumb of St. Peter, when he took the tribute money out of a fish of this species.

— Fish Pie —

Ingredients.–Any remains of cold fish, such as cod or haddock, pepper and salt to taste, breadcrumbs, ½ teaspoonful of grated nutmeg, 1 tablespoonful of finely chopped parsley.

Mode.–Clear the fish from the bones, and put a layer of it in a pie dish, which sprinkle with pepper and salt, then with a layer of breadcrumbs, nutmeg, and chopped parsley. Repeat this till the dish is quite full. You may form a covering either of breadcrumbs, which should be browned, or PUFF PASTE, which should be cut into long strips and laid in cross-bars over the fish, with a line of the paste first laid round the edge. Before putting on the top, pour in some plain melted butter, or a little thin WHITE SAUCE, and bake.

Time.–If made of cooked fish, ¼ hour; if made of fresh fish and puff paste, ¾ hour.

Note.–A nice little dish may be made by flaking any cold fish, adding a few oysters, seasoning with pepper and salt, and covering with mashed potatoes; 20 minutes will bake it.

— Baked Haddock —

Ingredients.–A small haddock, a nice FORCEMEAT, butter to taste, egg and breadcrumbs.

Mode.–Scale and clean the fish, without cutting it open much; put in a nice delicate forcemeat, and sew up the slit. Brush it over with egg, sprinkle over breadcrumbs, and bake, basting frequently with butter. Garnish with parsley and cut lemon, and serve with plain melted butter, or ANCHOVY SAUCE.

Time.–Large haddock, ¾ hour; moderate size, ½ hour.

Fresh Herring, Forcemeat for Baked Haddock, and Kedgeree

THE FINNAN HADDOCK.–This is the common haddock cured and dried, and takes its name from the fishing village of Findhorn, near Aberdeen, in Scotland, where the art has long attained to perfection. The haddocks are there hung up for a day or two in the smoke of peat, when they are ready for cooking, and are esteemed, by the Scotch, a great delicacy. In London, an imitation of them is made by washing the fish over with pyroligneous acid and hanging it up in a dry place for a few days.

— *Smoked Haddock* —

Ingredients.–2 lbs. of smoked haddock, 2 bayleaves, 1 small bunch of savoury herbs, not forgetting parsley, a little butter and pepper, boiling water.

Mode.–Skin and cut up the haddock into square pieces; make a basin hot by means of hot water, then pour the water out; lay in the fish, with the bayleaves and herbs; cover with boiling water; put a plate over to keep in the steam, and let it stand for 10 minutes. Take out the slices, put them in a hot dish, rub over with butter and pepper, and serve.

Time.–10 minutes. **Sufficient** for 4 or 5 persons.

— *Baked White Herrings* —

Ingredients.–12 small herrings, 4 bayleaves, 12 cloves, 12 allspice, 2 small blades of mace, cayenne pepper and salt to taste, sufficient vinegar to fill up the dish.

Mode.–Take the herrings, cut off the heads, and gut them. Put them in a pie dish, heads and tails alternately, and between each layer sprinkle over the above ingredients. Cover the fish with the vinegar, and bake for ½ hour, but do not serve till quite cold. The herrings may be cut down the front, the backbone taken out, and closed again. Sprats done in this way are very delicious.

Time.–½ hour. **Sufficient** for 6 persons.

Red Mullet and Grey Mullet

TO CHOOSE THE HERRING.–The more scales this fish has, the surer the sign of its freshness. It should also have a bright and silvery look; if red about the head, it is a sign that it has been dead for some time. The moment the herring is taken out of the water it dies, hence the origin of the common saying "dead as a herring".

— K e d g e r e e —

Ingredients.–Any cold fish, 1 teacupful of boiled rice, 1 oz. of butter, 1 teaspoonful of made mustard, 2 soft-boiled eggs, salt and cayenne to taste.

Mode.–Pick the fish carefully from the bones, mix with the other ingredients, and serve very hot. The quantities may be varied according to the amount of fish used.

Time.– ¼ hour after the rice is boiled. **Sufficient** for 2 persons.

— B r o i l e d   M a c k e r e l —

Ingredients.–4 small mackerel, pepper and salt, a little oil.

Mode.–Mackerel should never be washed when intended to be broiled or grilled, but merely wiped very clean and dry, after taking out the gills and insides. Open the back, and put in a little pepper, salt, and oil; broil under a hot grill, turning the fish over on both sides, and also on the back. When sufficiently cooked, the flesh can be detached from the bone, which will be in about 15 minutes for a small mackerel. Chop a little parsley, work it up in the butter, with pepper and salt to taste, and a squeeze of lemon juice, and put it in the back. Serve before the butter is quite melted, with MAITRE D'HOTEL SAUCE in a tureen.

Time.–Small mackerel 15 minutes. **Sufficient** for 4 persons.

— P i c k l e d   M a c k e r e l —

Ingredients.–4 mackerel, ½ pint of water, 12 peppercorns, 2 bayleaves, vinegar.

Mode.–Gently poach the mackerel after cleaning them and removing the heads; take half the liquor they were poached in, and add as much vinegar, with the peppercorns and bayleaves; boil for 10 minutes, and when cold, pour over the fish.

Time.– ½ hour. **Sufficient** for 4 persons.

— G r e y   M u l l e t —

Ingredients.–A grey mullet, ½ oz. of salt to each pint of water.

Mode.–If the fish be very large, it should be laid in cold salted water and gradually brought to a boil. Serve with ANCHOVY SAUCE and plain melted butter.

Time.–According to size, ¼ to ¾ hour.

— R e d   M u l l e t —

Ingredients.–4 red mullet, oiled paper, thickening of butter and flour, ½ teaspoonful of anchovy essence, 1 glass of sherry, cayenne and salt to taste.

Mode.–Clean the fish, take out the gills, but leave the inside, fold in oiled paper, and bake them in a moderate oven. When done, take the liquor that flows from the fish, add a thickening of butter kneaded with flour, put in the other ingredients, and let it boil for 2 minutes. Serve the sauce in a tureen, and the fish with or without the cases.

Time.–About 25 minutes. **Sufficient** for 4 persons.

TO CHOOSE MACKEREL.– In choosing this fish. purchasers should, to a great extent, be regulated by the brightness of its appearance. If it has a transparent, silvery hue, the flesh is good; if it be red about the head, it is stale. The mackerel is one of the most beautifully coloured fishes, when taken out of the sea, that we have. Death in some degree impairs the vivid splendour of its colours, but it does not entirely obliterate them.

THE STRIPED RED MULLET.– This fish was very highly esteemed by the ancients, especially by the Romans, who gave the most extravagant prices for it. Those of 2 pounds weight were valued at about £15 each; those of 4 pounds at £60, and, in the reign of Tiberius, three of them were sold for £209. To witness the changing loveliness of their colour during their dying agonies was one of the principal reasons that such a high price was paid for these fishes.

— Fish Scallop —

Ingredients.–Any cold fish, 1 egg, milk, 1 large blade of pounded mace, 1 tablespoonful of flour, 1 teaspoonful of anchovy essence, pepper and salt to taste, breadcrumbs, butter.

Mode.–Pick the fish carefully from the bones, and moisten with the milk and egg; add the other ingredients, and place in a deep dish or scallop shells; cover with breadcrumbs, butter the top, and brown in a hot oven; when quite hot, serve.

Time.–20 minutes.

MACE.–This is the membrane which surrounds the shell of the nutmeg. Its general qualities are the same as those of the nutmeg, producing an agreeable aromatic odour, with a hot and acrid taste. In *Beeton's Dictionary* we find that the four largest of the Banda Islands produce 150,000 pounds of it annually, which, with nutmegs, are their principal articles of export.

— Skate with Caper Sauce —
(A LA FRANÇAISE)

Ingredients.–2 or 3 lbs. of skate, ½ pint of vinegar, 2 oz. of salt, ½ teaspoonful of pepper, 1 sliced onion, a small bunch of parsley, 2 bayleaves, 2 or 3 sprigs of thyme, sufficient water to cover the fish, CAPER SAUCE.

Mode.–Put in a fish kettle all the above ingredients except the caper sauce, and simmer the skate in them till tender. When it is done, skin it neatly and pour over it some of the liquor in which it has been boiling. Drain it, put it on a hot dish, pour over it the caper sauce, and send some of the latter to table in a tureen.

Time.–½ hour. **Sufficient** for 5 or 6 people.

Note.–Skate may also be served with an onion sauce, or parsley and butter.

— To Bake Smelts —

Ingredients.–12 smelts, breadcrumbs, ¼ lb. of butter, 2 blades of pounded mace, salt and cayenne to taste, lemon juice.

Mode.–Wash the fish, then dry them thoroughly in a cloth, and arrange them nicely in a flat baking dish. Cover them with fine breadcrumbs, and place little pieces of butter all over them. Season, and bake for 15 minutes in a moderate oven. Just before serving, add a squeeze of lemon juice, and garnish with fried parsley and cut lemon.

Time.–¼ hour. **Sufficient** for 6 persons.

— Baked Soles —

Ingredients.–2 soles, ¼ lb. of butter, egg and breadcrumbs, minced parsley, 1 glass of sherry, lemon juice, cayenne and salt to taste.

Mode.–Clean, skin, and wash the fish, and dry them thoroughly in a cloth. Brush them over with egg, sprinkle with breadcrumbs mixed with a little minced parsley, and lay them in a large flat baking dish, white side uppermost; or if it will not hold the two soles, they may each be laid on a dish by itself, but they must not be put one on the top of the other. Melt the butter, and pour it over the whole, and bake for 20 minutes in a moderate oven. Take a portion of the liquor that flows from the fish, add the sherry, lemon juice, and seasoning, give it one boil, skim, pour it *under* the fish, and serve.

Time.–20 minutes. **Sufficient** for 4 or 5 persons.

TO CHOOSE SMELTS.–When good, this fish is of a fine silvery appearance, and when alive their backs are of a dark brown shade which, after death, fades to a light fawn. They ought to have a refreshing fragrance, resembling that of cucumber. This is a delicate little fish, and is in high esteem.

— Soles with Cream Sauce —

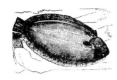

Ingredients.–2 soles, salt, cayenne, and pounded mace to taste, the juice of ½ lemon, salt and water, ½ pint of cream.

Mode.–Skin, wash, and fillet the soles, and divide each fillet in two pieces; lay them in cold salted water, which bring gradually to a boil. When the water boils, take out the fish, lay it in a clean stewpan, and cover with the cream. Add the seasoning, simmer very gently for 10 minutes and, just before serving, put in the lemon juice. The fillets may be rolled and secured by means of a skewer, but this is not so economical a way of dressing them, as double the quantity of cream is required.

Time.–10 minutes in the cream. **Sufficient** for 4 or 5 persons.

THE SOLE.–This fish should be both thick and firm. If the skin is difficult to take off, and the flesh looks grey, it is good. The sole ranks next to the turbot in point of excellence among our flat fish. It is abundant on the British coasts, but those of the western shores are much superior in size to those taken on the northern. The finest are caught in Torbay, and frequently weigh 8 or 10 pounds per pair. Its flesh, being firm, white, and delicate, is greatly esteemed.

Filleted Soles

— Fried Filleted Soles —

Ingredients.–2 large soles, egg and breadcrumbs, oil, lard, or clarified dripping.

Mode.–Soles for filleting should be large, as the flesh can be more easily separated from the bones, and there is less waste. The more usual way is to roll the fillets, after dividing each one in two pieces, and either bind them round with twine, or run a small skewer through them. Brush over with egg, and cover with breadcrumbs; put them in a deep pan, with plenty of heated fat so that it may neither scorch the fish nor make them sodden; when they are sufficiently cooked on one side, turn them carefully and brown them on the other. Lift them out carefully, and put them in a warm oven on soft paper to absorb the fat. Dish them on a hot napkin, and garnish with fried parsley and cut lemon.

Time.–About 10 minutes. **Sufficient** for 6 persons.

THE FLAVOUR OF THE SOLE.–This greatly depends on the nature of the ground and bait upon which the animal feeds. Its natural foods are small crabs and shellfish. Its colour also depends on the colour of the ground where it feeds, for if this be white, then the sole is called the white or lemon sole; but if the bottom be muddy, then it is called the black sole. Small-sized soles, caught in shallow water on the coasts, are the best in flavour.

— S p r a t s —

Ingredients.–2 dozen sprats, a little flour.

Mode.–Sprats should be cooked very fresh, which can be ascertained by their bright and sparkling eyes. Wipe them dry, fasten them in rows by a skewer run through the eyes, dredge with flour, and grill them under a hot grill, allowing them to cook for about 2 minutes on each side. Serve very hot.

Time.–3 or 4 minutes. **Sufficient** for 5 or 6 persons.

— S t e w e d T r o u t —

Ingredients.–2 middling-sized trout, ½ onion cut in thin slices, a little parsley, 2 cloves, 1 blade of mace, 2 bayleaves, a little thyme, salt and pepper to taste, 1 pint of MEDIUM STOCK, 1 glass of port, thickening of butter and flour.

Mode.–Wash the fish very clean, and wipe them quite dry. Lay them in a stewpan, with all the ingredients except the butter and flour, and simmer gently for ½ hour, or rather more should the fish be not quite done. Take them out, strain the liquor, add the thickening, and stir it over a high heat for 5 minutes; pour it over the trout, and serve.

Time.–According to size, ½ hour or more. **Sufficient** for 4 persons.

Note.–Trout may be served with ANCHOVY SAUCE or CAPER SAUCE, baked in buttered paper, or fried whole like smelts. Trout dressed à la Genevese is extremely delicate; for this proceed the same as with SALMON A LA GENEVESE.

— B a k e d F i l l e t s o f T u r b o t —

Ingredients.–The remains of cold turbot, LOBSTER SAUCE left from the preceding day, egg and breadcrumbs, cayenne and salt to taste, minced parsley, nutmeg, lemon juice, butter.

Mode.–After having cleared the fish from all skin and bone, divide it into square pieces of an equal size; brush them over with egg, and sprinkle with breadcrumbs mixed with a little minced parsley and seasoning. Lay the fish in a baking dish, with sufficient butter to baste with. Bake for ¼ hour in a moderate oven, and do not forget to keep the fish well moistened with the butter. Add a little lemon juice and grated nutmeg to the cold lobster sauce; make it hot, and pour over the fish, which must be well drained from the butter. Garnish with parsley and cut lemon.

Time.–Altogether, ½ hour.

— B o i l e d T u r b o t —

Ingredients.–A middling-sized turbot, ½ oz. of salt to each pint of water, lemon, lobster coral.

Mode.–Choose a moderate-sized turbot, for they are invariably the most valuable; if very large, the meat will be tough and thready. Three or four hours before dressing, soak the fish in salted water to take off the slime, then thoroughly wash it, and with a knife make an incision down the middle of the back, to prevent the skin of the belly from cracking. Rub it over with lemon, and be particular not to cut off the fins. Lay the fish in a very clean turbot kettle, with sufficient cold water to cover it, and salt in the above proportion. Let it gradually come to a boil, and skim very carefully; keep it gently simmering, and on no account let it boil fast, as the fish would have a very unsightly appearance. When the meat separates easily from the bone, it is done; then take it out, let it drain well, and dish it on a hot napkin. Rub a little lobster coral through a sieve, sprinkle it over the fish, and garnish with tufts of parsley and cut lemon. LOBSTER SAUCE or SHRIMP SAUCE, and plain melted butter, should be sent to table with it.

Time.–After the water boils, about ½ hour for a large turbot; about 20 minutes for one of middling size. **Sufficient**, if turbot is middling-sized, for 8 persons.

— *Whiting aux Fines Herbes* —

Ingredients.–6 small whiting, 1 bunch of sweet herbs chopped very fine, butter.

Mode.–Clean and skin the fish, fasten the tails in the mouths, and lay them in a baking dish. Mince the herbs very fine, strew them over the fish, and place small pieces of butter over; cover the dish, and let them cook in a moderate oven for ¼ hour or 20 minutes. Turn the fish once or twice, and serve with the butter and herbs poured over.

Time.–¼ hour or 20 minutes. **Sufficient** for 6 persons.

THE WHITING.– This fish forms a light, tender, and delicate food, easy of digestion, and should be chosen for the firmness of its flesh and the silvery hue of its appearance. It appears in our seas in the spring, within 3 miles of the shores, where it arrives in large shoals to deposit its spawn. It is usually between 10 and 12 inches long, and seldom exceeds 1 ½ pounds in weight. On the edge of the Dogger Bank, however, it has been caught so heavy as to weigh from 3 to 7 or 8 pounds.

Sprats, and Whiting aux Fines Herbes

WHITEBAIT.–
This highly esteemed little fish appears in innumerable multitudes in the river Thames, near Greenwich and Blackwall, during the month of July, when it forms, served with lemon and brown bread and butter, a tempting dish to vast numbers of Londoners, who flock to the various taverns of these places in order to gratify their appetites. The fish has been supposed be the fry of the shad, the sprat, the smelt, or the bleak. Mr. Yarrell, however, maintains that it is a species in itself, distinct from every other fish. When fried with flour, it is esteemed a great delicacy. The ministers of the crown have had a custom, for many years, of having a "whitebait dinner" just before the close of the session. It is invariably the precursor of the prorogation of Parliament, and the repast is provided by the proprietor of the Trafalgar at Greenwich.

— To Dress Whitebait —

Ingredients.–1 ½ lbs. of whitebait, a little flour, hot oil or lard, seasoning of salt.

Mode.–These little fish should be put into iced water as soon as bought, unless they are cooked immediately. Drain them from the water in a colander, and have ready a nice clean dry cloth, over which put 2 good handfuls of flour. Toss in the whitebait, shake them lightly in the cloth, and put them in a sieve to take away the superfluous flour. Throw them into a pan of boiling oil or lard, very few at a time, and let them fry till of a whitey-brown colour. Directly they are done, they must be taken out and laid in a warm oven for a minute or two on soft paper to absorb the fat. Dish them on a hot napkin, arranging the fish very high in the centre, and sprinkle a little salt over the whole.

Time.–3 minutes. **Sufficient** for 3 or 4 persons.

— To Dress Crab —

Ingredients.–A boiled crab, 2 tablespoonfuls of vinegar, 1 tablespoonful of oil, salt, white pepper, and cayenne to taste.

Mode.–Empty the shell and claws, thoroughly mix the meat with the above ingredients, and put it back in the shell. Garnish with slices of cut lemon and parsley. The quantity of oil may be increased if it is much liked.

Sufficient for 3 persons.

TO CHOOSE CRABS.–The middle-sized crab is the best and, like the lobster, should be judged by its weight; if light, it is watery.

Dressed Crab and Lobster Cutlets

THE CRAB TRIBE.–The whole of this tribe of animals have the body covered with a hard and strong shell, and live chiefly in the sea. Some, however, inhabit fresh waters, and a few live upon land. They feed variously, on aquatic or marine plants, small fish, molluscs, or dead bodies. The most remarkable feature in their history is the changing of their shells, and the regeneration of their broken claws. The former occurs once a year, usually between Christmas and Easter, when the crabs retire to cavities in the rocks, or conceal themselves under great stones.

— Hot Crab —

Ingredients.–A boiled crab, nutmeg, salt and pepper to taste, 3 oz. of butter, ¼ lb. of breadcrumbs, 3 tablespoonfuls of vinegar.

Mode.–Pick the meat out from the shell and claws, and mix with it the nutmeg and seasoning. Cut up the butter in small pieces, and add the breadcrumbs and vinegar. Mix all together, put the whole back in the shell, and brown in the oven.

Time.–20 minutes. **Sufficient** for 3 persons.

— To Boil Lobsters —

Ingredients.–Live lobsters, ¼ lb. of salt to each gallon of water.

Mode.–Buy the lobsters alive, and choose those that are heavy and full of motion, which is an indication of their freshness. When the shell is incrusted, it is a sign they are old. Medium-sized lobsters are the best. Have ready a stewpan of boiling water, salted in the above proportion; put in the lobsters, and keep them boiling quickly from 20 minutes to ¾ hour, according to size, and do not forget to skim well. If they boil too long, the meat becomes thready, and if not done enough, the shell is not red. Rub the shell over with a little butter or oil to make it brilliant.

Time.–Small lobsters, 20 minutes to ½ hour; large lobsters, ½ to ¾ hour.

— Lobster Cutlets —

Ingredients.–1 large hen lobster, boiled, 1 oz. of butter, a pinch of salt, pounded mace, grated nutmeg, cayenne and white pepper to taste, egg and breadcrumbs, BECHAMEL.

Mode.–Pick the meat from the head, body, and claws, and pound it in a mortar with the butter, and gradually add the mace and seasoning, well mixing the ingredients; beat all to a smooth paste, and add a little of the spawn; divide the mixture into pieces of an equal size, and shape them like cutlets. They should not be very thick. Brush them over with egg and sprinkle with breadcrumbs, and stick a short piece of small claw in the top of each; fry them a nice brown in hot oil or lard, and drain them in a warm oven on absorbent paper; arrange them nicely on a dish, and pour the béchamel in the middle, but not over the cutlets.

Time.–About 8 minutes after the cutlets are made. **Sufficient** for 5 or 6 persons.

— Hot Lobster —

Ingredients.–A hen lobster, boiled, 2 oz. of butter, grated nutmeg, salt, pepper, pounded mace, breadcrumbs, 2 eggs.

Mode.–Pound the meat of the lobster to a smooth paste with the butter and seasoning, and add a few breadcrumbs. Beat in the eggs, and make the whole mixture into the form of a lobster; pound the spawn, and sprinkle over it. Bake ¼ hour in a moderate oven, and just before serving, lay over it the tail and body shell, with the small claws underneath, to resemble a lobster.

Time.–¼ hour. **Sufficient** for 4 or 5 persons.

THE LOBSTER.– This is one of the crab tribe, and is found on most of the rocky coasts of Great Britain. Some are caught with the hand, but the larger number in pots, which serve all the purposes of a trap, being made of osiers and baited with garbage. They are shaped so that when the lobsters once enter them, they cannot get out again. They are fastened to a cord and sunk in the sea, and their place marked by a buoy.

Lobster Salad and Fried Oysters

BRILLAT-SAVARIN, in his clever and amusing volume, *The Physiology of Taste*, says that towards the end of the 18th century it was a most common thing for a well-arranged entertainment in Paris to commence with oysters, and that many guests were not contented without swallowing twelve dozen. Being anxious to know the weight of this advance guard, he ascertained that a dozen oysters, fluid included, weighed 4 ounces, thus the twelve dozen would weigh about 3 pounds. And there can be no doubt that the same persons who made no worse a dinner on account of having partaken of the oysters would have been completely satisfied if they had eaten the same weight of chicken or mutton.

— *Lobster Salad* —

Ingredients.–A hen lobster, boiled, lettuces, endive, small salad greens (whatever is in season), a little chopped beetroot, 2 hard-boiled eggs, a few slices of cucumber. For the dressing allow equal quantities of oil and vinegar, 1 teaspoonful of made mustard, the yolks of 2 eggs, cayenne and salt to taste, ¼ teaspoonful of anchovy essence; these ingredients should be mixed perfectly smooth and form a creamy-looking sauce.

Mode.–Wash the salad vegetables, and thoroughly dry them by shaking in a cloth. Cut up the lettuces and endive, pour the dressing on them, and lightly throw in the small salad greens. Mix all well together with the pickings from the body of the lobster; pick the meat from the tail, cut it up into nice square pieces, put half in the salad, and the other half reserve for garnishing. Separate the yolks from the whites of the hard-boiled eggs; chop the whites very fine and rub the yolks through a sieve, and afterwards the coral from the inside. Arrange the salad lightly on a glass dish, and garnish, first with a row of sliced cucumber, then with the pieces of lobster, the yolks and whites of the eggs, coral, and beetroot placed alternately, and arranged in small separate bunches.

Sufficient for 5 or 6 persons.

Note.–A few crayfish make a pretty garnishing to lobster salad.

TO CHOOSE LOBSTERS.–This shellfish, if it has been cooked alive, as it ought to have been, will have a stiffness in the tail, which, if gently raised, will return with a spring. In order to be good, lobsters should be weighty for their bulk; if light, they will be watery; and those of the medium size are always the best. Small-sized lobsters are cheapest, and answer very well for sauce.

THE EDIBLE
OYSTER.–This
shellfish is almost
universally distributed
near the shores of seas
in all latitudes, and
they especially abound
on the coasts of France
and Britain. The coasts
most celebrated, in
England, for them are
those of Essex and
Suffolk. Here they are
dredged up by means
of a net with an iron
scraper at the mouth,
that is dragged by a
rope from a boat over
the beds. As soon as
taken from their native
beds, they are stored in
pits, formed for the
purpose, furnished
with sluices, through
which, at the spring
tides, the water is
suffered to flow. This
water, being stagnant,
soon becomes green in
warm weather; and, in
a few days afterwards,
the oysters acquire the
same tinge, which
increases their value in
the market. They do
not, however, attain
their perfection and
become fit for sale till
the end of six or eight
weeks. Oysters are not
considered proper for
the table till they are
about a year and a
half old.

— Fried Oysters —

Ingredients.–3 dozen oysters, 2 oz. of butter, 1 tablespoonful of tomato paste, a little chopped lemon peel, ½ teaspoonful of chopped parsley.

Mode.–Boil the oysters for 1 minute in their own liquor and drain them; fry them with the butter, tomato paste, lemon peel, and parsley; lay them on a dish, and garnish with fried potatoes, toasted sippets of bread, and parsley. This is a favourite Italian dish.

Time.–5 minutes. **Sufficient** for 4 persons.

— Oysters Fried in Batter —

Ingredients.–3 dozen oysters, 2 eggs, ½ pint of milk, flour, pepper and salt to taste, a little nutmeg, hot oil.

Mode.–Prise open the shells and scoop out the oysters, which scald in their own liquor, and lay on a cloth to drain thoroughly. Break the eggs into a basin; mix the flour with them, adding the milk gradually, with nutmeg and seasoning, to make a batter; put the oysters in the batter. Make some oil hot in a deep frying-pan, and put in the oysters, one at a time; when done, take them up with a sharp-pointed skewer, and dish them on a napkin. Fried oysters are frequently used for garnishing boiled fish, and then a few breadcrumbs should be added to the flour.

Time.–5 or 6 minutes. **Sufficient** for 3 persons.

— Scalloped Oysters —

Ingredients.–5 or 6 dozen oysters, 1 oz. of butter, flour, 2 tablespoonfuls of WHITE STOCK, 2 tablespoonfuls of cream, pepper and salt to taste, breadcrumbs, plain melted butter, scallop shells.

Mode.–Prise open the shells, scoop out the oysters, scald them in their own liquor, and strain the liquor free from grit. Put 1 oz. of butter into a stewpan; when melted, dredge in sufficient flour to dry it up; add the stock, cream, and strained liquor, and give one boil. Put in the oysters and seasoning; let the oysters gradually heat through, but not boil. Have ready the scallop shells buttered; lay in the oysters and as much of the liquid as they will hold; cover them over with breadcrumbs, over which drop a little melted butter. Brown them in the oven or under the grill, and serve quickly, and very hot.

Time.–Altogether, ¼ hour. **Sufficient** for 5 or 6 persons.

Buttered Prawns or Shrimps

Ingredients.–1 pint of shelled prawns or shrimps, ¾ pint of MEDIUM STOCK, thickening of butter and flour, salt, cayenne, and nutmeg to taste.

Mode.–Put the prawns or shrimps in a stewpan with the stock; add a thickening of butter and flour, season, and simmer gently for 3 minutes. Serve on a dish garnished with fried bread or toasted sippets of bread. CREAM SAUCE may be substituted for the stock.

Time.–3 minutes. **Sufficient** for 3 persons.

TO KEEP
OYSTERS.–Put
the oysters, unopened,
in a tub, and cover
them with salt and
water. Let them
remain for 12 hours,
when they are to be
taken out and allowed
to stand for another
12 hours without
water. If left without
water every alternate
12 hours, they will be
much better than if
constantly kept in it.
Never put the same
water twice to them.

THE SHRIMP.–
This shellfish is
smaller than the
prawn, and is greatly
relished in London as a
delicacy. It inhabits
most of the sandy
shores of Europe, and
the Isle of Wight is
especially famous
for it.

CHAPTER 4

Sauces

Pickles, Gravies, and Forcemeats

THE PREPARATION AND APPEARANCE OF SAUCES AND GRAVIES are of the highest consequence, and in nothing does the talent and taste of the cook more display itself. Their special adaptability to the various viands they are to accompany cannot be too much studied, in order that they may harmonize and blend with them as perfectly, so to speak, as does a pianoforte accompaniment with the voice of the singer.

The general basis of most gravies and some sauces is the same stock as that used for soups, and, by the employment of this with perhaps an additional slice of ham, a little spice, a few herbs, and a slight flavouring from some cold sauce or ketchup, very nice gravies and sauces may be made for a very small expenditure.

Sauces should possess a decided character, and whether sharp or sweet, savoury or plain, they should carry out their names in a distinct manner, although of course not so much flavoured as to make them too piquant on the one hand, or too mawkish on the other. Brown sauces, generally speaking, should scarcely be so thick as white sauces.

Sauces should be sent to table very hot. Those sauces of which cream or eggs form a component part should be well stirred as soon as these ingredients are added to them, and must never be allowed to boil, as they would instantly curdle.

ALTHOUGH PICKLES MAY BE PURCHASED at shops at as low a price as they can usually be made for at home, or perhaps even for less, yet we would advise all housewives who have sufficient time and convenience to prepare their own. The only general rules worth stating here are that the vegetables and fruits used should be sound, and not over-ripe, and that the very best vinegar should be employed.

FOR FORCEMEATS, SPECIAL ATTENTION IS NECESSARY. The points which should be more particularly observed are the thorough chopping of the meat or suet, the complete mincing of the herbs, the careful grating of the breadcrumbs, and the perfect mixing of the whole. Nothing like a lump or fibre should be anywhere perceptible, and the flavour of no one spice or herb should be permitted to predominate.

Aspic

Ingredients.–4 lbs. of knuckle of veal, 1 cow heel, 3 or 4 slices of ham, any poultry trimmings, 2 carrots, 1 onion, 1 bunch of savoury herbs, 1 glass of sherry, 6 pints of water, seasoning to taste of salt and whole white pepper, 3 eggs.

Mode.–Lay the ham in the bottom of a stewpan, cut up the veal and cow heel into small pieces, and lay them on the ham; add the poultry trimmings, vegetables, herbs, sherry, and water, and let the whole simmer very gently for 4 hours, carefully taking away all scum that may rise to the surface; strain through a fine sieve, and pour into a pan to get cold. Have ready a clean stewpan, put in the jelly, and be particular to leave the sediment behind, or it will not be clear. Add the whites of 3 eggs, with salt and pepper, to clarify it; keep stirring over the heat till the whole becomes very white, then draw it to the side, and let it stand till clear. When this is the case, strain it through a cloth or jelly bag, and use it for moulding poultry, etc.

Time.–Altogether, 4½ hours.

Béchamel, or French White Sauce

Ingredients.–1 small bunch of parsley, 2 cloves, ½ bayleaf, a small bunch of savoury herbs, salt to taste, 3 or 4 mushrooms, when obtainable, 2 pints of WHITE STOCK, 1 pint of cream, 1 tablespoonful of arrowroot.

Mode.–Put the stock into a stewpan, with the parsley, cloves, bayleaf, herbs, and mushrooms; add a seasoning of salt, but no pepper, as that would give the sauce a dusty appearance. When it has boiled long enough to extract the flavour of the herbs, etc., strain it, and boil it up quickly again, until it is nearly half reduced. Now mix the arrowroot smoothly with the cream, and let it simmer very gently for 5 minutes over a very low heat; add to it the reduced stock, and continue to simmer slowly for 10 minutes. This is the foundation of many kinds of sauces, especially white sauces.

Time.–Altogether, 2 hours.

Béchamel Maigre
(WITHOUT MEAT)

Ingredients.–2 onions, 1 blade of mace, mushroom trimmings, a small bunch of parsley, 1 oz. of butter, 1 oz. of flour, ½ pint of water, 1 pint of milk, salt, the juice of ½ lemon, 2 eggs.

Mode.–Put in a stewpan the milk and water, with the onions, mace, mushrooms, parsley, and salt. Let these simmer gently for 20 minutes. In the meantime, rub together the flour and butter, add it to the liquor, and stir well till it boils up; then place it on a low heat and continue stirring until it is perfectly smooth. Now strain it through a sieve into a basin, after which put it back in the stewpan and add the lemon juice. Beat up the yolks of the eggs with about 4 dessertspoonfuls of milk; strain this into the sauce, stirring it all the while, but do not let it boil lest it curdle.

Time.–Altogether, ¾ hour.

— General Stock for Gravies —

MEDIUM STOCK or WHITE STOCK will be found to answer very well for the basis of many gravies, unless these are wanted very rich indeed. By the addition of various store sauces, thickening and flavouring, the stocks referred to above may be converted into very good gravies. It should be borne in mind, however, that the goodness and strength of spices, wines, flavourings, etc., evaporate, and that they lose a great deal of their fragrance if added to the gravy a long time before they are wanted. The remains of roast meat gravy should always be saved, as, when no meat is at hand, a very nice gravy in haste may be made from it, and added to hashes, ragoûts, etc.

The capsicum

CAYENNE.–This is the most acrid and stimulating spice with which we are acquainted, and is prepared from several varieties of the capsicum. It is from the ripe pods of *Capsicum baccatum*, the bird pepper, that the best cayenne is made.

— Melted Butter —

Ingredients.–¼ lb. of butter, 1 dessertspoonful of flour, 1 wineglassful of water, salt to taste.

Mode.–Cut the butter up into small pieces, put it in a saucepan over a low heat, dredge over the flour, and add the water and a seasoning of salt; stir it *one way* constantly till the whole of the ingredients are melted and thoroughly blended. Let it just boil, when it is ready to serve. If the butter is to be melted with cream, use the same quantity as of water, but omit the flour; keep stirring, but do not allow it to boil.

Time.–1 minute to simmer.

— Brown Roux —
(A FRENCH THICKENING FOR GRAVIES AND SAUCES)

Ingredients.–6 oz. of butter, 6 oz. of flour.

Mode.–Melt the butter in a stewpan over a low heat, and dredge in, very gradually, the flour; stir it till a light brown colour, but do this very slowly, otherwise the flour will burn and impart a bitter taste to any sauce it is mixed with. Pour in a jar and keep for use; it will remain good some time.

Time.–About ½ hour. **Sufficient**, if 1 tablespoonful is used, to thicken ¾ pint of sauce or gravy.

— White Roux —
(FOR THICKENING WHITE SAUCES)

Ingredients.–6 oz. of butter, 6 oz. of flour.

Mode.–Proceed in the same manner as for BROWN ROUX, but do not keep it on the heat too long, and take care not to let it colour. This is used for thickening white sauces. Pour it into a jar to use when wanted.

Time.–¼ hour. **Sufficient**, if 1 tablespoonful is used, to thicken ¾ pint of sauce or gravy.

— Anchovy Sauce for Fish —

Ingredients.–4 fresh anchovies, 1 oz. of butter, ½ pint of plain melted butter, cayenne to taste.

Mode.–Bone the anchovies, and pound them in a mortar to a paste with 1 oz. of butter. Make the melted butter hot, stir in the pounded anchovies and cayenne; simmer for 3 or 4 minutes, and if liked, add a squeeze of lemon juice. Serve hot.

Time.–5 minutes. **Sufficient**, this quantity, for a brill or a turbot.

— Apple Sauce —

Ingredients.–3 good-sized cooking apples, sugar to taste, a piece of butter the size of a walnut, water.

Mode.–Pare, core, and quarter the apples, and throw them into cold water to preserve their whiteness. Put them in a saucepan, with sufficient water to moisten them, and boil till soft enough to pulp. Beat them up, adding sugar to taste and a small piece of butter.

Time.–Depending on the size of the apples, about ¾ hour.

— Bread Sauce —

Ingredients.–1 pint of milk, ¼ lb. of stale white breadcrumbs, 1 onion, pounded mace, cayenne, and salt to taste, 1 oz. of butter.

Mode.–Peel and quarter the onion, and simmer it in the milk till perfectly tender. Put the breadcrumbs into a saucepan, strain the milk over them, cover them up, and let them stand for an hour to soak. Now beat them up with a fork very smoothly, add a seasoning of pounded mace, cayenne, and salt, and the butter, boil, and serve.

Time.–Altogether, 1¾ hours. **Sufficient** for a pair of fowls.

— Browned Butter —

Ingredients.–¼ lb. of butter, 1 tablespoonful of minced parsley, 3 tablespoonfuls of vinegar, salt and pepper to taste.

Mode.–Put the butter into a frying-pan over a high heat, and when it begins to smoke, throw in the parsley, and add the vinegar and seasoning. Let the whole simmer for a minute or two, when it is ready to serve. This is a very good sauce for skate.

Time.–¼ hour.

— Maître d' Hôtel Butter —

(FOR PUTTING INTO BROILED OR GRILLED FISH)

Ingredients.–¼ lb. of butter, 2 dessertspoonfuls of minced parsley, salt and pepper to taste, the juice of 1 large lemon.

Mode.–Work the above ingredients well together with a wooden spoon. If this is used as a sauce, melt it and pour either under or over the meat or fish it is intended to be served with.

Note.–4 tablespoonfuls of BECHAMEL, and 2 tablespoonfuls of WHITE STOCK with 2 oz. of the above butter stirred into it and allowed to simmer for 1 minute, make an excellent hot maître d'hôtel sauce.

PARSLEY.–This pretty aromatic herb was used in ancient times, as we learn from mythological narrative, to adorn the head of a hero, no less than Hercules. According to Homer's *Iliad*, warriors fed their chariot steeds on parsley; and Pliny acquaints us with the fact that, as a symbol of mourning, it was admitted to furnish the funeral tables of the Romans. Egypt, some say, first produced this herb; thence it was introduced, by some unknown voyager, into Sardinia, where the Carthaginians found it, and made it known to the inhabitants of Marseilles.

— Caper Sauce for Fish —

Ingredients.– ½ pint of MELTED BUTTER, 3 dessertspoonfuls of pickled capers, 1 dessertspoonful of their liquor, salt and pepper to taste, 1 tablespoonful of anchovy essence.

Mode.–Cut the capers once or twice, but do not chop them fine; put them in a saucepan with the melted butter, and add all the other ingredients. Keep stirring the whole until it just simmers, when it is ready to serve.

Time.–1 minute to simmer. **Sufficient** to serve with a skate or 1 ½ to 2 lbs. of salmon.

Celery Sauce for Boiled — Turkey, Poultry, etc. —

Ingredients.–6 heads of celery, 1 pint of WHITE STOCK, 2 blades of mace, 1 small bunch of savoury herbs, thickening of butter and flour, or arrowroot, ½ pint of cream, lemon juice.

Mode.–Boil the celery in salt and water until tender, and cut it into pieces 2 inches long. Put the stock into a stewpan with the mace and herbs, and let it simmer for ½ hour to extract their flavour. Then strain the stock, add the celery and a thickening of butter kneaded with flour or, what is still better, with arrowroot; just before serving, add the cream, boil it up, and squeeze in a little lemon juice. If necessary, add a seasoning of salt and white pepper.

Time.–25 minutes to boil the celery. **Sufficient** for a boiled turkey.

CAPERS.–These are the unopened buds of a low trailing shrub which grows wild among the crevices of the rocks in Greece, as well as in northern Africa; the plant, however, has come to be cultivated in Sicily, Italy, and the south of France, from whence the best capers are imported.

ARROWROOT.– This nutritious flour is obtained from the roots of a plant which is cultivated in both the East and West Indies. When the roots are about a year old, they are dug up and, after being well washed, are beaten to a pulp, which is afterwards, by means of water, separated from the fibrous part. After being passed through a sieve, once more washed, and then suffered to settle, the sediment is dried in the sun, when it becomes flour. The best is obtained from the West Indies, but a large quantity of what is sold in London is adulterated with potato starch.

Skate with Browned Butter, and Trout with Maître d'Hôtel Butter

Chestnut Sauce for Poultry

Ingredients.–½ lb. of fresh chestnuts, ½ pint of WHITE STOCK, 2 strips of lemon peel, cayenne to taste, ¼ pint of cream or milk.

Mode.–Peel off the outside skin of the chestnuts and put them into boiling water for a few minutes; take off the thin inside peel, and put them into a saucepan with the white stock and lemon peel, and let them simmer for 1½ hours, or until they are quite tender. Rub the whole through a fine sieve with a wooden spoon; add seasoning and the cream; let the sauce just simmer, but not boil, and keep stirring all the time. Serve very hot, and quickly. If milk is used instead of cream, a very small quantity of flour and butter thickening may be required.

Time.–Altogether, nearly 2 hours. **Sufficient** for a turkey.

Cream Sauce for Fish or — White Dishes —

Ingredients.–⅓ pint of cream, 2 oz. of butter, 1 teaspoonful of flour, salt and cayenne to taste, a small quantity of pounded mace or lemon juice when liked.

Mode.–Put the butter in a very clean saucepan, dredge in the flour, and keep shaking round till the butter is melted. Add the seasoning and cream, and stir the whole till it boils; let it just simmer for 5 minutes, when add either pounded mace or lemon juice to taste, to give it a flavour.

Time.–5 minutes to simmer.

— Dutch Sauce for Fish —

Ingredients.– ½ teaspoonful of flour, 2 oz. of butter, 4 tablespoonfuls of vinegar, the yolks of 2 eggs, the juice of ½ lemon, salt to taste.

Mode.–Put all the ingredients, except the lemon juice, into a stewpan; set it on the heat, and keep continually stirring. When it has thickened, take it off, as it should not boil. If, however, it happens to curdle, strain the sauce through a sieve. Add the lemon juice, and serve. Tarragon vinegar may be used instead of plain, and by many is considered far preferable.

Time.–10 minutes to thicken.

— Egg Sauce for Salt Fish —

Ingredients.–4 eggs, ½ pint of MELTED BUTTER, a little lemon juice if liked.

Mode.–Boil the eggs until quite hard, which will be in about 20 minutes, and put them into cold water for ½ hour. Strip off the shells, chop the eggs into small pieces, but not too fine. Make the melted butter very smoothly, and when it boils, stir in the eggs and serve very hot. Lemon juice may be added at pleasure.

Time.–20 minutes to boil the eggs. **Sufficient**, this quantity, for 3 or 4 lbs. of fish.

LEMON JUICE.– Citric acid is the principal component of lemon juice, which, in addition to the agreeableness of its flavour, is also particularly cooling and grateful. It is likewise an anti-scorbutic, and this quality enhances its value. In order to combat the fatal effects of scurvy amongst the crews of ships at sea, a regular allowance of lemon juice is served out to the men, and by this practice the disease has almost entirely disappeared. By putting the juice into bottles, and pouring on the top sufficient oil to cover it, it may be preserved for a considerable time. Italy and Turkey export great quantities of it in this manner.

Turbot with Cream Sauce, and Dutch Sauce

— E s p a g n o l e S a u c e —

Ingredients.–2 slices of lean ham, 1 lb. of pie veal, 1½ pints of WHITE STOCK, 2 or 3 sprigs of parsley, ½ bayleaf, 2 or 3 sprigs of savoury herbs, 6 spring onions, 3 shallots, 2 cloves, 1 blade of mace, 2 glasses of sherry or Madeira, thickening of butter and flour.

Mode.–Cut up the ham and veal into small square pieces, and put them into a stewpan. Moisten these with ½ pint of the stock, and simmer till the stock has reduced by half, when add the remainder of the stock, with the spices, herbs, shallots, and onions, and simmer very gently for 1 hour. Strain and skim off every particle of fat, and when required for use, thicken with butter and flour, or with a little BROWN ROUX. Add the wine, and if necessary a seasoning of cayenne, when it will be ready to serve.

Time.–1½ hours.

G r e e n S a u c e f o r Y o u n g — *G e e s e o r D u c k l i n g s* —

Ingredients.–¼ pint of sorrel or spinach juice, 1 glass of sherry, ½ lb. of green gooseberries, 1 teaspoonful of pounded sugar, 1 oz. of fresh butter.

Mode.–Boil the gooseberries in water until they are quite tender; mash them and press them through a sieve; put the pulp into a saucepan with the above ingredients; simmer for 3 or 4 minutes, and serve very hot.

Time.–3 or 4 minutes.

SORREL.–We gather from the pages of Pliny and Apicius that the Romans partook of sorrel, sometimes stewed with mustard and seasoned with a little oil and vinegar. The acid of sorrel is very *prononcé*.

H ORSERADISH has been, for many years, a favourite accompaniment of roast beef, and is a native of England. It grows wild in wet ground, but has long been cultivated in the garden, and is occasionally used in winter salads and in sauces. On account of the great volatility of its oil, it should never be preserved by drying, but should be kept moist by being stored in sand.

Mushroom Sauce for Fowls and Rabbits, and ingredients for Green Sauce

L EMON THYME.– Two or three tufts of this species of thyme usually find a place in the herb compartment of the kitchen garden. It is a trailing evergreen, is of smaller growth than the common kind, and is remarkable for its smell, which closely resembles that of the rind of a lemon, hence its distinctive name. It is used in dishes in which the fragrance of the lemon is desired to slightly predominate.

— *Horseradish Sauce* —
(TO SERVE WITH ROAST BEEF)

Ingredients.–4 tablespoonfuls of grated horseradish, 1 teaspoonful of sugar, 1 teaspoonful of salt, ½ teaspoonful of pepper, 2 teaspoonfuls of made mustard, vinegar.

Mode.–Grate the horseradish and mix it well with the sugar, salt, pepper, and mustard; moisten it with sufficient vinegar to give it the consistency of cream, and serve in a tureen. Added to the above, 3 or 4 tablespoonfuls of cream very much improve the appearance and flavour of this sauce. To heat it to serve with hot roast beef, put it in a *bain marie*, or in a jar, which place in a saucepan of boiling water; make it hot, but do not allow it to boil, or it will curdle.

Lemon Sauce for Boiled Fowls

Ingredients.–1 small lemon, ¾ pint of MELTED BUTTER.

Mode.–Cut the lemon into very thin slices, and these again into very small dice. Have ready ¾ pint of melted butter sauce; put in the lemon; let it just simmer, but not boil, and pour it over the fowls.

Time.–1 minute to simmer. **Sufficient** for a pair of large fowls.

S HALLOT.–This plant is supposed to have been introduced to England by the Crusaders, who found it growing wild in the vicinity of Ascalon. It is a bulbous root, and when full grown, its leaves wither. Taken up in the autumn and dried in the house, it will keep till spring. It is called by old authors the "barren onion", and is used in sauces and pickles, soups and made dishes, and as an accompaniment to chops and steaks.

— Lobster Sauce —
(TO SERVE WITH TURBOT, SALMON, BRILL, ETC.)

Ingredients.–1 middling-sized hen lobster, boiled, ¾ pint of MELTED BUTTER, 1 tablespoonful of anchovy essence, ½ oz. of butter, salt and cayenne to taste, a little pounded mace when liked, 2 or 3 tablespoonfuls of cream.

Mode.–Choose a hen lobster, as this is indispensable in order to render this sauce as good as it ought to be. Pick the meat from the body, tail, and claws, and cut it into small pieces; put the spawn, which will be found under the tail of the lobster, into a mortar with ½ oz. of butter, and pound it quite smooth; rub it through a sieve and cover up till wanted. Make the melted butter; add to it all the ingredients except the lobster meat, and well mix the sauce before the lobster is added to it as it should not come to table shredded and ragged. Put in the meat and let it get thoroughly hot, but do not allow it to boil, as the colour would immediately be spoiled; for it should be remembered that this sauce should always have a bright red appearance. If it is intended to be served with turbot or brill, a little of the spawn (dried and rubbed through a sieve without butter) should be saved to garnish with, but as the goodness, flavour, and appearance of the sauce so much depend on having a proper quantity of spawn, the less used for garnishing the better.

Time.–1 minute to simmer. **Sufficient** to serve with a small turbot, a brill, or a salmon for 6 persons.

— Mint Sauce —
(TO SERVE WITH ROAST LAMB)

Ingredients.–4 dessertspoonfuls of chopped mint, 2 dessertspoonfuls of sugar, ¼ pint of vinegar.

Mode.–Wash the mint, which should be young and freshly gathered, free from grit; pick the leaves from the stalks, mince them very fine, and put them into a tureen; add the sugar and vinegar, and stir till the former is dissolved. This sauce is better by being made 2 or 3 hours before wanted for table.

Sufficient to serve with a middling-sized joint of lamb.

A Very Rich and Good — Mushroom Sauce —
(TO SERVE WITH FOWLS OR RABBITS)

Ingredients.–½ lb. of mushroom buttons, salt to taste, a little grated nutmeg, 1 blade of pounded mace, 1 pint of cream, 2 oz. of butter, flour to thicken.

Mode.–Rub the buttons with a rough cloth and a little salt to take off the skin; put them in a stewpan with the above ingredients, previously kneading together the butter and flour; boil the whole for about 10 minutes, stirring all the time. Pour some of the sauce over the fowls or rabbits, and the remainder serve in a tureen.

Time.–10 minutes. **Sufficient** to serve with a pair of fowls.

MINT.–The common mint cultivated in our gardens is employed in different culinary processes, being sometimes boiled with certain dishes and afterwards withdrawn. It has an agreeable aromatic flavour, and forms an ingredient in soups, and sometimes is used in spring salads. It is valuable as a stomachic and anti-spasmodic, on which account it is generally served at table with pea soup.

HISTORY OF THE ONION.–It is not supposed that any variety of the onion is indigenous to Britain, as when the large and mild roots imported from warmer climates have been cultivated in these islands a few years they deteriorate both in size and sweetness.

French Onion Sauce, or Soubise

Ingredients.– ½ pint of BECHAMEL, 1 bayleaf, seasoning to taste of pounded mace and cayenne, 6 onions, a small piece of ham.

Mode.–Peel the onions and cut them in halves; put them in a stewpan, with just sufficient water to cover them, and add the bayleaf, ham, cayenne, and mace; be careful to keep the lid closely shut, and simmer them until tender. Take them out and drain them roughly; rub them through a sieve, and add them to the béchamel; stir over a moderate heat until it boils, when serve. If it should require any more seasoning, add it to taste.

Time.–¾ hour to boil the onions.

— White Onion Sauce —

Ingredients.–9 large onions, or 12 middling-sized ones, 1 pint of MELTED BUTTER made with milk rather than water, ½ teaspoonful of salt.

Mode.–Peel the onions and put them into water, to which a little salt has been added, to preserve their whiteness, and let them remain for ¼ hour. Then put them in a stewpan, cover them with water, and let them boil until tender; if they should be very strong, change the water after they have been boiling for ¼ hour. Drain them thoroughly, chop them, and rub them through a sieve. Make the melted butter, using milk instead of water, and when that boils, put in the onions, with a seasoning of salt; stir the sauce till it simmers, when it will be ready to serve. If these directions are carefully attended to, this onion sauce will be delicious.

Time.–From ¾ to 1 hour to boil the onions. **Sufficient** to serve with a roast shoulder of mutton, or a boiled rabbit.

— Orange Gravy —
(FOR WILDFOWL, WIDGEON, TEAL, ETC.)

Ingredients.– ½ pint of WHITE STOCK, 1 small onion, 3 or 4 strips of lemon or orange peel, a few leaves of basil, the juice of 1 Seville orange or 1 lemon, salt and pepper to taste, 1 glass of port.

Mode.–Put the onion, cut in slices, into a stewpan with the stock, orange peel, and basil, and let them simmer very gently for ¼ hour, or rather longer should the stock not taste sufficiently of the peel. Strain it, and add to the liquor the remaining ingredients; let the whole heat through and, when on the point of boiling, serve very hot in a tureen.

Time.–Altogether, ½ hour.

— Sauce Robert —

Ingredients.–2 oz. of butter, 3 onions, 1 teaspoonful of flour, 4 tablespoonfuls of gravy or MEDIUM STOCK, salt and pepper to taste, 1 teaspoonful of made mustard, 1 teaspoonful of vinegar, the juice of ½ lemon.

Mode.–Put the butter into a stewpan, set it on the heat and, when browning, throw in the onions, which must be cut into small slices. Fry them brown, but do not burn them; add the flour, shake the

Basil

onions in it, and give the whole another fry. Put in the gravy or stock, and seasoning, and boil gently for 10 minutes; skim off the fat, add the mustard, vinegar, and lemon juice; give it one boil, and pour round the steaks, or whatever dish the sauce has been prepared for.

Time.–Altogether, ½ hour. **Sufficient** for about 2 lbs. of steak.

Note.–This sauce will be found an excellent accompaniment to ROAST GOOSE, pork, mutton cutlets, and various other dishes.

— Shrimp Sauce —

Ingredients.–⅓ pint of MELTED BUTTER, ¼ pint of shelled shrimps, cayenne to taste.

Mode.–Make the melted butter very smoothly, shell the shrimps, and put them into the butter; season with cayenne, and let the sauce just simmer, but do not allow it to boil. When liked, a teaspoonful of ANCHOVY SAUCE may be added.

Time.–1 minute to simmer. **Sufficient** for 2 to 2½ lbs. of fish.

A Good Sauce for Steaks

Ingredients.–1 oz. of whole black pepper, ½ oz. of allspice, 1 oz. of salt, ½ oz. of grated horseradish, 2 or 3 pickled onions, 1 pint of MUSHROOM KETCHUP.

Mode.–Pound all the ingredients finely in a mortar, and put them into the ketchup. Let them stand for a fortnight, when strain off the liquor and bottle for use. Either pour a little of the sauce over the steaks or mix it in the gravy.

BLACK PEPPER.– This well-known aromatic spice is the fruit of a species of climbing vine, and is extensively cultivated in Malabar and the eastern islands of Borneo, Sumatra, and Java. It is generally employed as a condiment, but it should never be forgotten that even in small quantities it produces detrimental effects on inflammatory constitutions. Dr. Paris, in his work on Diet, says: "Foreign spices were not intended by Nature for the inhabitants of temperate climes; they are heating and highly stimulant. I am, however, not anxious to give more weight to this objection than it deserves. The dyspeptic invalid should be cautious in their use. The intrinsic goodness of meats should, however, always be suspected when they require spicy seasonings to compensate for their natural want of sapidity."

Gravy kettle

French Onion Sauce, Orange Gravy, and Hot Tomato Sauce

—Sweet Sauce for Venison—

Ingredients.–A small jar of REDCURRANT JELLY, 1 glass of port.

Mode.–Put the above ingredients into a stewpan, set them over the heat and, when melted, pour into a tureen and serve. This sauce should not be allowed to boil.

Time.–5 minutes to melt the jelly.

— Hot Tomato Sauce —
(TO SERVE WITH CUTLETS, ROAST MEATS, ETC.)

Ingredients.–6 tomatoes, 2 shallots, 1 clove, 1 blade of mace, salt and cayenne to taste, ½ pint of MEDIUM STOCK.

Mode.–Reduce the stock to half the quantity by boiling it briskly; cut the tomatoes in two, and squeeze the juice and seeds out; put them in a stewpan with the reduced stock and the other ingredients, and let them simmer *gently* until the tomatoes are tender enough to pulp; rub the whole through a sieve, boil for a few minutes, and serve.

Time.–1 hour to simmer the tomatoes.

THE OLIVE AND OLIVE OIL.-The olive tree is indigenous in the north of Africa, Syria, and Greece, and the Romans introduced it to Italy. In Spain and the south of France it is now cultivated; although it grows in England, its fruit does not ripen. Both in Greece and Portugal the fruit is eaten in its ripe state; to the Italian shepherd, bread and olives, with a little wine, form a nourishing diet; but in England, olives are usually only introduced by way of dessert, to destroy the taste of the viands which have been previously eaten, that the flavour of the wine may be the better enjoyed. The oil extracted from olives is, with the Continentals, in continual request, more dishes being prepared with than without it, we should imagine. With us, it is principally used in mixing a salad, and when thus employed tends to prevent fermentation and flatulency.

Rémoulade, and Fowl à la Mayonnaise

IN MAKING SALADS, the vegetables, etc. should never be added to the sauce very long before they are wanted for table; the dressing, however, may always be prepared some hours before required. Where salads are much in request, it is a good plan to bottle off sufficient dressing for a few days' consumption, as, thereby, much time and trouble are saved.

— Mayonnaise —

Ingredients.–The yolks of 2 eggs, 6 tablespoonfuls of salad oil, 4 tablespoonfuls of vinegar, salt and white pepper to taste, 1 tablespoonful of WHITE STOCK, 2 tablespoonfuls of cream.

Mode.–Put the yolks of the eggs into a basin, with a seasoning of pepper and salt; have ready the above quantities of oil and vinegar, in separate vessels, and add them *very gradually* to the eggs. In mixing the oil and vinegar with the eggs, put in first a few drops of oil, and then a few drops of vinegar, never adding a large quantity of either at one time. Continue beating the mixture with a wooden spoon, as herein consists the secret of having a nice smooth sauce. It cannot be beaten too frequently, and should be made in a very cool place or, if ice is at hand, it should be mixed over it. When the vinegar and oil are well incorporated with the eggs, add the stock and cream, stirring all the time, and it will then be ready for use.

For a fish mayonnaise, this sauce may be coloured with lobster spawn, pounded; and for poultry or meat, where variety is desired, a little parsley juice may be used to add to its appearance.

Rémoulade, or French — Salad Dressing —

Ingredients.–4 eggs, ½ tablespoonful of made mustard, salt and cayenne to taste, 3 tablespoonfuls of olive oil, 1 tablespoonful of tarragon or plain vinegar.

Mode.–Boil 3 eggs for about ¼ hour, put them into cold water, and let them remain in it for a few minutes; strip off the shells, put the yolks in a mortar, and pound them very smoothly; add to them, very gradually, the mustard, seasoning, and vinegar. Put in the oil drop by drop, and when this is thoroughly mixed with the other ingredients, add the yolk of a raw egg, and stir well, when it will be ready for use. To prevent this sauce from curdling, mix a little of everything at a time, and do not cease stirring. The quantities of oil and vinegar may be increased or diminished according to taste.

Green rémoulade is made by using tarragon vinegar instead of plain, and colouring with a little parsley juice.

Time.– ¼ hour to boil the eggs. **Sufficient** for a salad made for 4 to 6 persons.

— Salad Dressing —

Ingredients.–1 teaspoonful of made mustard, 1 teaspoonful of sugar, 2 tablespoonfuls of salad oil, 4 tablespoonfuls of milk, 2 tablespoonfuls of vinegar, cayenne and salt to taste.

Mode.–Put the mustard into a salad bowl with the sugar, and add the oil drop by drop, carefully stirring and mixing all well together. Proceed in this manner with the milk and vinegar, which must be added very gradually, or the sauce will curdle. Put in the seasoning, when the mixture will be ready for use. If this dressing is properly made, it will have a soft creamy appearance, and will be found very delicious with crab or cold fish as well as with salads.

Sufficient for a salad for 5 or 6 persons.

TARRAGON.–The leaves of this plant, known to naturalists as *Artemisia dracunculus*, are much used in France as a flavouring ingredient for salads. From it also is made the vinegar known as tarragon vinegar, which is employed by the French in mixing their mustard. It originally comes from Tartary.

— Pickled Beetroot —

Ingredients.–5 lbs. of small beets, sufficient vinegar to cover the beets, ½ oz. of whole pepper, and ½ oz. of allspice to every 2 pints of vinegar.

Mode.–Wash the beets free from dirt, and be very careful not to prick the outside skin, or they would lose their beautiful colour. Put them into boiling water, let them simmer gently, and when about three-quarters done, which will be in 1½ hours, take them out and let them cool. Peel them, cut them into slices about ½ inch thick, and put them into preserving jars. Boil the vinegar with the pepper and allspice, in the above proportion, for 10 minutes, and when cold, pour it on the beets. Cover the jars to exclude the air, and in a week the pickle will be fit for use.

— Pickled Cucumbers —

Ingredients.–6 cucumbers, 1 oz. of whole pepper, 1 oz. of fresh whole ginger, sufficient vinegar to cover the cucumbers.

Mode.–Cut the cucumbers in thick slices, sprinkle salt over them, and let them stand for 24 hours. The next day, drain them well for 6 hours, put them into preserving jars, pour boiling vinegar over them, and keep them in a warm place. A day later, boil up the vinegar again, add pepper and bruised ginger in the above proportion, return it to the cucumbers, and instantly cover the jars. In a few days the pickle will be fit for use.

— To Pickle Eggs —

Ingredients.–16 eggs, 2 pints of vinegar, ½ oz. of black peppercorns, ½ oz. of fresh ginger.

Mode.–Boil the eggs for 12 minutes, then dip them into cold water, and take off the shells. Put the vinegar, with the pepper and ginger, into a stewpan, and let it simmer for 10 minutes to absorb their flavour. Now place the eggs in a jar, strain over them the vinegar, boiling hot, and, when cold, tie down to exclude the air. This pickle will be ready for use in a month.

— Pickled Gherkins —

Ingredients.–5 lbs. of very young cucumbers, salt and water, 1 oz. of fresh ginger, ½ oz. of whole black pepper, ¼ oz. of whole allspice, 4 cloves, 2 blades of mace, a little horseradish, vine leaves, 2 pints of vinegar.

Mode.–Let the gherkins remain in salt and water for 3 or 4 days, when take them out, wipe perfectly dry, and put them into a jar. Boil sufficient vinegar to cover them, with spices and pepper, etc., in the above proportion, for 10 minutes, to draw out their flavour; strain the vinegar, boiling, over the gherkins, cover with vine leaves, and put over them a plate, setting the jar in a warm place, where they must remain all night. Next day drain off the vinegar, boil it up again with the spices, and strain it hot over the gherkins. Cover up with fresh vine leaves, and let the whole remain till quite cold. Now tie down the jar, and in a month or two the gherkins will be fit for use.

GINGER.–The ginger plant, known to naturalists as *Zingiber officinale*, is a native of the East and West Indies. It grows somewhat like the lily of the valley, but its height is about 3 feet. The fleshy creeping roots, which form the ginger of commerce, are in a proper state to be dug when the stalks are entirely withered. Ginger is generally considered as less pungent and heating to the system than might be expected from its effects on the organs of taste, and it is frequently used, with considerable effect, as an anti-spasmodic and carminative.

GHERKINS.– Gherkins are young cucumbers, and the only way in which they are used for cooking purposes is pickling them, as by the recipe here given. Not having arrived at maturity, they have not so strongly a developed flavour as cucumbers; as a pickle, they are very general favourites.

— Pickled Lemons —

Ingredients.–6 lemons, 4 pints of boiling water; to every 2 pints of vinegar allow ½ oz. of cloves, ½ oz. of whole white pepper, 1 oz. of fresh ginger, ¼ oz. each of mace and chillies, 1 oz. of mustard seed, a little sliced horseradish, a few cloves of garlic, salt.

Mode.–Put the lemons into water with sufficient salt in it that an egg may float therein; let them remain in it 6 days, stirring them every day; have ready 4 pints of boiling water, put in the lemons, and allow them to boil for ¼ hour; take them out, and let them lie in a cloth until perfectly dry and cold. Boil up sufficient vinegar to cover the lemons, with all the above ingredients, allowing the proportions stated to every 2 pints of vinegar. Pack the lemons in a jar, pour over the boiling vinegar, strained of the spices, etc., and tie down to exclude the air. They will be fit for use in about 12 months.

— Pickled Nasturtiums —

Ingredients.–To each pint of vinegar, allow 1 oz. of salt, 6 peppercorns, nasturtium pods.

Mode.–Gather the nasturtium pods on a dry day, and wipe them clean with a cloth; put them in a dry glass bottle, with vinegar, salt, and pepper in the above proportion. If you cannot find enough ripe to fill a bottle, cork up those you have until you have some more fit; they may be added from day to day. Seal the bottles. They will be fit for use in 10 to 12 months.

— Pickled Onions —

Ingredients.–5 lbs. of pickling onions, sufficient vinegar to cover the onions, ½ teaspoonful of allspice and ½ teaspoonful of whole black pepper to every 2 pints of vinegar.

Mode.–Take off the thin outside skin of the onions; then remove one more skin, when the onions will look quite clear. Have ready some very dry bottles or jars, and as fast as the onions are peeled, put them in. Pour over sufficient cold vinegar to cover them, with pepper and allspice in the above proportions, taking care that each jar has its share of the latter ingredients. Cover and put them in a dry place, and in a fortnight they will be fit for use. This is a most simple recipe and very delicious, the onions being nice and crisp. They should be eaten within 6 to 8 months after being done.

— Pickled Red Cabbage —

Ingredients.–Red cabbages weighing 6 lbs. altogether, salt; to every 2 pints of vinegar allow ½ oz. of fresh ginger, well bruised, 1 oz. of whole black pepper, and a little cayenne.

Mode.–Take off the outer leaves, cut the cabbages in quarters, remove the stalks, and cut them across in very thin slices. Lay them on a dish and strew them plentifully with salt, covering them with another dish. Let them stand for 24 hours, then turn into a colander to drain. Put them in a jar; boil up the vinegar, with spices in the above proportion, and, when cold, strain it over the cabbage and cover the jar. It will be fit for use in a week or two.

THE LEMON.– This fruit is a native of Asia, and is mentioned by Virgil, among others, as an antidote to poison. It is hardier than the orange and, as one of the citron tribe, was brought into Europe by the Arabians. The lemon was first cultivated in England in the beginning of the 17th century, and is now often to be found in our greenhouses. The kind commonly sold, however, is imported from Portugal, Spain, and the Azores. Some also come from St. Helena, but those from Spain are esteemed the best.

RED CABBAGE.– This plant, in its growth, is similar in form to that of the white, but is of a bluish-purple colour. It is principally from the white vegetable that the Germans make their *Sauerkraut*, a dish held in high estimation with the inhabitants of the Vaterland, but which requires, generally speaking, with strangers, a long acquaintance in order to become sufficiently impressed with its numerous merits.

NASTURTIUMS.– The elegant nasturtium plant came originally from Peru, but was easily made to grow in these islands. Its young leaves and flowers are of a slightly hot nature, and many consider them a good adjunct to salads, to which they certainly add a pretty appearance. When the beautiful blossoms, which may be employed with great effect in garnishing dishes, are past, then the fruit is used as described in the adjoining recipe. Nasturtium pods may be picked from the end of July to the end of August.

— Camp Vinegar —

Ingredients.–1 bulb of garlic, ½ oz. of cayenne, 2 teaspoonfuls of soy sauce, 2 teaspoonfuls of WALNUT KETCHUP, 1 pint of vinegar, cochineal to colour.

Mode.–Slice the garlic, and put it, with all the above ingredients, into a clean bottle. Let it infuse for a month, when strain it off quite clear, and it will be fit for use. Keep it in small bottles, well sealed to exclude the air.

— Chilli Vinegar —

Ingredients.–50 fresh red chillies, 1 pint of vinegar.

Mode.–Cut the chillies in half, and infuse them in the vinegar for a fortnight, when it will be fit for use. This will be found an agreeable relish to fish, as many people cannot eat it without the addition of an acid.

— Horseradish Vinegar —

Ingredients.–¼ lb. of grated horseradish, 1 oz. of minced shallot, a small pinch of cayenne, 2 pints of vinegar.

Mode.–Put all the ingredients into a corked bottle, which shake well every day for a fortnight. When they are thoroughly steeped, strain and bottle, and it will be fit for use immediately. This will be found an agreeable relish to cold beef, etc.

GARLIC.–The smell of this plant is generally considered offensive, and it is the most acrimonious in its taste of the whole of the alliaceous tribe. In 1548 it was introduced to England from the shores of the Mediterranean, where it is abundant; in Sicily it grows naturally. It was in greater repute with our ancestors than it is with ourselves, although it is still used as a seasoning herb. On the Continent, especially in Italy, it is much used, and the French consider it an essential in many made dishes.

Pickled Beetroot, and ingredients for Bengal Chutney

Bengal Recipe for making — Mango Chutney —

Ingredients.–1 ½ lbs. of moist brown sugar, ¾ lb. of salt, ¼ lb. of garlic, ¼ lb. of onions, ¾ lb. of powdered ginger, ¼ lb. of dried chillies, ¾ lb. of mustard seed, ¾ lb. of stoned raisins, 4 pints of vinegar, 30 large unripe sour apples.

Mode.–The sugar must be made into a syrup with 1 ½ pints of water; the garlic, onions, ginger, and mustard seed be finely pounded in a mortar; the apples be peeled, cored, and sliced, and boiled until tender in 3 pints of the vinegar. When all this is done, and the apples are quite cold, put them into a large pan, and gradually mix in all the other ingredients, including the remaining pint of vinegar. Stir until the whole is thoroughly blended, and then put into bottles or jars, and cover for use. This chutney is very superior to any which can be bought, and one trial will prove it to be delicious.

Note.–This recipe was given by a native to an English lady who had long been a resident in India, and who, since her return to her native country, has become quite celebrated amongst her friends for the excellence of this Eastern relish. The original recipe used unripe mangoes rather than apples.

— An Excellent Pickle —

Ingredients.–Equal quantities of medium-sized onions, cucumbers, and cooking apples, 1 ½ teaspoonfuls of salt, ¾ teaspoonful of cayenne, 1 wineglassful of soy sauce, 1 wineglassful of sherry, vinegar.

Mode.–Slice sufficient cucumbers, onions, and apples to fill a pint jar, taking care to cut the slices very thin; arrange them in alternate layers, shaking in as you proceed salt and cayenne in the above proportion; pour in the soy and wine, and fill up with vinegar. It will be fit for use the day it is made.

— Mixed Pickle —
(VERY GOOD)

Ingredients.–To each gallon of vinegar allow ¼ lb. of ground ginger, ¼ lb. of ground mustard, ¼ lb. of salt, 2 oz. of mustard seed, 1 ½ oz. of ground turmeric, 1 oz. of ground black pepper, ¼ oz. of cayenne; cauliflowers, onions, celery, sliced cucumbers, gherkins, French beans, nasturtium pods, bell peppers.

Mode.–Have ready a large jar, with a tightly fitting lid, in which put as much vinegar as required, reserving a little to mix the various powders to a smooth paste. Put into a basin the mustard, turmeric, pepper, and cayenne; mix them with vinegar, and stir well until no lumps remain; add all the ingredients to the vinegar, and mix well. Keep this liquor in a warm place, and thoroughly stir every morning for a month with a wooden spoon, when it will be ready for the different vegetables to be added to it. As these come into season, have them gathered on a dry day, and, after merely wiping them with a cloth to free them from moisture, put them raw into the pickle, store away in jars, and seal. As none of the ingredients are boiled, this pickle will not be fit to eat till 12 months have elapsed.

PICKLES.–The ancient Greeks and Romans held their pickles in high estimation. They consisted of flowers, herbs, roots, and vegetables preserved in vinegar, and which were kept, for a long time, in cylindrical vases with wide mouths. Their cooks prepared pickles with the greatest care, and the various ingredients were macerated in oil, brine, and vinegar, with which they were often impregnated drop by drop. Meat, also, after having been cut into very small pieces, was treated in the same manner.

SOY SAUCE.–This is a sauce frequently made use of for fish, and comes from Japan, where it is prepared from the seeds of a plant called *Dolichos soja*. The Chinese also manufacture it, but that made by the Japanese is said to be the best. All sorts of statements have been made respecting the very general adulteration of this article in England, and we fear that many of them are too true. When genuine, it is of an agreeable flavour, thick, and of a clear brown colour.

Mixed Pickle

— Mushroom Ketchup —

Ingredients.–To 8 lbs. of mushrooms allow ½ lb. of salt; to every 2 pints of mushroom liquor allow ¼ oz. of cayenne, ½ oz. of allspice, ½ oz. of ground ginger, 2 blades of pounded mace.

Mode.–Choose full-grown mushroom flaps, and take care they are perfectly fresh-gathered when the weather is tolerably dry, for if they are picked during very heavy rain the ketchup which is made from them is liable to get musty, and will not keep long. Put a layer of mushrooms in a deep pan, sprinkle salt over them, and then another layer of mushrooms, and so on, alternately. Let them stand for a few hours, when break them up with the hand; put them in a nice cool place for 3 days, occasionally stirring and mashing them well to extract from them as much juice as possible. Now measure the quantity of liquor, and to every 2 pints allow the above proportion of spices, etc. Put all into a jar, including the mushrooms, cover it up very tightly, put it in a saucepan of boiling water, set it over the heat, and let it boil for 3 hours. Have ready a nice clean stewpan; turn into it the contents of the jar, and let the whole simmer very gently for ½ hour; pour it into a jug, where it should stand in a cool place till the next day; then strain it off into another jug, taking care not to squeeze the mushrooms; be careful also to leave all the sediment behind in the jug. To each pint of ketchup add a few drops of brandy, then strain again into very dry clean bottles; cork well so as to exclude the air perfectly.

MUSHROOM KETCHUP, if genuine and well prepared, is one of the most useful store sauces to the experienced cook, and no trouble should be spared in its preparation. Double ketchup is made by reducing the liquor to half the quantity. This goes farther than ordinary ketchup, as so little is required to flavour a good quantity of gravy.

CINNAMON.–The cinnamon tree (*Laurus cinnamomum*) is a valuable and beautiful species of the laurel family, and grows to the height of 20 or 30 feet. The trunk is short and straight, with wide spreading branches, and it has a smooth ash-like bark. The leaves are upon short stalks, and are of an oval shape, and 3 to 5 inches long. The flowers are in panicles, with six small petals, and the fruit is about the size of an olive, soft, insipid, and of a deep blue. This encloses a nut, the kernel of which germinates soon after it falls. The wood of the tree is white and not very solid, and its root is thick and branching, exuding a great quantity of camphor. The inner bark of the tree forms the cinnamon of commerce.

Burnt Onions for Gravies

Ingredients.– ½ lb. of onions, ½ pint of water, ½ lb. of moist brown sugar, ⅓ pint of vinegar.

Mode.–Peel and chop the onions fine, and put them into a stewpan with the water; let them boil for 5 minutes, then add the sugar, and simmer gently until the mixture becomes nearly black and throws out bubbles of smoke. Have ready the boiling vinegar, strain the liquor gradually to it, and keep stirring with a wooden spoon until it is well incorporated. When cold, bottle for use.

Time.–Altogether, 1 hour.

Tomato Sauce for Keeping

Ingredients.–To every pint of tomato pulp allow ½ pint of CHILLI VINEGAR, ½ oz. of shallots, ½ oz. of garlic, peeled and cut in slices, salt to taste; to every 3 pints of liquor allow ¼ pint of soy sauce, ¼ pint of anchovy essence.

Mode.–Gather the tomatoes quite ripe; bake them in a slow oven till tender; rub them through a sieve, and to every pint of pulp add chilli vinegar, shallots, garlic, and salt, in the above proportion; boil the whole together till the garlic and shallots are quite soft, then rub it through a sieve; put it again into a saucepan and, to every 3 pints of the liquor, add ¼ pint of soy sauce and the same quantity of anchovy essence, and boil together for about 20 minutes; bottle off for use, and carefully seal. This sauce will keep good for 2 or 3 years, but will be fit for use in a week. A useful and less expensive sauce may be made by omitting the anchovy and soy.

Time.–Altogether, 1 hour.

— Walnut Ketchup —

Ingredients.–100 green walnuts, 1 handful of salt, 2 pints of vinegar, ¼ oz. of ground mace, ¼ oz. of grated nutmeg, ¼ oz. of cloves, ¼ oz. of ground ginger, ¼ oz. of whole black pepper, a small piece of horseradish, 20 shallots, ¼ lb. of anchovies, 1 pint of port.

Mode.–Procure the walnuts green, before the shell inside hardens, when a pin may be run through them; slightly bruise them, and put them into a jar with the salt and vinegar; let them stand for 8 days, stirring every day; then drain the liquor from them, and boil it, with the above ingredients, for about ½ hour. It may be strained or not, as preferred, and if required a little more vinegar or port can be added, according to taste. Bottle and seal well.

— Hot Spice —
(A DELICIOUS ADJUNCT TO CHOPS, GRAVIES, ETC.)

Ingredients.–3 pinches each of ground ginger, black pepper, and cinnamon, 7 cloves, ½ oz. of ground mace, ¼ oz. of cayenne, 1 oz. of grated nutmeg, 1½ oz. of ground white pepper.

Mode.–Mix the spices thoroughly together, taking care that everything is well blended; put in a very dry glass bottle for use. The quantity of cayenne may be increased, should the above not be enough to suit the palate.

TOMATO, OR LOVE-APPLE.– The plant which bears this fruit is a native of South America, and takes its name from a Portuguese word. The tomato fruit is about the size of a small potato, and is chiefly used in soups, sauces, and gravies. It is sometimes served to table roasted or boiled, and when green makes a good ketchup or pickle. In its unripe state, it is esteemed as excellent sauce for roast goose or pork.

THE WALNUT.– This nut is a native of Persia, and was introduced into England from France. As a pickle, it is much used in the green state, and grated walnuts in Spain are much employed both in tarts and other dishes. On the Continent it is occasionally employed as a substitute for olive oil in cooking, but it is apt, under such circumstances, to become rancid. The matter which remains after the oil is extracted is considered highly nutritious for poultry. It is called *mare*, and in Switzerland is eaten under the name of *pain amer* by the poor. The oil is frequently manufactured into a kind of soap, and the leaves and green husks yield brown dye which is used to stain hair, wool, and wood.

MARJORAM is a native of Portugal, and when its leaves are used as a seasoning herb, they have an agreeable aromatic flavour.

—Forcemeat for Fish—

Ingredients.–1 oz. of butter, 1 oz. of suet, 1 oz. of fat bacon, 1 small teaspoonful of minced savoury herbs, including parsley, a little onion, when liked, shredded very fine, salt, nutmeg, and cayenne to taste, 4 oz. of breadcrumbs, 1 egg.

Mode.–Mix all the ingredients well together, carefully mincing them very finely; beat up the egg, moisten the other ingredients with it, and work the whole very smoothly together. Oysters or anchovies, minced and added to this forcemeat, will be found a great improvement.

Sufficient for a moderate-sized haddock or pike.

Forcemeat for Veal, —Fowls, Hare, etc.—

Ingredients.–2 oz. of ham or lean bacon, ¼ lb. of suet, the rind of ½ lemon, 1 teaspoonful of minced parsley, 1 teaspoonful of minced sweet herbs, salt, cayenne, and pounded mace to taste, 6 oz. of breadcrumbs, 2 eggs.

Mode.–Shred the ham or bacon, lemon peel, and herbs, taking particular care that all be very finely minced; add the suet and a seasoning to taste, of salt, cayenne, and mace, and blend all thoroughly together with the breadcrumbs. Now beat and strain the eggs, work these into the other ingredients, and the forcemeat will be ready for use. When it is made into balls, fry of a nice brown, in oil or clarified dripping, or put them on a tin and bake for ½ hour in a moderate oven.

Sufficient for a turkey, a moderate-sized fillet of veal, or a hare.

SWEET HERBS.– Those most usually employed for the flavouring of soups, sauces, forcemeats, etc., are thyme, sage, mint, marjoram, savory, and basil. In town, sweet herbs have to be procured at the greengrocers' or herbalists', whilst, in the country, the garden should furnish all that are wanted, the cook taking great care to have some dried in the autumn for her use throughout the winter months.

Roast Breast of Veal with Forcemeat, Sausagemeat Stuffing for Turkey, and blades of mace

Sage and Onion Stuffing — for Poultry and Pork —

Ingredients.–4 large onions, 10 sage leaves, ¼ lb. of breadcrumbs, 1½ oz. of butter, salt and pepper to taste, 1 egg.

Mode.–Peel the onions, put them into boiling water, let them simmer for 5 minutes or rather longer; just before they are taken out, put in the sage leaves for a minute or two to take off their rawness. Chop the onions and sage very fine, add the breadcrumbs, seasoning, and butter, and work the whole together with the egg yolk, when the stuffing will be ready for use. It should be rather highly seasoned. Many cooks do not parboil the onions in the manner just stated, but merely use them raw. The stuffing then, however, is not nearly so mild. When made for a goose, a portion of the liver of the bird, simmered for a few minutes and very finely minced, may be added to this stuffing.

Time.–Rather more than 5 minutes to simmer the onions.

Sufficient for a goose, or a pair of ducks.

SAGE.–This was originally a native of the south of Europe, but it has long been cultivated in the English garden. There are several kinds of it, known as the green, the red, the small-leaved, and the broad-leaved balsamic. In cookery, its principal use is for stuffings and sauces, for which purpose the red is the most agreeable, and the green the next. The others are used for medicinal purposes.

— Sausagemeat Stuffing —

Ingredients.–6 oz. of lean pork, 6 oz. of fat pork, both weighed after being chopped (beef suet may be substituted for the latter), 2 oz. of breadcrumbs, 1 small tablespoonful of minced sage, 1 blade of mace pounded, salt and pepper to taste, 1 egg.

Mode.–Chop the meat and fat very finely, and mix with them the other ingredients, taking care that the whole is thoroughly incorporated. Moisten with the egg, and the stuffing will be ready for use. Equal quantities of this stuffing and of the forcemeat given above will be found to answer very well, as the herbs, lemon peel, etc., in the latter impart a very delicious flavour to the sausagemeat.

Sufficient for a small turkey.

— Fried Sippets of Bread —
(FOR GARNISHING MANY DISHES)

Mode.–Cut the bread into thin slices, and stamp them out in whatever shape you like–rings, crosses, diamonds, etc. Fry them in clear boiling oil, lard, or clarified dripping, and drain them in the oven until thoroughly crisp.

— Fried Parsley —
(FOR GARNISHING)

Mode.–Gather some young parsley; wash, pick, and dry it thoroughly in a cloth; put it into a wire basket and hold it in the boiling fat for a minute or two; the quicker it is fried the better. Directly it is done, lift out the basket, and let it stand in a warm oven, that the parsley may become thoroughly crisp.

Wire basket

CHAPTER 5

Meat

IT IS NATURAL THAT MAN SHOULD SEEK TO FEED ON FLESH; he has too small a stomach to be supported alone by fruit, which has not sufficient nourishment to renovate him; it is possible he might subsist on vegetables, but their preparation needs the knowledge of art, only to be obtained after the lapse of many centuries.

Fire having been discovered, mankind endeavoured to make use of it for drying, and afterwards for cooking, their meat, but they were a considerable time before they hit upon proper and commodious methods of employing it. Meat placed on burning fuel was found better than when raw; it had more firmness, was eaten with less difficulty, and had a pleasing perfume and flavour. Still, however, the meat cooked thus would become somewhat befouled. This disadvantage was remedied by passing spits through it and placing it at a suitable height above the burning fuel; thus grilling was invented.

WHITE MEATS, AND THE MEAT OF YOUNG ANIMALS, require to be very well cooked, both to be pleasant to the palate and easy of digestion. Thus veal, pork, and lamb should be thoroughly done to the centre. Mutton and beef, on the other hand, do not, generally speaking, require to be so thoroughly done, and they should be cooked to the point that, in carving them, the gravy should just run, but not too freely.

BOILING, or the preparation of meat by hot water, though one of the easiest processes in cookery, requires skilful management. Boiled meat should be tender, savoury, and full of its own juice, or natural gravy, but through carelessness and ignorance, it is too often sent to table hard, tasteless, and innutritious. To ensure a successful result in boiling meat, the proper quantity of water must be maintained in the pot, and the scum which rises to the surface must be carefully removed. As a general rule, 20 minutes, reckoning from the moment when the boiling commences, may be allowed for every pound of meat.

Many writers on cookery assert that meat to be boiled should be put into *cold water*, and that the pot should be heated gradually, but Liebig, the highest authority on all matters connected with the chemistry of food, has shown that meat so treated loses some of its most nutritious constituents.

Stewpan

I N STEWING, it is not requisite to have so great a heat as in boiling. A gentle simmering in a small quantity of water, so that the meat is stewed almost in its own juices, is all that is necessary. It is a method much used on the Continent, and is wholesome and economical.

BROILING, OR GRILLING, is, generally speaking, a mode of preparing small dishes, amongst which the beefsteak and mutton chop of the solitary English diner may be mentioned as celebrated all the world over. In order to succeed in a broil, or grill, the cook must have a bright, clear heat so that the surface of the meat may be quickly sealed. The result of this is the same as that obtained in roasting, namely that a crust is formed outside, and thus the juices of the meat are retained.

FRYING may be accurately described as boiling in fat or oil. The great point to be borne in mind in frying is that the fat must be hot enough to act instantaneously on the articles placed in it. All dishes fried in fat should be placed in a warm oven on a piece of absorbent paper and there left for a few minutes so that any superfluous greasy moisture may be removed.

OF THE VARIOUS METHODS OF PREPARING MEAT, ROASTING is that which most effectually preserves its nutritive qualities. Meat is roasted by being exposed to the direct influence of the heat. When meat is properly roasted, the outer layer is coagulated, and thus presents a barrier to the exit of the juice. In roasting meat, the heat must be strongest at first, and it should then be much reduced. The juice that is squeezed out, in the most careful roasting, evaporates on the surface of the meat, and gives it a dark brown colour, a rich lustre, and a strong aromatic taste.

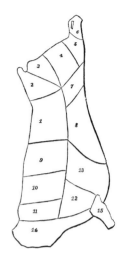

Side of beef, showing the several joints

B EEF JOINTS.–The joints of the hindquarter are:–
1. Sirloin (the two sirloins together form a baron). 2. Rump (the finest part for steaks). 3. Aitch bone (boiling piece). 4. Buttock, round, or topside (prime boiling piece, pot roasting).
5. Silverside (boiling or pot roasting). 6. Hock (stewing). 7. Thick flank or skirt (primest boiling piece). 8. Thin flank or skirt (boiling, stewing). The joints of the forequarter are:–
9. Fore-ribs (primest roasting piece).
10. Back and top ribs (the most economical joints for roasting).
11. Chuck and bladebone (for second quality steaks).
12. Leg-of-mutton cut (the shoulder dissected from the breast).
13. Brisket or breast (for salting and boiling). 14. Neck or sticking piece, and clod (for soups, gravies, stocks, pies, and sausages). 15. Shin (stewing).

Baked Beefsteak Pudding and Beef Olives

Boiling pot

BEEF.–The quality of beef depends on various circumstances, such as the age, the sex, the breed of the animal, and also on the food upon which it has been raised. Bull beef is, in general, dry and tough, and by no means possessed of an agreeable flavour, whilst the flesh of the ox is not only highly nourishing and digestible, but, if not too old, extremely agreeable. The flesh of the cow is also nourishing, but it is not so agreeable as that of the ox, although that of a heifer is held in high estimation. The flesh of the smaller breeds is much sweeter than that of the larger, which is best when the animal is about seven years old. That of the smaller breeds is best at about five years.

— Baked Beef —

Ingredients.–About 2 lbs. of cold roast beef, 2 small onions, 1 large carrot or 2 small ones, 1 turnip, a small bunch of savoury herbs, salt and pepper to taste, 4 tablespoonfuls of gravy or rich stock, 3 tablespoonfuls of ale, COMMON CRUST or mashed potatoes.

Mode.–Cut the beef in slices, allowing a small amount of fat to each slice; place a layer in the bottom of a pie dish, with a portion of the onions, carrots, and turnips, which must be sliced; mince the herbs, strew them over the meat, and season with pepper and salt. Then put in another layer of meat, vegetables, and seasoning, and proceed in this manner until all the ingredients are used. Pour in the gravy and ale (water may be substituted for the former, but it is not so nice), cover with a pie crust or mashed potatoes, and bake in a moderate oven for ½ hour, or rather longer.

Time.–Rather more than ½ hours. **Sufficient** for 5 or 6 persons.

Note.–It is as well to parboil the carrots and turnips before adding them to the meat, and to use some of the liquor in which they were boiled as a substitute for gravy when there is no gravy at hand.

Baked Beefsteak Pudding

Ingredients.–6 oz. of flour, 2 eggs, not quite 1 pint of milk, salt to taste, 1½ lbs. of rump steak, ½ lb. of beef kidney, pepper and salt.

Mode.–Cut the steak into nice square pieces, with a small quantity of fat, and divide the kidney into small pieces. Make a batter of flour, eggs, and milk in the above proportions; lay a little of it at the bottom of a pie dish; then put in the steak and kidney, which should be well seasoned with pepper and salt, pour over the remainder of the batter, and bake for 1½ hours in a brisk but not fierce oven.

Time.–1½ hours. **Sufficient** for 4 or 5 persons.

— Boiled Round of Beef —

Ingredients.–12 lbs. of silverside, water, salt, 1 lb. each of carrots, turnips, parsnips, and onions.

Mode.–As a whole round of beef, generally speaking, is too large for small families, we here give the recipe for dressing a portion of the silverside of the round. Skewer it up in a nice round-looking form, and bind it with string to keep the skewers in their places. Put it in a saucepan of boiling water, set it on a good heat, and when it begins to simmer, carefully remove any scum from the surface. When it is well skimmed, draw the pot a little off the heat, add salt, and let it simmer very gently for about 3 hours, adding the sliced carrots, turnips and parsnips, and the sliced and browned onions, about 1 hour before it is done. Serve garnished with the vegetables, and with suet dumplings when liked. The liquor should be saved, and converted into pea soup, and the outside slices, which are generally hard and of an uninviting appearance, may be cut off before being sent to table, and potted as a relish for breakfast or luncheon.

Time.–About 3 hours after the water boils. **Sufficient** for a dinner for 16 persons.

Note.–The brisket and rump may also be boiled by the above recipe.

A ROUND OF BEEF is not so easily carved as many other joints of beef, and to manage it properly, a thin-bladed and very sharp knife is necessary. Off the outside of the joint, at its top, a thick slice should first be cut, so as to leave the surface smooth; then thin and even slices should be cleverly carved in a horizontal direction.

— To Dress Beef Kidney —

Ingredients.–1 lb. of kidney, 1 dessertspoonful of minced parsley, 1 teaspoonful of minced shallot, salt and pepper to taste, ¼ pint of roast beef gravy, 3 tablespoonfuls of sherry.

Mode.–Take off a little of the kidney fat, mince it very fine, and put it in a frying-pan; slice the kidney, sprinkle over it parsley and shallots in the above proportion, add a seasoning of pepper and salt, and fry it a nice brown. When it is done enough, dredge over a little flour, and pour in the gravy and sherry. Let it just simmer, but not boil any more, or the kidney would harden; serve very hot, and garnish with croûtons.

Time.–From 5 to 10 minutes. **Sufficient** for 3 or 4 persons.

— Beef Olives —

Ingredients.–2 lbs. of rump steak, 1 egg, 1 tablespoonful of minced savoury herbs, pepper and salt to taste, 1 pint of MEDIUM STOCK, 2 or 3 slices of bacon, 2 tablespoonfuls of any bottled sauce, thickening of butter and flour.

Mode.–Have the steak cut rather thin, slightly beat it to make it of a uniform thickness, cut it into 6 or 7 pieces, brush over with the beaten egg, and sprinkle with the herbs, which should be very finely minced; season with pepper and salt, and roll up the pieces tightly, and fasten with small skewers. Put the stock in a stewpan that will exactly hold the olives, for by being pressed together, they will keep their shape better; lay in the olives, cover them with the bacon, cut in thin slices, and a piece of buttered paper, and stew them very gently for a full 2 hours, for the slower they are done the better. Take them out, remove the skewers, thicken the gravy with butter and flour, and flavour it with any bottled sauce that may be liked. Give one boil, pour over the meat, and serve.

Time.–2 hours. **Sufficient** for 4 or 5 persons.

TO CLARIFY BEEF DRIPPING.– Good and fresh dripping answers very well for basting everything except game and poultry, and when well clarified serves for frying; it should be kept in a cool place, and will remain good some time. To clarify it, put the dripping into a basin, pour over it boiling water, and keep stirring the whole to wash away the impurities. Let it stand to cool, when the water and dirty sediment will settle at the bottom of the basin. Remove the dripping, and put it away in jars or basins for use.

Roast Ribs of Beef with Grated Horseradish

Roast Ribs or Sirloin of Beef

TO CARVE A SIRLOIN.–First cut some slices from the underside, in the direction 1 to 2, as the fillet is very much preferred by some eaters. The upper part should be cut in the direction 5 to 6, and care should be taken to carve it evenly and in thin slices. It will be found a great assistance, in carving this joint well, if the knife be first inserted just above the bone at the bottom, and run sharply along between the bone and meat. The slices will then come away more readily. Some carvers cut the upper side of the sirloin across, as shown by the line 3 to 4, but this is a wasteful plan, and not one to be recommended.

Ingredients.–A rib joint or a sirloin weighing 10 lbs., a little flour and salt.

Mode.–The fore-rib is considered the primest roasting piece, but the back and top ribs are considered the most economical. The sirloin resembles a rib cut, except that it has a fillet or undercut and comes from that portion of the back adjoining the rump; it is, in consequence, more expensive. Dredge the joint with a little flour before putting it in the oven; to have it in perfection and the juices kept in, put it first into a hot oven, and when the outside is set and firm reduce the heat and leave the joint to roast very slowly, allowing 20 minutes per pound for meat on the bone, and 25 minutes per pound for a boned joint. When it is done, take it from the roasting pan and sprinkle some fine salt over it (this must never be done until the joint is dished, as it draws the juices from the meat); pour the dripping from the pan, put in a little boiling water slightly salted, and strain the gravy over the meat. Garnish with tufts of grated horseradish, and send HORSERADISH SAUCE to table with it. A YORKSHIRE PUDDING sometimes accompanies this dish and, if lightly made and well cooked, will be found a very agreeable addition

Time.–3½ to 4½ hours. **Sufficient** for a dinner for 16 persons.

— To Salt Beef —

Ingredients.– ½ round of beef weighing about 10 lbs., 4 oz. of sugar, 1 oz. of powdered saltpetre, 2 oz. of ground black pepper, ¼ lb. of sea salt, ½ lb. of common salt.

Mode.–Rub the meat well with the sea salt, and let stand for a day, to disgorge and clear it from slime. The next day, rub it well with the other ingredients on every side, and let it stand for about a week, turning it every day. It may be boiled fresh from the pickle, or smoked.

Note.–The aitch bone, flank, or brisket may be salted and pickled by this recipe, allowing less time for small joints to remain in the pickle; for instance, a joint of 8 or 9 lbs. will be sufficiently salt in 5 or 6 days.

— Spiced Beef —

Ingredients.–7 lbs. of the thick flank or rump of beef, ¼ lb. of sugar, ½ oz. of saltpetre, 2 oz. of pounded allspice, ½ lb. of common salt, flour and water.

Mode.–Rub the sugar well into the beef, and let it stand for 12 hours; then rub the saltpetre and allspice, both of which should be pounded, over the meat, and let it stand for another 12 hours; then rub in the salt. Turn daily in the liquor for a fortnight, then soak it for a few hours in water, dry it with a cloth, cover it with a coarse paste made of flour and water, put a little water at the bottom of the pan, and bake in a moderate oven for 2½ hours. If it is not covered with a paste, be careful to put the beef into a deep vessel and cover it with a plate, or it will be too crisp. During the time the meat is in the oven it should be turned once or twice. Serve cold with a salad.

Time.–2½ hours.

ORIGIN OF THE WORD "SIRLOIN".–The loin of beef is said to have been knighted by King Charles II, at Friday Hall, Chingford. The "Merry Monarch" returned to this hospitable mansion from Epping Forest literally "as hungry as a hunter", and beheld with delight a huge loin of beef steaming upon the table. "A noble joint!" exclaimed the king. "By St. George, it shall have a title!" Then drawing his sword, he raised it above the meat and cried, with mock dignity: "Loin, we dub thee knight. Henceforward be Sir Loin!" It is, perhaps, a pity to spoil so noble a story, but the interests of truth demand that we declare that *sirloin* is probably a corruption of *surloin*, which signifies the upper part of a loin, the prefix *sur* being equivalent to *over* or *above*. In French we find this joint called *surlonge*, which so closely resembles our *sirloin* that we may safely refer the two words to a common origin.

Beefsteaks with Fried Potatoes

FRENCH BEEF.–It has been all but universally admitted that the beef of France is greatly inferior in quality to that of England, owing to inferiority of pasturage. Monsieur Curmer, however, one of the latest writers on the culinary art, tells us that this is a vulgar error, and that French beef is far superior to that of England. This is mere vaunting on the part of our neighbours, who seem to want *la gloire* in everything. No, M. Curmer, we are ready to acknowledge the superiority of your cookery, but we have long since made up our minds as to the inferiority of your raw material.

Beefsteaks with Fried — Potatoes —
(A LA MODE FRANÇAISE)

Ingredients.–2 lbs. of sirloin steak, 8 potatoes, ¼ lb. of butter, salt and pepper to taste, 1 teaspoonful of minced herbs.

Mode.–Put the butter into a frying- or *sauté* pan, set it over the heat, and let it get very hot; peel and cut the potatoes into long thin slices; put them into the hot butter, and fry them till of a nice brown colour. Now broil the steaks under a nice hot grill, turning them frequently, that every part may be equally done; as they should not be thick, 5 minutes will suffice. Put the herbs and seasoning in the butter the potatoes were fried in, pour it under the steaks, and place the fried potatoes round, as a garnish. To have this dish in perfection, a portion of the fillet of the sirloin should be used, as the meat is generally so much more tender than that of the rump, and the steaks should be cut about ⅓ inch in thickness.

Time.–5 minutes to grill the steaks, and about the same time to fry the potatoes. If the fillet of sirloin is cooked whole, fry it for 8 to 10 minutes on each side. **Sufficient** for 4 persons.

— T o a d - i n - t h e - H o l e —

Ingredients.–1½ lbs. of rump steak, 1 sheep's kidney, pepper and salt to taste; for the batter allow 3 eggs, 1 pint of milk, 4 tablespoonfuls of flour, a pinch of salt.

Mode.–Cut up the steak and kidney into convenient sized pieces, and put them into a buttered pie dish, with a good seasoning of salt and pepper; mix the flour with a small quantity of milk at first, to prevent its being lumpy, then add the remainder, and the 3 eggs, which should be well beaten; put in the salt, stir the batter for about 5 minutes, and pour it over the steak. Place it in a moderately hot oven immediately, and bake for 1½ hours.

Time.–1½ hours. **Sufficient** for 4 or 5 persons.

To Pickle and Dress a Tongue

Ingredients.–1 ox tongue weighing about 6 lbs., 6 oz. of common salt, 2 oz. of sea salt, 1 oz. of saltpetre, 3 oz. of sugar, seasoning of cloves, mace, and allspice, butter, common crust of flour and water.

Mode.–Lay the tongue for a fortnight in the above pickle, turning it every day, and be particular that the spices are well pounded; put it into a small pan just large enough to hold it, place some pieces of butter on it, and cover with a common crust made of flour and water. Bake in a slow oven until so tender that a straw would penetrate it; take off the skin, fasten it down to a piece of board by running a fork through the root and another through the tip, at the same time straightening it and putting it into shape. When cold, glaze it with ASPIC, put a paper ruche round the root, which is generally very unsightly, and garnish with tufts of parsley.

Time.–3 to 4 hours in a slow oven, according to size.

— To Dress Tripe —

Ingredients.–Tripe, WHITE ONION SAUCE, milk and water.

Mode.–Ascertain that the tripe is quite fresh, and have it cleaned and dressed. Cut away the coarsest fat, and boil it in equal proportions of milk and water for ¾ hour. Have ready some white onion sauce, dish the tripe, smother it with the sauce, and the remainder send to table in a tureen.

Time.–¾ hour.

— China Chilo —

Ingredients.–1½ lbs. of leg, loin, or neck of mutton, 2 onions, 2 lettuces, 1 lb. of green peas, 1 teaspoonful of salt, 1 teaspoonful of pepper, ¼ pint of water, ¼ lb. of CLARIFIED BUTTER, a little cayenne, when liked.

Mode.–Mince the above quantity of leg, loin, or neck of mutton, adding a little of the fat, also minced; put it into a stewpan with the remaining ingredients, previously shredding the lettuce and onion rather fine; tightly cover the stewpan, after the ingredients have been well stirred, and simmer gently for rather more than 2 hours. Serve in a dish, with a border of rice round, the same as for curry.

Time.–Rather more than 2 hours. **Sufficient** for 3 or 4 persons.

THE LATE MR. MATTHEWS, the comedian, told the following story of a Frenchman and an Englishman: a Frenchman was one day blandly demonstrating against the supercilious scorn expressed by Englishmen for the beef of France, which he, for his part, did not find so inferior to that of England: "I have been two times in England," he remarked, "but I nevère find the bif so supérieur to ours. I find it vary conveenient that they bring it you on leetle pieces of stick, for one penny; but I do not find the bif supérieur." On hearing this, the Englishman, red with astonishment, exclaimed: "Good heavens, sir! you have been eating cat's meat."

— Irish Stew —

Ingredients.–3 lbs. of loin or neck of mutton, 5 lbs. of potatoes, 5 large onions, pepper and salt to taste, rather more than 1 pint of water.

Mode.–Trim off some of the fat from the mutton, and cut it into chops of a moderate thickness. Peel and halve the potatoes, and cut the onions into thick slices. Put a layer of potatoes at the bottom of a stewpan, then a layer of mutton and onions, and season with pepper and salt; proceed in this manner until the stewpan is full, taking care to have plenty of vegetables at the top. Pour in the water, and let it stew very gently for 2½ hours, keeping the lid of the stewpan shut the whole time, and occasionally shaking it to prevent its burning.

Time.–2½ hours. **Sufficient** for 5 or 6 persons.

Irish Stew

THE ORDER OF THE GOLDEN FLEECE.–This order of knighthood was founded by Philip the Good, Duke of Burgundy, in 1429, on the day of his marriage with the Princess Isabella of Portugal. The number of the members was originally fixed at 31, including the sovereign, as the head and chief of the institution. In 1516, Pope Leo X consented to increase the number to 52, including the head. In 1700 the German emperor Charles VI and King Philip of Spain both laid claim to the order. The dispute, though subsequently settled by the intercession of France, England, and Holland, was frequently renewed, until the order was tacitly introduced into both countries, and it now passes by the respective names of the Spanish or Austrian "Order of the Golden Fleece", according to the country where it is issued.

Breast of Lamb and — Green Peas —

Ingredients.–1 breast of lamb, a few slices of bacon, ½ pint of MEDIUM STOCK, 1 lemon, 1 onion, 1 bunch of savoury herbs, fresh green peas.

Mode.–Remove the skin from the breast of lamb, put it into a saucepan of boiling water, and let it simmer for 5 minutes. Take it out and lay it in cold water. Line the bottom of a stewpan with a few thin slices of bacon; lay the lamb on these; peel the lemon, cut it into slices, and put these on the meat, to keep it white and make it tender; cover with 1 or 2 more slices of bacon; add the stock, onion, and herbs, and set it on a low heat to simmer very gently until tender. Have ready some green peas, put these on a dish, and place the lamb on the top of them.

Time.–1½ hours. **Sufficient** for 3 persons.

— Lamb Chops —

Ingredients.–8 loin chops, pepper and salt to taste.

Mode.–Ask the butcher to trim off the flap from a fine loin of lamb and cut the chops about ¾ inch in thickness. Have ready a hot grill; lay the chops on the gridiron, and broil them a nice pale brown, turning them when required. Season them with pepper and salt; serve very hot and quickly, and garnish with FRIED PARSLEY, or place them on mashed potatoes. Asparagus, spinach, or green peas are the favourite accompaniments to lamb chops.

Time.–About 8 or 10 minutes. **Sufficient** for 4 persons.

Lamb Cutlets and Spinach

Ingredients.–8 cutlets from the best end of neck, egg and breadcrumbs, salt and pepper, a little CLARIFIED BUTTER, spinach.

Mode.–Brush the cutlets over with beaten egg, sprinkle them with breadcrumbs, and season with pepper and salt. Now dip them into clarified butter, sprinkle over a few more breadcrumbs, and fry them over a high heat, turning them when required. Lay them in a warm oven to drain, then arrange them on a dish with the spinach in the centre, which should be previously well washed, boiled, drained, chopped, and seasoned.

Time.–About 7 or 8 minutes. **Sufficient** for 4 persons.

Note.–Peas, asparagus, or French beans may be substituted for the spinach; or lamb cutlets may be served with STEWED CUCUMBERS, SOUBISE sauce, etc.

— Lamb's Fries —

Ingredients.–1 lb. of lamb's fries, 3 pints of water, egg and breadcrumbs, 1 teaspoonful of chopped parsley, salt and pepper.

Mode.–To clean the fries, cut through the outer skins, push the fries out and discard the sacs. Boil the fries for ¼ hour in the above proportion of water, take them out, and dry them in a cloth; grate some bread down finely, mix with it a teaspoonful of chopped parsley and a high seasoning of pepper and salt; brush the fries lightly over with the yolk of an egg, sprinkle over the breadcrumbs, and fry for 5 minutes. Serve very hot on a napkin in a dish, with FRIED PARSLEY.

Time.–¼ hour to simmer the fries, 5 minutes to fry them. **Sufficient** for 2 or 3 persons.

— Fried Kidneys —

Ingredients.–6 kidneys, butter, pepper and salt to taste.

Mode.–Cut the kidneys open without quite dividing them, remove the skin, and put a small piece of butter in the frying-pan. When the butter is melted, lay in the kidneys the flat side downwards, and fry them for 7 or 8 minutes, turning them when they are half done. Serve on a piece of dry toast, season with pepper and salt, and put a small piece of butter in each kidney; pour the juices from the pan over them, and serve very hot.

Time.–7 or 8 minutes. **Sufficient** for 6 persons.

Roast Leg of Lamb with Mint Sauce

Saddle of lamb

Ribs of lamb

Leg of lamb

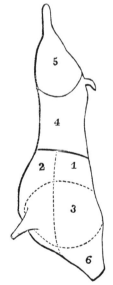

Side of lamb showing the several joints

JOINTING A LAMB.–1. Middle neck and best end of neck. 2. Breast. 3. Shoulder. 4. Loin. 5. Leg. 6. Scrag end. 1,2, and 3. Forequarter.

Roast Leg or Saddle of Lamb

Ingredients.–A leg or saddle of lamb weighing 5 to 6 lbs., a little salt.

Mode.–Place the joint in a moderately hot oven, and baste well the whole time it is cooking. When nearly done make the oven very hot so that the joint acquires a nice brown colour. Take the joint out of the roasting pan and sprinkle a little fine salt over it. Add a little boiling water to the roasting juices and strain over the meat. Serve with MINT SAUCE, and peas, spinach, or cauliflowers.

Time.–About 2 hours, allowing 20 to 25 minutes per lb.
Sufficient for 7 or 8 persons.

— Braised Loin of Lamb —

Ingredients.–1 loin of lamb weighing about 3 lbs., a few slices of fat bacon, 1 bunch of spring onions, 5 or 6 young carrots, a bunch of savoury herbs, 2 blades of pounded mace, 1 pint of stock, salt.

Mode.–Bone the meat, and line the bottom of a stewpan just capable of holding it with a few thin slices of fat bacon; add the remaining ingredients, cover the meat with a few more slices of bacon, pour in the stock, and simmer very gently for 2 hours; take out the meat, dry it, strain and reduce the gravy to half the quantity by boiling, with which glaze the meat; serve either on STEWED GREEN PEAS, boiled spinach, or STEWED CUCUMBERS.

Time.–2 hours. **Sufficient** for 4 or 5 persons.

Stuffed Shoulder of Lamb

Ingredients.–A shoulder of lamb, FORCEMEAT, trimmings of veal or beef, 2 onions, ½ head of celery, a bunch of savoury herbs, a few slices of fat bacon, 2 pints of MEDIUM STOCK.

Mode.–Ask the butcher to take the blade-bone out of a shoulder of lamb; fill up its place with forcemeat, and sew it up with coarse thread. Put it into a stewpan with a few slices of bacon under and over it, and add the remaining ingredients. Stew very gently for rather more than 2 hours. Pour off the stock, reduce it to half the quantity, then return it to the meat; serve with peas, STEWED CUCUMBERS, or a sorrel sauce.

Time.–Rather more than 2 hours. **Sufficient**, a shoulder weighing 5 lbs., for 4 or 5 persons.

Lamb's Sweetbreads, —larded, and Asparagus—

Ingredients.–1 ½ lbs. of sweetbreads, thin strips of bacon for larding, ½ pint of WHITE STOCK, white pepper and salt to taste, a small bunch of spring onions, 1 blade of pounded mace, thickening of butter and flour, 2 eggs, nearly ½ pint of cream, 1 teaspoonful of minced parsley, a very little grated nutmeg. 1 teacupful of asparagus tops.

Mode.–Soak the sweetbreads in lukewarm water, put them into a saucepan with sufficient boiling water to cover them, and let them simmer for 10 minutes; then take them out and put them into cold water. Now lard them with strips of bacon 2 inches in length, using a larding needle to thread them through, lay them in a stewpan, add the stock, seasoning, onions, mace, and a thickening of butter and flour, and stew gently for ¼ hour or 20 minutes. Beat up the egg with the cream, to which add the minced parsley and a very little grated nutmeg. Add this to the other ingredients; stir well till quite hot, but do not boil after the cream is added, or it will curdle. Have ready some tender asparagus tops, boiled; add these to the sweetbreads, and serve.

Time.–Altogether, ½ hour. **Sufficient** for 4 or 5 persons.

Bacon for larding, and larding needle

Bacon for larding should be cut into strips about 2 inches in length and about ¼ inch in width, and drawn through the meat with a larding needle. The ends of the bacon strips should show by about ¼ inch.

— Boiled Bacon —

Ingredients.–Piece of bacon weighing 2 lbs., water.

Mode.–As bacon is frequently excessively salt, let it be soaked in warm water for an hour or two before cooking it; then pare off the rusty parts, and scrape the underside and rind as clean as possible. Put it into a saucepan of cold water, let it come gradually to a boil, and as the scum rises to the surface of the water, remove it. Let it simmer very gently for 1 ½ hours; then take it up, strip off the skin, and sprinkle over the bacon a few toasted breadcrumbs, and garnish with tufts of boiled cauliflower or Brussels sprouts. When served alone, young and tender broad beans or green peas are the usual accompaniments.

Time.–1 ½ hours. **Sufficient** for 4 or 5 persons.

Boiled bacon

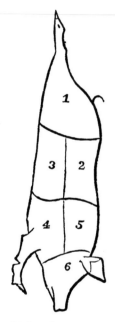

Side of a pig, showing the several joints

— Pork Cheese —

Ingredients.–2 lbs. of cold roast pork, pepper and salt to taste, 1 dessertspoonful of minced parsley, 4 leaves of sage, a very small bunch of savoury herbs, 2 blades of pounded mace, a little nutmeg, ½ teaspoonful of minced lemon peel, sufficient good strong gravy or stock to fill the mould.

Mode.–Cut the pork into fine pieces, allowing ¼ lb. of fat to each pound of lean. Season with pepper and salt; pound well the spices, and chop finely the parsley, sage, herbs, and lemon peel, and mix the whole nicely together. Put it into a mould, fill up with good strong gravy or stock, and bake in a moderate oven for rather more than 1 hour. When cold, turn it out of the mould and serve up with parsley as a garnish.

Time.–Rather more than 1 hour.

— Pork Cutlets or Chops —

Ingredients.–6 loin or foreloin cutlets of pork, egg and breadcrumbs, salt and pepper to taste; to every tablespoonful of breadcrumbs allow ½ teaspoonful of minced sage; CLARIFIED BUTTER, a little oil.

Mode.–Brush the cutlets over with egg, and sprinkle them with breadcrumbs, with which have been mixed minced sage and a seasoning of pepper and salt; drop a little clarified butter on them, and press the crumbs well down. Put the frying-pan on the heat and put in some oil; when this is hot, lay in the cutlets, and fry them a light brown on both sides. Take them out, put them in a warm oven to dry the greasy moisture from them, and dish them on mashed potatoes. Serve with them TOMATO SAUCE or SAUCE ROBERT, or PICKLED GHERKINS.

Time.–From 15 to 20 minutes. **Sufficient** for 6 persons.

— To boil a Ham —

Ingredients.–A ham, water, ASPIC or toasted breadcrumbs.

Mode.–In choosing a ham, ascertain that it is perfectly sweet by running a sharp knife into it, close to the bone; if, when the knife is withdrawn, it has an agreeable smell, the ham is good; if, on the contrary, the blade has a greasy appearance and offensive smell, the ham is bad. If it has been long hung, and is very dry and salt, let it soak in water for 24 hours, changing the water frequently. This length of time is only necessary in the case of its being very hard. Wash it thoroughly clean, and trim away from the underside all the rusty and smoked parts, which would spoil the appearance. Put it into a boiling pan, with sufficient cold water to cover it; bring it gradually to a boil, and as the scum rises, carefully remove it. Keep it simmering very gently until tender, and be careful that it does not stop boiling, nor boil too quickly. When done, take it out of the pan, strip off the skin, glaze it with ASPIC or sprinkle over it some toasted breadcrumbs, put a frill of cut paper round the knuckle, and serve. If to be eaten cold, let the ham remain in the water until nearly cold; by this method the juices are kept in, and it will be found infinitely superior to one taken out of the water hot.

NUTMEG.–This is a native of the Moluccas, and was long kept from being spread in other places by the monopolizing spirit of the Dutch, who endeavoured to keep it wholly to themselves. The plant, through the enterprise of the British, has now found its way into Penang and Bencoolen, where it flourishes and produces well. It has also been naturalized in the West Indies, where it bears fruit all the year round. Nutmeg ought to be used with caution by those who are of paralytic or apoplectic habits.

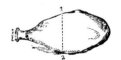

IN CUTTING A HAM, the carver will commence at the knuckle end, and cut off thin slices towards the thick part of the ham. To reach the choicer portion, the knife, which must be very sharp and thin, should be carried quite down to the bone, in the direction of the line 1 to 2. The slices should be thin and even, and always cut down to the bone.

Boiled Ham and Pork Cheese

THE HOG IN ENGLAND.–In the Anglo-Saxon period, the flesh of the hog was the staple article of consumption in every family, and a large portion of the wealth of the rich freemen of the country consisted of hogs. Hence it was common to make bequests of swine, with lands for their support, and to these were attached rights and privileges in connection with their feeding and the extent of woodland to be occupied by a given number.

R o a s t   L e g   o r   L o i n   o f   P o r k

Ingredients.–A leg or loin of pork weighing 4 to 5 lbs., SAGE AND ONION STUFFING, a little oil.

Mode.–Score the skin across in narrow strips, about ¼ inch apart, and brush it with a little oil (this makes the crackling crisper and a better colour); put it in a hot oven for the first 20 minutes, then reduce the heat a little and roast for a further 2 hours, or a little longer, taking care to baste it well. The sage and onion stuffing may be made separately and baked in a dish or, if a leg of pork is cooked, the knuckle skin may be loosened and the inside filled with stuffing. Do not omit to send to table with it a tureen of APPLE SAUCE.

Time.–About 2 hours for a loin, 2½ hours for a leg. **Sufficient** for 7 or 8 persons.

L i t t l e   R a i s e d   P o r k   P i e s

Ingredients.–2 lbs. of flour, ½ lb. of butter, ½ lb. of mutton suet, salt and white pepper to taste, 4 lbs. of boned foreloin of pork, 1 dessertspoonful of powdered sage, 1 egg.

Mode.–Mince the suet, and put it with the flour and butter into a saucepan to be made hot, and add a little salt. When melted, mix it up into a stiff paste and keep it warm; chop the pork into small pieces, season it with white pepper, salt, and the powdered sage; divide the paste into small pieces, raise it in a round or oval form, fill with the meat, cover with lids of paste, brush with a little beaten egg, and bake in a moderate oven.

Time.–If made small, about 1½ hours. **Sufficient** for about 20 small pies.

THE LEARNED PIG.–That the pig is capable of education is a fact long known to the world. The best modern evidence of his docility is the instance of the learned pig, first exhibited about a century since, who put together all the letters or figures that composed the day, month, hour, and date of the exhibition, besides many other unquestioned evidences of memory.

TO SMOKE HAMS AT HOME.– Take an old hogshead, stop up all the crevices, and fix a cross-stick near the top on which to hang the articles to be smoked. Next, in the side, cut a hole near the bottom, to introduce an iron pan filled with oak sawdust and small pieces of green wood. Hang the articles upon the cross-stick, introduce the iron pan in the opening, and place a piece of red-hot iron in the pan, cover it with sawdust, and all will be complete. Let a large ham remain 40 hours, and keep up a good smoke.

— *To Make Sausages* —

(AUTHOR'S OXFORD RECIPE)

Ingredients.–1 lb. of pork, fat and lean, without skin or gristle, 1 lb. of lean veal, 1 lb. of beef suet, ½ lb. of breadcrumbs, the rind of ½ lemon, 1 small nutmeg, 6 sage leaves, 1 teaspoonful of pepper, 2 teaspoonfuls of salt, ½ teaspoonful each of savory and marjoram.

Mode.–Chop the pork, veal, and suet finely together, add the breadcrumbs, lemon peel (which should be well minced), and the nutmeg grated. Wash and chop the sage leaves very finely, add these, with the remaining ingredients, to the sausagemeat, and when thoroughly mixed, either put the meat into skins or form it into little cakes, which should be floured and fried.

Sufficient for about 30 moderate-sized sausages.

— *Roast Sucking Pig* —

Ingredients.–A sucking pig, 6 oz. of breadcrumbs, 16 sage leaves, pepper and salt to taste, a piece of butter the size of an egg, salad oil or butter to baste with, about ½ pint of stock or gravy, 1 tablespoonful of lemon juice.

Mode.–A sucking pig, to be eaten in perfection, should not be more than three weeks old. After preparing the pig, stuff it with fine breadcrumbs, minced sage, pepper, salt, and a piece of butter the size of an egg, all of which should be well mixed together, and put into the body of the pig. Sew up the slit neatly, and truss the legs back, to allow the inside to be roasted and the underpart to be crisp. Rub the skin all over with oil, and put it into a moderate oven. Baste with oil

TO PREPARE A
SUCKING PIG
FOR COOKING.–
Immerse the pig in
boiling water for
2 minutes, then pull off
the hair. When the
skin is clean, make a
slit down the belly,
take out the entrails,
clean the nostrils and
ears, wash the pig in
cold water, and wipe it
thoroughly dry. Take
off the feet at the first
joints, leaving sufficient
skin to turn neatly
over.

TO CARVE A
SUCKING PIG.–
The first point to be
attended to is to
separate the shoulder
from the carcase, by
carrying the knife
quickly and neatly
round the circular line
1, 2, 3. The next step
is to take off the leg, by
cutting round this joint
in the same way as the
shoulder. The ribs
then stand fairly open
to the knife, which
should be carried down
in the direction of the
line 4 to 5, and two or
three helpings will
dispose of these.

*Roast Loin of
Pork with Apple
Sauce and Sage
and Onion
Stuffing*

Foreloin of pork

Hind loin of pork

Roast leg of pork

the whole of the time it is roasting, and do not allow the crackling to become blistered or burnt. Before it is taken out of the oven, cut off the head, and divide that and the body down the middle. Chop the brains and mix them with the stuffing; add ½ pint of good stock or gravy, and a tablespoonful of lemon juice to the gravy that flowed from the pig; put a little of this on the dish with the pig, and the remainder send to table in a tureen. APPLE SAUCE is a traditional accompaniment to roast pig.

Time.–2 to 2½ hours for a small pig. **Sufficient** for 10 persons.

— Pig's Trotters —

Ingredients.–4 pig's trotters or pettitoes, ½ lb. of pig's liver, ½ lb. of pig's heart, a thin slice of bacon, 1 onion, 1 blade of mace, 6 peppercorns, 3 or 4 sprigs of thyme, 1 pint of gravy, pepper and salt to taste, thickening of butter and flour.

Mode.–Put the liver, heart, and pettitoes into a stewpan with the bacon, mace, peppercorns, thyme, onion, and gravy, and simmer these gently for ¼ hour; then take out the heart and liver, and mince them very fine. Keep stewing the feet until quite tender, which will be in 20 minutes to ½ hour, reckoning from the time that they boiled up first; then put back the minced liver and heart, thicken the gravy with a little butter and flour, season with pepper and salt, and simmer over a gentle heat for 5 minutes, occasionally stirring. Dish the mince, split the feet, and arrange them round alternately with sippets of toasted bread, and pour the gravy in the middle.

Time.–Altogether 40 minutes. **Sufficient** for 3 or 4 persons.

— Veal à la Bourgeoise —

Ingredients.–2 to 3 lbs. of loin or neck of veal, 10 to 12 young carrots, a bunch of spring onions, 2 slices of lean bacon, 2 blades of mace pounded, 1 bunch of savoury herbs, pepper and salt to taste, a few new potatoes, 1 lb. of shelled green peas, bottled TOMATO SAUCE or MUSHROOM KETCHUP to flavour, butter.

Mode.–Cut the veal into cutlets, trim them, and put the trimmings into a stewpan with a little butter; lay in the cutlets and fry them a nice brown colour on both sides. Add the bacon, carrots, onions, mace, herbs, and seasoning; pour in about a pint of boiling water, and stew gently for 2 hours over a low heat. When done, skim off the fat, take out the herbs, and flavour the liquor with a little tomato sauce or mushroom ketchup. Have ready the peas and potatoes, boiled separately; put them with the veal, and serve.

Time.–2 hours. **Sufficient** for 5 or 6 persons.

— Roast Breast of Veal —

Ingredients.–3 lbs. of breast of veal, a little flour, butter.

Mode.–Wash the veal, wipe it, and dredge it with flour; put it in a moderately hot oven. Baste it plentifully until done; dish it, pour over it some plain melted butter, and send to table with it a piece of boiled bacon and a cut lemon.

Time.–From 40 to 45 minutes per lb. **Sufficient** for 6 persons.

HOW TO SILENCE A PIG.–When the emperor Charles V was one day walking in the neighbourhood of Vienna, he was much annoyed by the noise of a pig, which a country youth was carrying a little way before him. At length, irritated by the unmitigated noise, he demanded: "Have you not learned how to quiet a pig?" "Noa," replied the ingenuous peasant, ignorant of the quality of his interrogator, "and I should very much like to know how to do it." "Why, take the pig by the tail," said the emperor, "and you will see how quiet he will become." Struck by the novelty of the suggestion, the countryman at once dangled his noisy companion by the tail, and soon discovered that the pig had indeed become silent. Looking with admiration on his august adviser, he exclaimed: "Ah, you must have learned the trade much longer than I, for you understand it a great deal better."

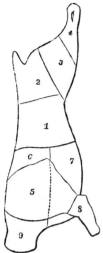

Side of a calf, showing the several joints

JOINTING A CALF. —1. Loin. 2. Chump, or rump. 3. Fillet. 4. Hock, or hind knuckle. 5. Shoulder and middle neck. 6. Best end of neck. 7. Breast. 8. Fore knuckle. 9. Scrag.

THE BREAST OF VEAL consists of two parts, the rib bones and the gristly brisket. These two parts should first be separated by sharply passing the knife in the direction of the line 1 to 2; when they are entirely divided, the rib bones should be carved in the direction of the line 5 to 6; and the brisket can be helped by cutting pieces in the direction 3 to 4.

— V e a l   C a k e —

(A CONVENIENT DISH FOR A PICNIC)

Ingredients.–A few slices of cold roast veal, a few slices of cold ham, 2 hard-boiled eggs, 2 tablespoonfuls of minced parsley, a little pepper, good gravy or stock.

Mode.–Cut off all the roast outside from the veal, and cut the eggs into slices. Procure a pretty mould; lay the veal, ham, eggs, and parsley in layers, with a little pepper between each, and when the mould is full, fill up the shape with the gravy or stock. Bake for ½ hour in a moderate oven and, when cold, turn it out.

Time.– ½ hour.

— V e a l   C o l l o p s —

(AN ENTREE)

Ingredients.–About 2 lbs. of the prime part of a leg of veal, a few slices of bacon, FORCEMEAT, cayenne to taste, egg and breadcrumbs, butter, gravy or stock, seasoning of salt, pepper, and pounded mace.

Mode.–Cut the veal into long thin collops, flatten them, and lay on each a piece of thin bacon of the same size; have ready some forcemeat, which spread over the bacon, sprinkle over all a little cayenne, roll the collops up tightly, and do not let them be more than 2 inches long. Skewer each one firmly, egg and breadcrumb them, and fry them a nice brown in a little butter, turning them occasionally, and shaking the pan about. When done, place them on a dish in a warm oven; put a small piece of butter in the pan, dredge in a little flour, add ¼ pint of gravy, or stock, or water, 2 tablespoonfuls of lemon juice, salt, pepper, and pounded mace; let the whole boil up, and pour it over the collops.

Time.–From 10 to 15 minutes. **Sufficient** for 5 or 6 persons.

— V e a l   C u t l e t s —

Ingredients.–About 3 lbs. of the prime part of a leg of veal, egg and breadcrumbs, 3 tablespoonfuls of minced savoury herbs, salt and pepper to taste, a small piece of butter, flour and lemon juice.

Mode.–Have the veal cut into slices about ¾ inch in thickness, and, if not cut perfectly even, level the meat with a cutlet bat or rolling pin. Shape and trim the cutlets, and brush them over with egg. Sprinkle with breadcrumbs, with which have been mixed the minced herbs and a seasoning of pepper and salt, and press the crumbs down. Fry them a delicate brown in oil or butter, and be careful not to burn them. They should be very thoroughly done, but not dry. Lay the cutlets in a dish, keep them hot, and make a gravy in the pan as follows: dredge in a little flour, add a piece of butter the size of a walnut, brown it, then pour ¼ pint of boiling water over it, season with pepper and salt, add a little lemon juice, give one boil, and pour it over the cutlets. These should be garnished with slices of grilled bacon; a few balls of FORCEMEAT will be found a very excellent addition to this dish.

Time.–For cutlets of a moderate thickness, about 12 minutes. **Sufficient** for 6 persons.

Boiled Calf's Feet with — Parsley and Butter —

Ingredients.–2 calf's feet, 2 slices of bacon, 2 oz. of butter, 2 tablespoonfuls of lemon juice, salt and whole pepper to taste, 1 onion, a bunch of savoury herbs, 4 cloves, 1 blade of mace, water, parsley and butter.

Mode.–Procure 2 calf's feet; bone them as far as the first joint, and put them into warm water to soak for 2 hours. Then put the bacon, butter, lemon juice, onion, herbs, spices, and seasoning into a stewpan; lay in the feet, and pour in just sufficient water to cover the whole. Stew gently for about 3 hours; take out the feet, dish them, and cover with melted butter with finely minced parsley in it. The liquor they were boiled in should be strained and put by in a clean basin; it will be found very good as an addition to gravies, etc.

Time.–Rather more than 3 hours. **Sufficient** for 4 persons.

Stewed Knuckle of Veal — and Rice —

Ingredients.–6 lbs. of knuckle of veal, 1 onion, 2 blades of mace, 1 teaspoonful of salt, ½ lb. of rice.

Mode.–Break the shank bone so that the knuckle will fit into the stewpan; put in sufficient water to cover it. Let it gradually come to a boil, put in the salt, and remove the scum as it rises. When it has simmered gently for about ¾ hour, add the remaining ingredients, and stew the whole gently for 2¼ hours. Put the meat into a deep dish, pour over it the rice, etc., and send boiled bacon and a tureen of melted butter and parsley to table with it.

Time.–3 hours' gentle stewing. **Sufficient** for 5 or 6 persons.

Note.–Macaroni, instead of rice, boiled with the veal, will be found good.

— Calf's Liver and Bacon —

Ingredients.–2 or 3 lbs. of liver, bacon, pepper and salt to taste, a small piece of butter, flour, 2 tablespoonfuls of lemon juice, ¼ pint of water.

Mode.–Cut the liver in thin slices, and cut as many slices of bacon as there are of liver; fry the bacon first, and keep it hot. Fry the liver in the fat which comes from the bacon, after seasoning it with pepper and salt and dredging over it a very little flour. Turn the liver occasionally to prevent its burning and, when done, lay it round the dish with a piece of bacon between each slice. Pour away the bacon fat, put in a small piece of butter, dredge in a little flour, add the lemon juice and water, give one boil, and pour it in the middle of the dish. It may be garnished with slices of cut lemon or balls of FORCEMEAT.

Time.–According to the thickness of the liver, 5 to 10 minutes. **Sufficient** for 6 or 7 persons.

WHEN A CALF SHOULD BE KILLED.–The age at which a calf ought to be killed should not be under four weeks; before that time the flesh is certainly not wholesome, wanting firmness, due development of muscular fibre, and those animal juices on which the flavour and nutritive properties of the flesh depend, whatever the unhealthy palate of epicures may deem to the contrary. In France, a law exists to prevent the slaughtering of calves under six weeks of age. The calf is considered in prime condition at ten weeks, when he will weigh from 16 to 18 stone, and sometimes even 20.

Calf's Liver and Bacon, and Veal à la Bourgeoise

— Calf's Liver aux Fines Herbes —

Ingredients.–2½ to 3 lbs. of calf's liver, flour, a bunch of savoury herbs, including parsley, 2 minced shallots, when liked, 1 teaspoonful of flour, 1 tablespoonful of vinegar, 1 tablespoonful of lemon juice, pepper and salt to taste, ¼ pint of water, butter.

Mode.–Procure a calf's liver as pale as possible, and cut it into slices of a good and equal shape. Dip them in flour, and fry them a good colour in a little butter. When they are done, put them on a dish, which keep hot in the oven. Mince the herbs very fine, put them in the frying-pan with a little more butter, add the remaining ingredients, simmer gently until the herbs are done, and pour over the liver.

Time.–According to the thickness of the slices, 5 to 10 minutes. **Sufficient** for 7 or 8 persons.

— Roast Loin of Veal —

Ingredients.–4 lbs. of loin of veal, butter.

Mode.–Wrap the kidney fat in paper, roll in and skewer the flap, which makes the joint a good shape, dredge it well with flour, and put it into a moderate oven. Keep it well basted, and a short time before serving, remove the paper from the kidney and allow it to acquire a nice brown colour. Have ready some melted butter, stir it into the juices in the dripping pan after taking out the meat, pour it over the veal, and serve. Garnish the dish with slices of lemon and balls of FORCEMEAT, and send to table with it boiled bacon, ham, pickled pork, or pig's cheek.

Time.–3 hours. **Sufficient** for 7 or 8 persons.

A VERY VEAL DINNER.–At a dinner given by Lord Polkemmet, a Scotch nobleman and judge, his guests saw, when the covers were removed, that the fare consisted of veal broth, a roasted fillet of veal, veal cutlets, a veal pie, a calf's head, and calf's-foot jelly. The judge, observing the surprise of his guests, volunteered an explanation: "Ou, ay, it's a' cauf; when we kill a beast, we just eat up ae side and doun the tither."

— *Minced Veal and Macaroni* —
(A PRETTY SIDE OR CORNER DISH)

Ingredients.– ¾ lb. of minced cold roast veal, 3 oz. of lean ham, 1 tablespoonful of gravy or stock, pepper and salt to taste, grated nutmeg, 1 teacupful of breadcrumbs, ¼ lb. of macaroni, 1 or 2 eggs to bind, a small piece of butter.

Mode.–Cut some nice slices from a cold fillet of veal, trim off the brown outside, and mince the meat finely with the above proportion of ham; should the meat be very dry, add a spoonful of gravy or stock. Season highly with pepper and salt, add the grated nutmeg and breadcrumbs, and mix these ingredients with 1 or 2 eggs well beaten, which should bind the mixture and make it like forcemeat. In the meantime, boil the macaroni in salt and water, and drain it; butter a mould, put some of the macaroni at the bottom and sides, mix the remainder with the forcemeat, fill the mould up to the top, put a plate or small dish on it, and steam for ½ hour. Turn it out carefully, and serve with a good gravy poured round, but not over, the meat.

Time.– ½ hour. **Sufficient** for 3 or 4 persons.

Note.–To make a variety, boil some carrots and turnips separately in a little salt and water; when done, cut them into pieces about ⅛ inch in thickness, butter an oval mould, and place the pieces in it, in white and red stripes alternately, at the bottom and sides. Proceed to fill the mould with macaroni and minced veal in the manner detailed in the recipe above, and be very careful in turning it out of the mould.

— *Veal and Ham Pie* —

Ingredients.–2 lbs. of best end of neck of veal, ½ lb. of boiled ham, 2 tablespoonfuls of minced savoury herbs, ¼ teaspoonful of grated nutmeg, 2 blades of mace pounded, pepper and salt to taste, a strip of lemon peel finely minced, the yolks of 2 hard-boiled eggs, ½ pint of water, nearly ½ pint of good strong stock or gravy, PUFF PASTE.

Mode.–Cut the veal into nice square pieces, and put a layer of them at the bottom of a pie dish; sprinkle over these a portion of the herbs, spices, seasoning, lemon peel, and the yolks of the eggs cut in slices; cut the ham very thin, and put a layer of this in. Proceed in this manner until the dish is full, so arranging it that the ham comes at the top. Lay a line of puff paste around the rim of the dish, and pour in about ½ pint of water; cover with a lid of paste, ornament it with leaves, brush it over with the yolk of an egg, and bake in a moderately hot oven for 1 to 1½ hours, or longer should the pie be very large. When it is taken out of the oven, pour in at the top, through a funnel, nearly ½ pint of strong stock or gravy; this should be made sufficiently good that, when cold, it may cut in a firm jelly. This pie may be very much enriched by adding a few mushrooms, oysters, or sweetbreads, but it will be found very good without any of the last-named additions.

Time.–1½ hours, or longer should the pie be very large.
Sufficient for 5 or 6 persons.

TO CARVE A LOIN OF VEAL.– As with a loin of mutton, the careful jointing of a loin of veal is more than half the battle in carving it. If the butcher be negligent in this matter, he should be admonished. When the jointing is properly performed, there is little difficulty in carrying the knife down in the direction of the line 1 to 2. To each guest should be given a piece of the kidney and kidney fat, which lie underneath and are considered great delicacies.

THE CALF'S-HEAD CLUB.– When the restoration of Charles II took the strait waistcoat off the minds and morose religion of the Commonwealth period, there still remained a large section of society wedded to the former state of things. The young bloods of this school adopted a novel expedient to keep alive their republican sentiments: they met, in considerable numbers, at some convenient inn, on the 30th of January in each year, the anniversary of Charles I's death, and dined off a feast prepared from calves' heads dressed in every possible variety of way, and drank toasts of defiance and hatred to the house of Stuart, and glory to the memory of old Holl Cromwell. This odd custom was continued for some time, and even down to the early part of this century it was customary for men of republican politics always to dine off calf's head on the 30th of January.

CHAPTER 6

❦ *Poultry* ❦

THE DIVISIONS OF BIRDS are founded principally on their habits of life and the natural resemblance which their external parts, especially their bills, bear to each other; there are five orders, respectively designated as BIRDS OF PREY, PERCHERS, WALKERS, WADERS, and SWIMMERS. Whereas the quadrupeds, that are formed to tread the earth in common with man are muscular and vigorous, birds are generally feeble, and therefore timid. Accordingly, wings have been given them to enable them to fly through the air and thus elude the forces which, by nature, they are unable to resist.

The mechanisms which enable birds to wing their course through the air are both singular and instructive. Their bodies are covered with feathers, so placed as to overlap each other, and arranged from the forepart backwards; their bones are tubular or hollow, and extremely light compared with those of terrestrial animals; their heads are comparatively small, their bills shaped like a wedge, their bodies slender, sharp below and round above; their eyes are much larger in proportion to the bulk of the head than in any other order of animals; their wings are capable of great expansion when struck in a downward direction, and the muscles which move them are exceedingly large—all these present a union of conditions favourable to cutting their way through the aerial element.

The food of birds varies, as it does in quadrupeds, according to the species. Some are altogether carnivorous; others, as so many of the web-footed tribes, subsist on fish; others, again, on insects and worms; and others on grain and fruit. The extraordinary powers of the gizzard of the granivorous tribes appear to exceed all credibility. Tin tubes full of grain have been forced into the stomachs of turkeys, and in twenty-four hours have been found broken, compressed, and distorted into every shape.

All birds being oviparous, the eggs which they produce are in the various species different both in figure and colour, as well as in point of number. Birds, however, do not lay eggs before they have some place to put them; accordingly, they construct nests for themselves with astonishing art. This art of nidification is one of the most wonderful contrivances which the wide field of Nature can show, and ought, of itself, to be sufficient to compel mankind to the belief that they and every other part of the creation are constantly under the protecting power of a superintending Being.

AGE AND FLAVOUR OF CHICKENS.–It has been the opinion of the medical faculty that the flesh of the young chicken is the most delicate and easy to digest of all animal food. In no animal, however, does age work such a change, in regard to the quality of its flesh, as it does in domestic fowls. In their infancy, cocks and hens are equally tender and toothsome; but as time overtakes them it is the cock whose flesh toughens first. A year-old cock, indeed, is fit for little else than to be converted into soup, while a hen at the same age, although sufficiently substantial, is not callous to the insinuations of a carving knife. As regards capons, however, the rule respecting age does not hold good. There is scarcely to be found a more delicious animal than a well fed, well dressed capon. Age does not dry up his juices; indeed, like wine, he seems but'to mellow. At three years old, even, he is as tender as a chick, with the additional advantage of his proper chicken flavour being fully developed.

— Boiled Fowls or Chickens —

Ingredients.–A pair of fowls, water, a few slices of lemon.

Mode.–Truss the fowls and put them into a stewpan with plenty of hot water; bring it to boil, and carefully remove all the scum as it rises. Simmer very gently until the fowls are tender, and bear in mind that the slower they boil, the plumper and whiter they will be. Many cooks wrap them in a floured cloth to preserve the colour and to prevent the scum from clinging to them; in this case, a few slices of lemon should be placed on the breasts, over these a sheet of buttered paper, and then the floured cloth; cooking them in this manner renders the flesh very white. Boiled ham, bacon, boiled tongue, or pickled pork, are the usual accompaniments to boiled fowls, and they may be served with BECHAMEL, WHITE SAUCE, LEMON SAUCE, MUSHROOM SAUCE, CELERY SAUCE, oyster or liver sauce, or parsley and butter. A little should be poured over the fowls, after the skewers are removed, and the remainder sent in a tureen to table.

Time.–Large birds, 1 hour; moderate-sized ones, ½ to ¾ hour. **Sufficient** for 8 to 10 persons.

— Fowl à la Mayonnaise —

Ingredients.–A cold roast fowl, MAYONNAISE, 4 or 5 young lettuces, 4 hard-boiled eggs, a bunch of watercress, endive.

Mode.–Cut the fowl into neat joints, lay them in a deep dish, piling them high in the centre, spoon mayonnaise over them, and garnish the dish with young lettuces cut in halves, watercress, endive, and hard-boiled eggs; the latter may be sliced in rings, or laid on the dish whole, cutting off at the bottom a piece of the white to make them stand. All kinds of cold meat and fish may be dressed à la mayonnaise, and make excellent luncheon or supper dishes. The sauce should not be spooned over the fowls until the moment of serving.

Sufficient for a salad for 6 or 7 persons.

— Chicken Cutlets —

Ingredients.–2 chickens, seasoning to taste of salt, white pepper, and cayenne, 1 pint of water, 2 blades of pounded mace, egg and breadcrumbs, CLARIFIED BUTTER, 1 strip of lemon rind, 2 carrots, 1 onion, 2 tablespoonfuls of MUSHROOM KETCHUP, thickening of butter and flour, 1 egg.

Mode.–Remove the breast and leg bones of the chickens; cut the meat into convenient portions or cutlets after having skinned it, and season with pepper, salt, pounded mace, and cayenne. Put the bones, trimmings, etc., into a stewpan with the water, adding the sliced carrots and onions, and lemon peel, in the above proportion; stew gently for 1½ hours, and strain the liquor. Thicken it with butter and flour, add the ketchup and the egg, well beaten; stir it over the heat, and bring it to the simmering point, but do not allow it to boil. In the meantime, egg and breadcrumb the cutlets, and sprinkle over them a few drops of clarified butter; gently fry them a delicate brown, occasionally turning them; arrange them pyramidically on the dish, and pour over them the sauce.

Time.–15 minutes to fry the cutlets. **Sufficient** for 8 persons.

TO TRUSS A FOWL FOR BOILING.–Cut the feet off to the first joint, tuck the stumps into a slit made on each side of the belly, twist the wings over the back of the fowl, and secure the top of the leg and the bottom of the wing together by running a skewer through them and the body. Make a slit in the apron of the fowl large enough to admit the parson's nose, and tie a string on the tops of the legs to keep them in their proper place. Should the fowl be very large and old, draw the sinews of the legs before tucking them in.

THE FEATHER-LEGGED BANTAM.–Since the introduction of the bantam into Europe, it has ramified into many varieties, none of which are destitute of elegance, and some, indeed, remarkable for their beauty. All are, or ought to be, of small size, but lively and vigorous, exhibiting in their movements both grace and stateliness. The variety shown in the engraving is remarkable for the tarsi, or beams of the legs, being plumed to the toes with stiff, long feathers which brush the ground. A pure white bantam is bred in the royal aviary at Windsor.

Boiled Chicken with Lemon Sauce

Fricasséed Fowl or Chicken

Ingredients.–2 small fowls or 1 large one, with the giblets, 3 oz. of butter, a bunch of parsley and of spring onions, 1 clove, 2 blades of mace, 1 shallot, 1 bayleaf, salt and white pepper to taste, ¼ pint of cream, the yolks of 3 eggs, flour.

Mode.–Choose plump birds; after washing them, skin them and carve them into joints; blanch these in boiling water for 2 or 3 minutes; take them out, and immerse them in cold water to render them white. Put the giblets, with the necks and legs, into a stewpan; add the parsley, onions, clove, mace, shallot, bayleaf, and a seasoning of pepper and salt; add to these the water that the chickens were blanched in, and simmer gently for rather more than 1 hour. Have ready another stewpan; put in the joints of fowl, with the above proportion of butter; dredge them with flour, let them get hot, but do not brown them too much; then moisten the fricassée with the stock made from the giblets, etc., and stew very gently for ½ hour. Lift the joints into another stewpan, skim the sauce, reduce it quickly over the fire by letting it boil fast, and strain it over them. Add the cream, and a seasoning of pounded mace and cayenne; let it boil up, and when ready to serve, stir in the well beaten yolks of the eggs; these should not be put in till the last moment, and the sauce should be made hot, but must not boil, or it will instantly curdle. A few mushroom buttons stewed with the fricassée are by many persons considered an improvement.

Time.–1 hour to make the gravy, ½ hour to simmer the fowl.
Sufficient for 5 or 6 persons.

— Chicken or Fowl Pie —

Ingredients.–2 small fowls or 1 large one, 1 onion, a bunch of savoury herbs, 1 blade of mace, white pepper and salt to taste, ½ teaspoonful of grated nutmeg, ½ teaspoonful of pounded mace, FORCEMEAT, a few slices of ham, 3 hard-boiled eggs, ½ pint of water, ½ lb. of PUFF PASTE.

Mode.–Skin and cut up the fowls into joints, and put the neck, legs, and backbones in a stewpan, with a little water, the sliced onion, herbs, and mace; let these stew for about 1 hour; when done, strain off the liquor (this is reserved for the gravy). Put a layer of fowl at the bottom of a pie dish, then a layer of ham, then one of forcemeat and hard-boiled eggs cut in rings; between the layers put a seasoning of pounded mace, nutmeg, pepper, and salt. Proceed in this manner until the dish is full, then pour in about ½ pint of water; border the edge of the dish with puff paste, put on a cover of paste, ornament the top, and glaze it by brushing over it the yolk of an egg. Bake from 1¼ to 1½ hours, should the pie be very large; when done, pour in, at the top, the gravy made from the bones.

Time.–1¼ to 1½ hours. **Sufficient** for 6 or 7 persons.

— Fowl Pilaff —
(BASED ON MONSIEUR SOYER'S RECIPE)

Ingredients.–1 lb. of Patna rice, 2 oz. of butter, a plump fowl, 4 pints of stock or good broth, 40 cardamom seeds, ½ oz. of coriander seeds, ¼ oz. of cloves, ¼ oz. of allspice, ¼ oz. of mace, ¼ oz. of cinnamon, ½ oz. of peppercorns, 4 onions, 6 thin slices of bacon, 2 hard-boiled eggs.

Mode.–Well wash the rice, put it into a frying-pan with the butter, and stir over a low heat until the rice is lightly browned. Truss the fowl as for boiling, put it into a stewpan with the stock or broth; pound the spices and seeds thoroughly in a mortar, tie them in a piece of muslin, and put them in with the fowl. Let it simmer slowly until it is nearly done; then add the rice, which should stew until quite tender and almost dry; cut the onions into slices, sprinkle them with flour, and fry a nice brown colour without breaking them. Have ready the slices of bacon, rolled up and grilled, and the eggs boiled hard. Lay the fowl in a dish, smother with the rice, after removing the spices, garnish with the bacon, fried onions, and the hard-boiled eggs cut into quarters, and serve very hot.

Time.–½ hour to boil a small fowl, with the rice. **Sufficient** for 5 or 6 persons.

— Roast Fowl —

Ingredients.–A large fowl, FORCEMEAT, a little flour.

Mode.–Select a large plump fowl, fill the breast with forcemeat, truss it firmly, the same as for a plain roast fowl, dredge it with flour, and put it in a moderately hot oven, basting frequently. Roast it for nearly or quite 1 hour; remove the skewers, and serve with a gravy made from the roasting juices, and BREAD SAUCE. SAUSAGEMEAT STUFFING may be substituted for the above.

Time.–A large fowl, 1 hour. **Sufficient** for 5 or 6 persons.

CHOOSING AND TRUSSING FOWLS FOR ROASTING.–Fowls, to be tender, should be killed a couple of days before they are dressed. In drawing them, be careful not to break the gall bag, as this would impart a very bitter taste; the liver and gizzard should be preserved. After having carefully plucked them, cut off the head, and skewer the skin of the neck down over the back. Cut off the claws, dip the legs in boiling water, and scrape them; turn the wings under, run a skewer through them and the middle of the legs, which should be passed through the body to the wing and leg on the other side, one skewer securing the limbs on both sides. The liver and gizzard should be placed in the wings, the liver on one side and the gizzard on the other. Tie the legs together by passing a trussing needle, threaded with twine, through the backbone, and secure it on the other side.

THE WINGS, BREAST, AND MERRYTHOUGHT [wishbone] are esteemed the prime parts of a fowl, and are usually served to the ladies of the company, to whom legs, except as a matter of paramount necessity, should not be given. Byron gave it as one reason why he did not like dining with ladies, that they always had the wings of the fowls, which he himself preferred. We heard a gentleman who, when he might have had a wing, declared his partiality for a leg, saying that he had been obliged to eat legs for so long a time that he had at last come to like them better than the other more prized parts.

Fowl Pilaff

THE AYLESBURY DUCK is, deservedly, a universal favourite. Its snowy plumage and comfortable comportment make it a credit to the poultry yard, while its broad and deep breast, and its ample back, convey the assurance that your satisfaction will not cease at its death. In parts of Buckinghamshire, this member of the duck family is bred on an extensive scale, not on plains and commons but in the abodes of the cottagers. Round the walls of the living rooms, and of the bedroom even, are fixed rows of wooden boxes lined with hay; and it is the business of the wife and children to nurse and comfort the feathered lodgers, to feed the little ducklings, and to take the old ones out for an airing. Sometimes the "stock" ducks are the cottager's own property, but it more frequently happens that they are entrusted to his care by a wholesale breeder, who pays him so much per score for all ducklings properly raised. To be perfect, the Aylesbury duck should be plump, pure white, with yellow feet and a flesh-coloured beak.

CHOOSING AND TRUSSING DUCKS.—Choose ducks with plump bellies, and with thick and yellowish feet. They should be trussed with the feet on, which should be scalded, and the skin peeled off and then turned up close to the legs. Run a skewer through the middle of each leg, after having drawn them as close as possible to the body to plump up the breast, passing the same quite through the body. Cut off the heads and necks, and the wings at the first joint, and bring these close to the sides; twist the feet round and truss them at the back of the bird. After the duck is stuffed, both ends should be secured with string.

To ensure ducks being tender, never dress them the same day they are killed; if the weather permits, they should hang a day or two.

— Roast Ducks —

Ingredients.—A pair of ducks, SAGE AND ONION STUFFING, flour.

Mode.—Make a stuffing of sage and onion sufficient for one duck, and leave the other unseasoned, as the flavour is not liked by everybody. Put them into a moderately hot oven, and keep them well basted the whole of the time they are cooking. A few minutes before serving, dredge them lightly with flour to make them froth and look plump; send them to table hot and quickly, with a good gravy made from the roasting juices; pour a little of this round but not over the ducks, and put the rest in a tureen. When in season, green peas should invariably accompany this dish.

Time.—Full-grown ducks, ¾ to 1 hour; ducklings, 25 to 35 minutes. **Sufficient** for 6 or 7 persons.

— Stewed Duck and Turnips —

Ingredients.—The remains of 2 roast duck, ½ pint of good gravy, 4 shallots, a few slices of carrot, a small bunch of savoury herbs, 1 blade of pounded mace, 1 lb. of turnips, weighed after being peeled, 2 oz. of butter, pepper and salt to taste.

Mode.—Cut up the duck into joints, fry the shallots, carrots, and herbs, and put them, with the duck, into the gravy; add the pounded mace, and stew gently for 20 minutes to ½ hour. Cut the turnips into ½-inch cubes, put the butter into a stewpan, and stew them till quite tender, which will be in about ½ hour, or rather more; season with pepper and salt, and serve in the centre of the dish, with the duck, etc. laid round.

Time.—½ hour to stew the duck, rather more than ½ hour to stew the turnips.

— Roast Goose —

CHOOSING AND TRUSSING A GOOSE.–Select a goose with a clean white skin, plump breast, and yellow feet; if these latter are red, the bird is old. Should the weather permit, let it hang for a few days to improve the flavour. Carefully wash and wipe the goose; cut off the neck close to the back, leaving the skin long enough to turn over; cut off the feet and also the wings at the first joint. Beat the breastbone flat with a rolling pin, put a skewer through the underpart of each wing, and having drawn up the legs closely, put a skewer into the middle of each and pass the same quite through the body. Insert another skewer into the small of the leg, bring it close down to the side bone, run it through, and do the same to the other side.

Ingredients.–A goose, 4 large onions, 10 sage leaves, ¼ lb. of breadcrumbs, 1½ oz. of butter, salt and pepper to taste, 1 egg.

Mode.–Make a sage and onion stuffing of the above ingredients, put it into the body of the goose, and secure it firmly at both ends, by passing the rump through a hole made in the skin, and the other end by tying the skin of the neck to the back; by this means the seasoning will not escape. Should a very highly-flavoured stuffing be preferred, the onions should not be parboiled, but minced raw; of the two methods, the mild seasoning is far superior. Put the goose into a moderately hot oven, keep it well basted, and roast for 1½ to 2 hours, according to the size. Remove the skewers, and serve with a tureen of gravy made from the roasting juices, and one of APPLE SAUCE. A ragoût, or pie, should be made of the giblets, or they may be stewed down to make gravy. Be careful to serve the goose before the breast falls, or its appearance will be spoiled by coming flattened to table. As this is rather a troublesome bird to carve, a large quantity of gravy should not be poured round it, but sent in a tureen.

Time.–A large goose, 1¾ hours; a moderate-sized one, 1¼ to 1½ hours. **Sufficient** for 8 or 9 persons.

Note.–A teaspoonful of made mustard, a saltspoonful of salt, and a few grains of cayenne, mixed with a glass of port, are sometimes poured into the goose by a slit made in the apron. This sauce is, by many persons, considered an improvement.

TO CARVE A GOOSE.–Evenly cut slices, not too thick or too thin, should be carved from the breast in the direction of 2 to 3; after the first slice has been cut, a hole should be made with the knife in the part called the apron, passing it round the line 1, 1, 1; here the stuffing is located, and some of this should be served on each plate. The shape of the leg and wing, when disengaged from the body of the goose, should be like that shown in the engravings below. It will be necessary, perhaps, in taking off the leg, to turn the goose on its side, and then, pressing down the small end of the leg, the knife should be passed under it from the top quite down to the joint; the leg being now turned back by the fork, the knife must cut through the joint, loosening the thigh bone from its socket.

Emden goose

Leg and wing of goose

Croquettes of Turkey, and Pigeon Pie

Raised pie of pigeons

THE GOOSE.–The best geese are found on the borders of Suffolk, and in Norfolk and Berkshire, but the largest flocks are reared in the fens of Lincolnshire and Cambridge. They thrive best where they have an easy access to water, and large herds of them are sent every year to London to be fattened by the metropolitan poulterers. "A Michaelmas goose," says Dr. Kitchener, "is as famous in the mouths of the millions as the mince pie at Christmas; yet for those who eat with delicacy, it is, at that time, too full-grown. The true period when the goose is in the highest perfection is when it has just acquired its full growth, and not begun to harden; if the March goose is insipid, the Michaelmas goose is rank. The fine time is between both, from the second week in June to the first in September." It is said that the Michaelmas goose is indebted to Queen Elizabeth for its origin on the table at that season. Her majesty happened to dine on one at the table of an English baronet, when she received the news of the discomfiture of the Spanish Armada. In commemoration of this event, she commanded the goose to make its appearance at table on every Michaelmas.

— *Pigeon Pie* —
(EPSOM GRANDSTAND RECIPE)

Ingredients.–1 ½ lbs. of rump steak, 2 or 3 pigeons, 3 slices of ham, pepper and salt to taste, 2 oz. of butter, 4 eggs, ½ lb. of PUFF PASTE, ½ pint of MEDIUM STOCK.

Mode.–Cut the steak into pieces about 3 inches square, and with them line the bottom of a pie dish, seasoning them well with pepper and salt. Clean the pigeons, rub them with pepper and salt inside and out, and put into the body of each rather more than ½ oz. of butter; lay them on the steak, with a piece of ham on each pigeon. Add the yolks of 4 eggs, and half fill the dish with the stock; place a border of puff paste round the edge of the dish, put on the cover, and ornament it in any way that may be preferred. Clean three of the feet, and place them in a hole made in the crust at the top; this shows what kind of pie it is. Glaze the crust, that is to say, brush it over with the yolk of an egg, and bake it in a moderate oven for about 1 ¼ hours. When liked, a seasoning of pounded mace may be added.

Time.–1 ¼ hours. **Sufficient** for 5 or 6 persons.

— *Croquettes of Turkey* —

Ingredients.–The remains of a turkey; to every ½ lb. of meat allow 2 oz. of ham or bacon, 2 shallots, 1 oz. of butter, 1 tablespoonful of flour, the yolks of 2 eggs, egg and breadcrumbs.

Mode.–The smaller pieces of turkey, that will not do for a fricassée or hash, answer very well for this dish. Mince the meat finely with ham or bacon in the above proportion; make a stock of the bones and trimmings, well seasoning it; mince the shallots, put them into a stewpan with the butter, and add the flour; put into the stewpan the minced meat, and about ½ pint of the stock made from the bones and trimmings. When just boiled, add the yolks of 2 eggs; allow the mixture to cool, and then shape it in a wineglass. Cover the croquettes with egg and breadcrumbs, and fry them a delicate brown. Put small pieces of parsley stems for stalks, and serve with rolls of grilled bacon.

Time.–8 minutes to fry the croquettes.

— *Roast Turkey* —

Ingredients.–Turkey, FORCEMEAT, a little flour, butter.

Mode.–Fasten a sheet of buttered paper to the breast of the bird, put it into a moderately hot oven, and keep it well basted the whole of the time it is cooking. About ¼ hour before serving, remove the paper, dredge the turkey lightly with flour, and put a piece of butter into the basting ladle; as the butter melts, baste the bird with it. When of a nice brown and well frothed, serve with a tureen of gravy made from the roasting juices and one of BREAD SAUCE. Fried sausages are a favourite addition to roast turkey; they make a pretty garnish, besides adding very much to the flavour. Turkey may also be cooked with SAUSAGEMEAT STUFFING or served with a chestnut forcemeat and CHESTNUT SAUCE.

Time.–A small turkey, 1 ½ hours; a moderate-sized one, about 10 lbs., 2 hours; a large one, 2 ½ hours, or longer.

THE PIGEON.– The blue house-pigeon is the variety principally reared for the table in this country. When young, and still fed by their parents, they are most preferable for the table, and are called squabs; under six months they are denominated squeakers, and at six months they begin to breed. Their flesh is accounted savoury, delicate, and stimulating, and the dark-coloured birds are considered to have the highest flavour, whilst the light are esteemed to have the more delicate flesh.

ENGLISH TURKEYS.–These are reared in great numbers in Suffolk, Norfolk, and several other counties, whence they were wont to be driven to the London market in flocks of several hundreds; the improvements in our modes of travelling now, however, enable them to be brought by railway. Their drivers used to manage them with great facility by means of a bit of red rag tied to the end of a long stick, which, from the antipathy these birds have to that colour, effectually answered the purpose of a scourge.

CHAPTER 7

Game

THE COMMON LAW OF ENGLAND has a maxim that goods in which no person can claim any property belong, by his or her prerogative, to the king or queen. Accordingly, those animals, those *ferae naturae*, which come under the denomination of game are, in our laws, styled his or her majesty's, and may therefore, as a matter of course, be granted by the sovereign to another. From this circumstance arose the right of lords of manors or others to the game within their respective liberties, and to protect these species of animals the game laws were originated and still remain in force. There are innumerable acts of parliament inflicting penalties on persons who illegally kill game, and some of them are very severe.

THE PURSUIT OF FOUR-FOOTED BEASTS OF GAME is called hunting, which to this day is followed in the field and the forest, with gun and greyhound. Birds, on the contrary, are not hunted, but shot in the air or taken with nets and other devices, which is called fowling, or they are pursued and taken by birds of prey, which is called hawking, a species of sport now fallen almost entirely into desuetude in England.

William the Norman and his two sons who succeeded him were passionately fond of hunting, and greatly circumscribed the liberties of their subjects in reference to the killing of game. The privilege of hunting in the royal forests was confined to the king and his favourites. King John was likewise especially attached to the sports of the field, whilst Edward III was so enamoured of the exercise that even during his absence at the wars in France he took with him sixty couples of stag hounds and as many hare hounds. Great in wisdom as the Scotch Solomon, James I, conceited himself to be, he was much addicted to the amusements of hunting, hawking, and shooting. Yea, it is even asserted that his precious time was divided between hunting, the bottle, and his inkstand; to the first he gave his fair weather, to the second his dull, and to the third his cloudy. From his days down to the present, the sports of the field have continued to hold their high reputation, not only for the promotion of health, but for helping to form that manliness of character which enters so largely into the composition of the sons of the British soil.

— R o a s t   B l a c k c o c k —

Ingredients.–A brace of blackcock, butter, toast.

Mode.–Let these birds hang for a few days, or they will be tough and tasteless. Pluck and draw them, and wipe the insides and outsides with a damp cloth, as washing spoils the flavour. Truss them in the same manner as roast fowl, cutting off the toes, and scalding and peeling the feet; the head may be cut off or left on and skewered to the side. Put them into a moderate oven, baste them well with butter, and serve with a piece of toast under, and a good gravy and BREAD SAUCE. After trussing, some cooks cover the breast with vine leaves and slices of bacon, and then roast them.

Time.–45 to 50 minutes. **Sufficient** for 5 or 6 persons.
Seasonable from the middle of August to the end of December.

THE BLACKCOCK, HEATHCOCK, MOORFOWL, OR HEATH POULT.–This bird sometimes weighs as much as 4 pounds, and the hen about 2. It is at present confined to the more northern parts of Britain, culture and extending population having united in driving it into more desolate regions. The males are hardly distinguishable from the females until they are about half grown, when the black feathers begin to appear, first about the sides and breast. Their food consists of the tops of birch and heath, except when the mountain berries are ripe, at which period they eagerly pick the bilberries and cranberries from the bushes.

Jugged Hare with Redcurrant Jelly and Forcemeat Balls

— R o a s t   W i l d   D u c k —

Ingredients.–A brace of wild duck, flour, butter.

Mode.–Carefully pluck and draw the ducks; cut off the heads close to the necks, leaving sufficient skin to turn over, but leave the feet on; twist each leg at the knuckle, and rest the claws on each side of the breast. Roast the birds in a moderately hot oven; let them remain for 5 minutes without basting when they are first put in (this will keep the juices in), and afterwards baste plentifully with butter; a few minutes before serving, dredge them lightly with flour, baste well, and send them to table nicely frothed and full of gravy. If overdone, the birds will lose their flavour. Serve with a good gravy made from the roasting juices or ORANGE GRAVY, and a cut lemon.

Time.–When liked underdone, 20 to 25 minutes; well done, 25 to 35 minutes. **Sufficient** for 6 persons. **Seasonable** from November to February.

— Grouse Pie —

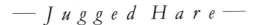

Ingredients.–A brace of grouse, cayenne, salt, and pepper to taste, 1 lb. of rump steak, ½ pint of well-seasoned CHICKEN BROTH, ½ lb. of PUFF PASTE, 1 egg yolk.

Mode.–Pluck and draw the birds; line the bottom of a pie dish with the rump steak cut into neat pieces; should the birds be large, cut them into joints, but if small they may be laid in the pie whole; season highly with salt, cayenne, and black pepper; pour in the broth, line the rim of the dish with puff paste, cover with a round of paste brushed over with the yolk of an egg, and bake in a moderate oven for ¾ to 1 hour. If the grouse is cut into joints, the backbones and trimmings will make the broth, by stewing them with an onion, a little sherry, a bunch of herbs, and a blade of mace.

Time.–¾ to 1 hour. **Sufficient** for 4 or 5 persons. **Seasonable** from August 12 to the beginning of December.

— Jugged Hare —

Ingredients.–A hare, 1½ lbs. of shin of beef, ½ lb. of butter, 1 onion, 1 lemon, 6 cloves, pepper, cayenne, and salt to taste, ½ pint of port, flour.

Mode.–Skin, paunch, and wash the hare, cut it into pieces, dredge them with flour, and fry in butter. Have ready 1½ pints of gravy, made from the above proportion of beef and thickened with a little flour. Put this into a jar; add the pieces of fried hare, an onion stuck with the cloves, a lemon peeled and cut in half, and a good seasoning of pepper, cayenne, and salt; cover the jar down tightly, put it up to the neck into a stewpan of boiling water, and let it stew until the hare is quite tender, taking care to keep the water boiling. When nearly done, pour in the port, and add a few balls of FORCEMEAT; these must be fried or baked in the oven for a few minutes before they are put into the gravy. Serve with REDCURRANT JELLY.

Time.–3½ to 4 hours. If the hare is old, allow 4½ hours. **Sufficient** for 7 or 8 persons.

— Roast Hare —

Ingredients.–A hare, FORCEMEAT, a little milk, butter and flour.

Mode.–Wash the hare in several waters, wipe it dry, fill the belly with forcemeat, and sew it up. Put it in a moderate oven at first, or the outside will become dry and hard before the inside is done. Baste it well with milk for a short time, and afterwards with butter; particular attention must be paid to the basting, so as to preserve the meat on the back juicy and nutritive. When it is almost roasted enough, flour the hare, and baste well with butter. When nicely frothed, dish it, remove the skewers, and send it to table with a little gravy made from the roasting juices, and a tureen of the same. REDCURRANT JELLY must also not be forgotten, as this is an indispensable accompaniment to roast hare. If the liver is fresh and sound, it may be parboiled, minced, and mixed with the stuffing.

Time.–A middling-sized hare, 1¼ hours; a large hare, 1½ to 2 hours. **Sufficient** for 5 or 6 persons. **Seasonable** from September to the end of February.

THE WILD DUCK. –The male of the wild duck is called a mallard, and the young ones are called flappers. The time to try to find a brood of these is about the month of July, among the rushes of the deepest and most retired parts of some brook or stream. When once found, flappers are easily killed, as they attain their full growth before their wings are fledged. Consequently, the sport is more like hunting water-rats than shooting birds. When the flappers take wing, they assume the name of wild ducks, and about the month of August repair to the corn fields, where they remain until they are disturbed by harvesting. They then frequent the rivers pretty early in the evening, and give excellent sport to those who have patience to wait for them. In order to know a wild duck, it is necessary only to look at the claws, which should be black.

GROUSE.–These birds are divided into wood grouse, black grouse, red grouse, and white grouse. The wood grouse is further distinguished as the cock of the wood, or capercaillie, and is as large as the turkey. Black grouse is also distinguished as black-game, or the blackcock. The red grouse, gorcock, or moorcock, weighs about 19 ounces, and the female somewhat less. In the wild heathy tracts of the northern counties of England it is plentiful, also in Wales and the highlands of Scotland. White grouse, or ptarmigan, is nearly the same size as the red grouse, and is found in lofty situations, where it supports itself in the severest weather.

—Roast Partridge—

Ingredients.–A brace of partridges, butter, a little flour.

Mode.–When the birds are firmly and plumply trussed, roast them in a moderately hot oven; keep them well basted with butter, and a few minutes before serving, flour and froth them well. Dish them, and serve with gravy made from the roasting juices and BREAD SAUCE, and send to table hot and quickly. A little of the gravy should be poured over the birds.

Time.–25 to 35 minutes. **Sufficient** for 4 or 5 persons.
Seasonable from September 1 to the beginning of February.

CHOOSING AND TRUSSING PARTRIDGES.–Choose young birds, with dark-coloured bills and yellowish legs, and let them hang a few days, or there will be no flavour to the flesh, nor will it be tender. They may be trussed with or without the head. Pluck, draw, and wipe the partridge carefully inside and out; cut off the head, leaving sufficient skin on the neck to skewer back; bring the legs close to the breast, between it and the side bones, and pass a skewer through the pinions and the thick part of the thighs. When the head is left on, it should be brought round and fixed onto the point of the skewer.

THE PHEASANT.– This beautiful bird is said to have been discovered by the Argonauts on the banks of the Phasis, near Mount Ararat, in their expedition to Colchis. It is common, however, in almost all the southern parts of the European continent, and has been long naturalized in the warmest and most woody counties of England. The cock bird is generally reckoned the best, except when the hen is with egg. They should hang some time before they are dressed, as, if they are cooked fresh, the flesh will be exceedingly dry and tasteless.

Roast Pheasant with Bread Sauce and Stewed Celery à la Crème

—Roast Pheasant—

Ingredients.–A brace of pheasants, a little flour and butter, ¼ pint of WHITE STOCK.

Mode.–After the birds are plucked and drawn, wipe the insides with a damp cloth, place a walnut of butter in each, and truss in the same manner as partridge. If the head is left on, bring it round under the wing and fix it with a skewer. Roast the birds in a moderately hot oven, keeping them well basted and turning them occasionally. Ten minutes before they are done, dredge a little flour over them to froth and brown the skin. Thicken the cooking juices with a little butter and flour, adding a few tablespoonfuls of stock, and serve poured round the birds, with a tureen of BREAD SAUCE. Several of the best tail feathers are sometimes stuck in the tail as an ornament.

Time.– ½ to 1 hour, according to the size of the birds. **Sufficient** for 4 or 5 persons. **Seasonable** from October 1 to early February.

— R a b b i t   P i e —

Ingredients.–1 rabbit, a few slices of ham, salt and white pepper to taste, 2 blades of pounded mace, ½ teaspoonful of grated nutmeg, FORCEMEAT, 3 hard-boiled eggs, ½ pint of gravy, ½ lb. of PUFF PASTE.

Mode.–Cut up the rabbit (which should be young), remove the breastbone, and bone the legs. Put the rabbit, slices of ham, forcemeat balls, and hard-boiled eggs in layers, and season each layer with pepper, salt, pounded mace, and grated nutmeg. Pour in about ½ pint of water, cover with puff paste, and bake in a moderate oven for about 1½ hours. Should the crust acquire too much colour, place a piece of paper over it to prevent its burning. When done, pour in at the top, by means of the hole in the middle of the crust, a little good gravy made of the breast and leg bones of the rabbit and 2 or 3 shin bones of beef, flavoured with onion, herbs, and spices.

Time.–1½ hours. **Sufficient** for 5 or 6 persons.

Note.–The liver of the rabbit may be boiled, minced, and mixed with the forcemeat if the flavour is liked.

THE COMMON OR WILD RABBIT.– Warrens, or enclosures, are frequently made in favourable localities, and some of them are so large as to comprise 2,000 acres. The common wild rabbit is of a grey colour, and is esteemed the best for the purposes of food. Its skin is valuable as an article of commerce, being used for the making of hats. Another variety of the rabbit, however, called the "silver-grey", has been lately introduced to this country, and is still more valuable.

— R a g o û t   o f   R a b b i t   o r   H a r e —

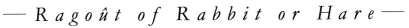

Ingredients.–A rabbit, 3 teaspoonfuls of flour, 3 sliced onions, 2 oz. of butter, a few thin slices of bacon, pepper and salt to taste, 2 slices of lemon, 1 bayleaf, 1 glass of port.

Mode.–Slice the onions, and put them into a stewpan with the flour and butter; place the pan near the fire, stir well as the butter melts, till the onions become a rich brown colour, and add, by degrees, a little water or gravy till the mixture is of the consistency of cream. Cut some thin slices of bacon; lay these in the pan with the rabbit, cut into neat joints; add a seasoning of pepper and salt, the lemon and bayleaf, and let the whole simmer until tender. Pour in the port, give one boil, and serve.

Time.–About ½ hour to simmer the rabbit. **Sufficient** for 4 or 5 persons.

CHOOSING AND TRUSSING A HARE.–Choose a young hare, which may be known by its smooth and sharp claws, and by the cleft in the lip not being much spread. To be eaten in perfection, it must hang for several days. It is better to hang without being paunched, but should it be emptied, wipe the inside every day, and sprinkle over it a little pepper and ginger to prevent the musty taste which long keeping in the damp occasions, and which also affects the stuffing. After it is skinned, wash it well, and soak it for an hour in warm water to draw out the blood; if old, let it lie in vinegar for a short time, but wash it well afterwards in several waters. After filling the belly with forcemeat, bring the hind and fore legs close to the body towards the head, run a skewer through each, fix the head between the shoulders by means of another skewer, and be careful to leave the ears on. Put a string round the body from skewer to skewer, and tie it above the back.

— S t e w e d   V e n i s o n —

Ingredients.–A shoulder of venison, a few slices of mutton fat, 2 glasses of port, pepper and allspice to taste, 1½ pints of weak stock or gravy, ½ teaspoonful of pepper, ½ teaspoonful of allspice, whole allspice and peppercorns to taste.

Mode.–Hang the venison till tender; take out the bone, flatten the meat with a rolling pin, and place over it a few slices of mutton fat, which have been previously soaked for 2 or 3 hours in port; sprinkle these with a little fine allspice and pepper, roll the meat up, and bind and tie it securely. Put it into a stewpan with the bone and the above proportion of weak stock or gravy, the port, and whole allspice and black pepper to taste; cover tightly, and simmer very gently for 3½ to 4 hours. When quite tender, take off the string and dish the meat; strain the gravy over it, and send it to table with REDCURRANT JELLY. Unless the joint is very fat, the above is the best mode of cooking it.

Time.–3½ to 4 hours. **Sufficient** for 10 to 12 persons.

Seasonable– Buck venison, from June to Michaelmas; doe venison, from November to the end of January.

VENISON.–This is the name given to the flesh of some kinds of deer, which is esteemed as very delicious. About a century back, deer were found wild in some of the rough and mountainous parts of Wales, as well as in the forests of Exmoor, in Devonshire, and the woods on the banks of the Tamar. In the middle ages, the deer formed food for the not over-abstemious monks, as represented by Friar Tuck in the admirable fiction of *Ivanhoe*; and at a later period it was a deer-stealing adventure that drove the "ingenious" William Shakespeare to London, to become a common player, and the greatest dramatist that ever lived.

CHAPTER 8

Vegetables

Strange there should be found
Who, self-imprison'd in their proud saloons,
Renounce the odours of the open field
For the unscented fictions of the loom;
Who, satisfied with only pencilled scenes,
Prefer to the performance of a God,
Th' inferior wonders of an artist's hand!
Lovely, indeed, the mimic works of art,
But Nature's works far lovelier.—COWPER.

"IF OUR POWERS OF OBSERVATION were limited to the highest orders of animals and plants," says Hogg in his *Natural History of the Vegetable Kingdom*, "if there were only mammals, birds, reptiles, fishes, and insects in the one, and trees, shrubs, and herbs in the other, we should then be able with facility to define the bounds of the two kingdoms; but as we descend the scale of each, and arrive at the lowest forms of animals and plants, we there meet with bodies of the simplest structure, sometimes a mere cell, whose organization, modes of development and reproduction, are so anomalous that we cannot distinguish whether they are plants or animals."

Whilst it is thus difficult to determine where the animal begins and the vegetable ends, it is as difficult to account for many of the singularities by which numbers of plants are characterized. This, however, can hardly be regarded as a matter of surprise when we recollect that the vegetable kingdom is composed of many thousands of species of plants.

IN ACCORDANCE WITH THE PLAN OF THIS WORK, special notices of culinary vegetables will accompany the various recipes in which they are spoken of. But here we cannot resist the opportunity of declaring it as our conviction that he or she who introduces a useful or an ornamental plant into our island ought justly to be considered a benefactor to the country. No one can calculate the benefits which may spring from this very vegetable, after its qualities have become thoroughly known. If viewed in no other light, it is pleasing to consider it as bestowing upon us a share of the blessings of other climates, and enabling us to participate in the luxury which a more genial sun has produced.

*Asparagus
Pudding*

ARTICHOKES.–
Wash artichokes
well in several waters;
see that no insects
remain about them,
and trim away the
leaves at the bottom.
Cut off the stems and
put them into boiling
water, to which has
been added a little
salt and lemon juice.
Keep the saucepan
uncovered, and let
them boil quickly until
tender; ascertain when
they are done by
thrusting a fork in
them, or by trying if
the leaves can be easily
removed.

— Fried Artichokes —

Ingredients.–5 or 6 globe artichokes, salt and water; for the batter, ¼ lb. of flour, a little salt, the yolk of 1 egg, milk.

Mode.–Trim and boil the artichokes, and rub them over with lemon juice, to keep them white. When they are quite tender, take them up, remove the chokes, and divide the bottoms; dip each piece into batter, fry them in hot oil, and garnish the dish with FRIED PARSLEY . Serve with plain melted butter.

Time.–20 minutes to boil the artichokes, 5 to 7 minutes to fry them. **Sufficient** for 4 or 5 persons.

— Boiled Asparagus —

Ingredients.–To each pint of water allow ½ teaspoonful of salt; 50 to 60 stems of asparagus.

Mode.–Asparagus should be dressed as soon as possible after it is cut, although it may be kept for a day or two by putting the stalks into cold water; yet, to be good, like every other vegetable, it cannot be cooked too fresh. Scrape the white part of the stems, beginning from the head, and throw them into cold water; then tie them into bundles of about 20 each, keeping the heads all one way, and cut the stalks evenly, that they may all be the same length; put them into boiling water, with salt in the above proportion; keep them boiling

Asparagus tongs

ASPARAGUS.–This plant belongs to the order Liliaceae, which, in the temperate regions of both hemispheres, is most abundant, and, between the tropics, gigantic in size and arborescent in form. Asparagus is a native of Great Britain, and is found on various parts of the seacoast, and in the fens of Lincolnshire. At Kynarve Cove, in Cornwall, there is an island called Asparagus Island, from the abundance in which it is there found.

quickly until tender, with the saucepan uncovered. When the asparagus is done, dish it upon toast, and leave the white ends outwards each way, with the points meeting in the middle. Serve with a tureen of plain melted butter.

Time.–15 to 18 minutes. **Sufficient** for 4 or 5 persons.

— A s p a r a g u s   P u d d i n g —

Ingredients.– ½ lb. of asparagus "peas", 4 eggs, 2 tablespoonfuls of flour, 1 tablespoonful of very finely minced ham, 1 oz. of butter, pepper and salt to taste, milk.

Mode.–Cut up the nice green tender parts of asparagus about the size of peas; put them into a basin with the eggs, which should be well beaten, and the flour, ham, butter, pepper, and salt. Mix all these ingredients well together, and moisten with sufficient milk to make the pudding of the consistency of thick batter; put it into a buttered basin, tie it down tightly with a floured cloth, place it in boiling water, and let it boil for 2 hours; turn it out of the basin on to a hot dish, and pour plain melted butter round, but not over, the pudding.

Time.–2 hours. **Sufficient** for 4 or 5 persons.

— B r o a d   B e a n s   à   l a   P o u l e t t e —

Ingredients.–4 lbs. of broad beans, shelled, ½ pint of stock or broth, a small bunch of savoury herbs, including parsley, a small lump of sugar, the yolk of 1 egg, ¼ pint of cream, pepper and salt to taste.

Mode.–Procure the beans young and freshly gathered, and shell sufficient to make 1 ½ lbs. Boil them, in lightly salted water, until nearly done; then drain them and put them into a stewpan, with the stock, finely minced herbs, and sugar. Stew the beans until perfectly tender, and the liquor has evaporated a little; then beat up the egg yolk with the cream and seasoning, add this to the beans, let the whole get thoroughly hot and, when on the point of simmering, serve.

Time.–10 minutes to boil the beans, 15 minutes to stew them in the stock. **Sufficient** for 4 persons.

— B o i l e d   B e e t r o o t —

Ingredients.–Beetroot, boiling water.

Mode.–When large, young, and juicy, this vegetable makes a very excellent addition to winter salads, and may easily be converted into PICKLED BEETROOT. Beetroot is more frequently served cold than hot, but when the latter mode is preferred, plain melted butter should be sent to table with it. It may also be stewed with button onions, or boiled and served with roasted onions. Wash the beets thoroughly, but do not prick or break the skin, or they would lose their beautiful colour in boiling. Put them into boiling water, and let them boil until tender, keeping them well covered. If to be served hot, remove the peel quickly, and cut the beetroot into thick slices. For salads, let the root cool, then peel and cut it into slices.

Time.–Small beetroot, 1 ½ to 2 hours; large, 2 ½ to 3 hours.

BEETROOT.–The geographical distribution of the order to which beetroot belongs is most common in extra-tropical and temperate regions, where they are common weeds, frequenting waste places, among rubbish, and on marshes by the seashore. Many of them are used as potherbs, and some are emetic and vermifuge in their medicinal properties. The root of garden or red beet is exceedingly wholesome and nutritious, and Dr. Lyon Playfair has recommended that a good brown bread may be made by rasping down this root with an equal quantity of flour.

Boiled Broccoli, and Stewed Red Cabbage with Sausages

— Boiled Broccoli —

Ingredients.–To each pint of water allow ½ teaspoonful of salt; 2 lbs. of broccoli.

Mode.–Strip off the outer leaves, and cut off the others level with the flower; put into cold salted water, with the heads downwards. When they have remained in this for about ¾ hour, and they are perfectly free from insects, put them into a saucepan of boiling water, salted in the above proportion, and keep them boiling briskly, with the saucepan uncovered. Take them up with a slice the moment they are done, drain them well, and serve with a tureen of melted butter, a little of which should be poured over the broccoli. If left in the water after it is done, its colour will be spoiled and its crispness gone.

Time.–Small heads, 10 to 15 minutes; large ones, 20 minutes. **Sufficient** for 5 or 6 persons.

— Boiled Brussels Sprouts —

Ingredients.–To each pint of water allow ½ teaspoonful of salt; 2 lbs. of Brussels sprouts.

Mode.–Nicely wash the sprouts and pick off the outer leaves; put them into a saucepan of boiling water, with salt in the above proportion; keep the pan uncovered, and let them boil briskly until tender; drain, dish, and serve with a tureen of MELTED BUTTER, or with MAITRE D'HOTEL BUTTER poured over them. Another mode of serving, when they are dished, is to stir in about 1½ oz. of butter and a seasoning of pepper and salt. They must, however, be sent to table very quickly, as they soon cool. Where the cook is very expeditious, they may be arranged on the dish in the form of a pineapple, giving a very pretty appearance.

Time.–From 9 to 12 minutes after the water boils. **Sufficient** for 5 or 6 persons.

Brussels sprouts

THE CABBAGE TRIBE.–Of all the tribes of the *Cruciferae* this is by far the most important. It contains a collection of plants which, both in themselves and their products, occupy a prominent position in agriculture, commerce, and domestic economy. On the cliffs of Dover, and in many places on the coasts of Dorsetshire, Cornwall, and Yorkshire, there grows a wild plant, with variously-indented, much-waved, and loose-spreading leaves, of a sea-green colour, and large yellow flowers. In spring, the leaves of this plant are collected by the inhabitants, who, after boiling them in two waters to remove the saltness, use them as a vegetable along with their meat. This is the *Brassica oleracea* of science, the wild cabbage or colewort from which have originated all the varieties of cabbage, cauliflower, greens, and broccoli.

—Stewed Red Cabbage—

Ingredients.–1 large red cabbage, a small slice of ham, ½ oz. of butter, 1 pint of weak stock or broth, ¼ pint of vinegar, salt and pepper to taste, 1 teaspoonful of sugar.

Mode.–Trim and wash the cabbage and cut it into very thin slices; put it into a stewpan, with the ham cut in dice, the butter, half the stock, and the vinegar; cover the pan closely, and let it stew for 1 hour. When it is very tender, add the remainder of the stock, a seasoning of salt and pepper, and the sugar; mix all well together, stir over the heat until nearly all the liquor has dried away, and serve. Fried sausages are usually sent to table with this dish; they should be laid round and on the cabbage, as a garnish.

Time.–Rather more than 1 hour. **Sufficient** for 5 or 6 persons.

To Dress Carrots in —the German Way—

Ingredients.–8 large carrots, 3 oz. of butter, salt to taste, a very little grated nutmeg, 1 tablespoonful of finely-minced parsley, 1 dessertspoonful of minced onion, rather more than 1 pint of weak stock or broth, 1 tablespoonful of flour.

Mode.–Wash and scrape the carrots, and cut them into rings of about ¼ inch in thickness. Put the butter into a stewpan; when it is melted, lay in the carrots, with salt, nutmeg, parsley, and onion in the above proportions. Toss the stewpan over the fire for a few minutes, and when the carrots are well saturated with the butter, pour in the stock and simmer gently until they are nearly tender. Then put into another stewpan a small piece of butter; dredge in about a tablespoonful of flour; stir this over the fire, and when a nice brown colour, add the liquor that the carrots have been boiling in; let this just boil up, pour it over the carrots in the other stewpan, and let them finish simmering until quite tender. Serve very hot. This vegetable, dressed as above, is a favourite accompaniment of roast pork, sausages, etc.

Time.–About ¾ hour. **Sufficient** for 6 or 7 persons.

ORIGIN OF THE CARROT.–In its wild state, this vegetable is found plentifully in Britain, both in cultivated lands and by waysides, and is known by the name of bird's nest, from its umbels of fruit becoming incurved from a hollow cup, like a bird's nest. In this state its root is whitish, slender, and hard, with an acrid, disagreeable taste, and a strong aromatic smell, and was formerly used as an aperient. When cultivated, it is reddish, thick, fleshy, with a pleasant odour, and a peculiar, sweet, mucilaginous taste.

Cauliflowers with — Parmesan Cheese—

CAULIFLOWER AND BROCCOLI.– These are only forms of the wild cabbage in its cultivated state. They are both well known, but the purple and white broccoli are only varieties of the cauliflower.

Choose cauliflowers that are close and white; cut off the stalk close at the bottom, leaving a few of the tender, inside leaves on.

Ingredients.–2 or 3 small cauliflowers, rather more than ½ pint of MELTED BUTTER, 2 tablespoonfuls of grated Parmesan cheese, 2 oz. of butter, 3 tablespoonfuls of breadcrumbs.

Mode.–Cleanse and boil the cauliflowers, putting them in fast-boiling water with a little salt in it; drain them and dish them with the flowers standing upright. Have ready the above proportion of melted butter; pour sufficient of it over the cauliflowers just to cover the top; sprinkle over this some of the Parmesan cheese and the breadcrumbs, and drop on these the butter, which should be melted but not oiled. Brown in a hot oven or under the grill, and pour round, but not over, the cauliflowers the remainder of the melted butter, with which should be mixed the rest of the grated Parmesan.

Time.–Altogether, ½ hour. **Sufficient** for 5 or 6 persons.

Cauliflower

— Stewed Celery à la Crème —

Ingredients.–6 heads of celery; to each pint of water allow ½ teaspoonful of salt, 1 blade of mace pounded, ⅓ pint of cream.

Mode.–Wash and trim the celery thoroughly, and boil it in salt and water until tender. Put the cream and pounded mace into a stewpan; stir it over the heat until the cream thickens, dish the celery, pour over the sauce, and serve.

Time.–Large heads of celery, 25 minutes; small ones, 15 to 20 minutes. **Sufficient** for 7 or 8 persons.

— Fried Cucumbers —

Ingredients.–2 cucumbers, pepper and salt, flour, oil or butter.

Mode.–Peel the cucumbers and cut them into slices of an equal thickness. Wipe the slices dry with a cloth, dredge them with flour, and put them into a pan of hot oil or butter; keep turning them about until brown; lift them out of the pan, let them drain, and serve.

Time.–5 minutes. **Sufficient** for 4 or 5 persons.

— Stewed Cucumbers —

Ingredients.–6 cucumbers, 3 moderate-sized onions, not quite 1 pint of WHITE STOCK, cayenne and salt to taste, the yolks of 2 eggs, a very little grated nutmeg.

Mode.–Peel and slice the cucumbers, take out the seeds, and cut the onions into thin slices; put both vegetables into a stewpan, with the stock, and let them boil for ¼ hour, or longer should the cucumbers be very large. Beat up the yolks of the eggs, stir these into the cucumbers, and add the cayenne, salt, and grated nutmeg; bring to the point of boiling, and serve with lamb chops or steaks.

Time.–Altogether, 20 minutes. **Sufficient** for 6 or 7 persons.

ORIGIN OF CELERY.–In the marshes and ditches of this country there is to be found a wild form of celery; in this state, it has a peculiar rank, coarse taste and smell, and its root was reckoned by the ancients as one of the "five greater aperient roots". There is a variety in which the root becomes turnip-shaped and large; it is called celeriac, and is extensively used by the Germans, and preferred by them to celery.

Cucumber

Rump Steak with Fried Cucumbers, and Haricot Beans and Minced Onions

HARICOTS AND LENTILS.– Although these vegetables are not much used in this country, yet in France and other Catholic countries they form an excellent substitute for animal food during Lent and *maigre* days. At the time of the prevalence of the Roman religion in this country, they were probably much more generally used than at present. As reformations are often carried beyond necessity, they may have fallen into disuse as an article of diet amongst Protestants for fear the use of them might be considered a sign of popery.

Haricot Beans and Minced — Onions —

Ingredients.–2 lbs. of white haricot beans, 4 middling-sized onions, ½ pint of MEDIUM STOCK, pepper and salt to taste, flour.

Mode.–Peel and mince the onions not too finely, and fry them in butter till a light brown colour; dredge over them a little flour, and add the stock, reduced to ¼ pint by boiling, and a seasoning of pepper and salt. Have ready the haricot beans, well boiled and drained; put them with the onions and stock, mix all well together, and serve.

Time.–2 to 2½ hours to boil the beans; 5 minutes to fry the onions. **Sufficient** for 7 or 8 persons.

Jerusalem Artichokes with — White Sauce —

Ingredients.–12 to 15 artichokes, 12 to 15 Brussels sprouts, salt and water, ½ pint of BECHAMEL.

Mode.–Peel and cut the artichokes in the shape of a pear, and cut a piece off the bottom of each that they may stand upright in the dish; boil them in salted water until tender. Have ready the béchamel, warmed; dish the artichokes, pour over them the sauce, and place between each a fine Brussels sprout; these should be boiled separately, and not with the artichokes.

Time.–About 20 minutes. **Sufficient** for 6 or 7 persons.

— Baked Mushrooms —

Ingredients.–16 to 20 mushroom flaps, butter, pepper to taste.

Mode.–For this mode of cooking, mushroom flaps are better than buttons, and should not be too large. Cut off a portion of the stalk, peel the top, and wipe the mushrooms carefully with a piece of cloth and a little fine salt. Put them into a baking tin, with a very small piece of butter placed on each mushroom; sprinkle over a little pepper, and let them bake for about 20 minutes, or longer should the mushrooms be very large. Have ready a very hot dish, pile the mushrooms high in the centre, pour the cooking liquor round, and send them to table quickly, with very hot plates.

Time.–20 minutes; large mushrooms, ½ hour. **Sufficient** for 5 or 6 persons.

— Baked Spanish Onions —

Ingredients.–4 or 5 large Spanish onions, salt and water.

Mode.–Put the onions, with their skins on, into a saucepan of boiling water, slightly salted, and let them boil quickly for 1 hour. Then take them out, wipe them thoroughly, wrap each one in a piece of buttered paper separately, and bake them in a moderate oven for 2 hours. They may be served in their skins, and eaten with a piece of cold butter and a seasoning of pepper and salt, or they may be peeled, and a good brown gravy poured over them.

Time.–1 hour to boil, 2 hours to bake. **Sufficient** for 4 persons.

THE JERSUALEM ARTICHOKE.– This being a tuberous-rooted plant, with leafy stems from 4 to 6 feet high, it is alleged that its tops will afford as much fodder per acre as a crop of oats, or more, and its roots half as many tubers as an ordinary crop of potatoes. The fibres of the stems may be separated by maceration and manufactured into cordage or cloth; this is said to be done in some parts of the north and west of France, as about Hagenau.

VARIETIES OF MUSHROOM.– The common mushroom found in our pastures is the *Agaricus campestris* of science, but *A. primulus* is affirmed to be the most delicious. The morel is *Morchella esculenta*, and *Tuber cibarium* is the common truffle.

THE ONION, like the leek, garlic, and shallot, belongs to the genus *Allium*, which is a numerous tribe of vegetables; every one of them possesses, more or less, a volatile and acrid penetrating principle, pricking the thin transparent membrane of the eyelids, and all are very similar in their properties. In the whole of them the bulb is the most active part, and any one of them may supply the place of the other, for they are all irritant, excitant, and vesicant. With many, the onion is a very great favourite, and is considered an extremely nutritive vegetable. The Spanish kind is frequently taken for supper, it being simply boiled and then seasoned with salt, pepper, and butter. Some dredge on a little flour, but many prefer it without this.

— Stewed Green Peas —

Ingredients.–3 lbs. of shelled peas, 1 lettuce, 1 onion, 2 oz. of butter, pepper and salt to taste, 1 egg, ½ teaspoonful of sugar.

Mode.–Shell the peas, and cut the onion and lettuce into slices; put all into a stewpan, with the butter, pepper, and salt, but with no more water than that which hangs round the lettuce from washing. Stew the whole very gently for rather more than 1 hour; then stir in a well beaten egg, and the sugar. When the peas, etc., are nicely thickened, serve; after the egg is added, do not allow them to boil.

Time.–1 ¼ hours. **Sufficient** for 3 or 4 persons.

Green pea

— Baked Potatoes —

Ingredients.–Large potatoes.

Mode.–Choose large potatoes, as much of a size as possible; wash them in lukewarm water, and scrub them well, for the browned skin of a baked potato is by many persons considered the better part of it. Put them into a moderate oven, and bake them for about 2 hours, turning them three or four times whilst they are cooking. Serve them in a napkin immediately they are done, as if kept over-long in the oven, they have a shrivelled appearance. Do not forget to send to table with them a piece of cold butter.

Time.–Large potates, 1½ to 2 hours in a hot oven; 2 to 2½ hours in a cool oven.

A CASSEROLE OF POTATOES, which is often used for ragoûts instead of rice, is made by mashing potatoes rather thickly, placing them on a dish, and making an opening in the centre. After having browned the potatoes in the oven, the dish should be wiped clean, and the ragoût or fricassée poured in.

THE POTATO AS AN ARTICLE OF HUMAN FOOD.–This valuable esculent, next to wheat, is of the greatest importance in the eye of the political economist. From no other crop that can be cultivated does the public derive so much benefit; and it has been demonstrated that an acre of potatoes will feed double the number of people that can be fed from an acre of wheat.

— Fried Potatoes —

(FRENCH FASHION)

Ingredients.–Potatoes, hot butter or oil, salt.

Mode.–Peel and cut the potatoes into thin slices, as nearly the same size as possible; make some butter or oil quite hot in a frying-pan, put in the potatoes, and fry them on both sides of a nice brown. When they are crisp and done, take them up, place them on absorbent paper and put them into a warm oven to drain them from grease, and serve very hot, after sprinkling them with salt. These are delicious with rump steak.

Time.–5 minutes.

— Purée de Pommes de Terre —

Ingredients.–To every lb. of mashed potatoes allow ¼ pint of good broth or stock, 2 oz. of butter.

Mode.–Peel and boil the potatoes, drain them well, and mash them smooth; add the stock or broth, and rub the whole through a sieve. Put the purée into a saucepan with the butter; stir it well over the fire until thoroughly hot, and it will then be ready to serve. A purée should be rather thinner than mashed potatoes, and is a delicious accompaniment to delicately grilled mutton cutlets. Cream or milk may be substituted for the broth when the latter is not at hand.

Time.–About ½ hour to boil the potatoes, 6 or 7 minutes to warm the purée.

— Potato Rissoles —

Ingredients.–Mashed potatoes, salt and pepper to taste, a very little minced parsley, egg, and breadcrumbs, oil or lard.

Mode.–Boil and thoroughly mash the potatoes, and add a seasoning of pepper and salt, and a little minced parsley. Roll the potatoes into small balls, cover them with egg and breadcrumbs, and fry in hot oil or lard for about 10 minutes; let them drain in a warm oven, dish them on a napkin, and serve.

Time.–10 minutes to fry the rissoles.

Note.–The flavour of these rissoles may be very much increased by adding finely minced tongue or ham, or even chopped onions.

— To Dress Salsify —

TO USE COLD POTATOES.– Mash the potatoes with a fork until perfectly free from lumps, stir in a little flour, minced onion, butter, and seasoning, and add sufficient milk to moisten; press the mixture into a buttered mould, and bake in a moderate oven until nicely brown.

Ingredients.–Salsify; to each pint of water allow ½ teaspoonful of salt, 1 oz. of butter, 2 tablespoonfuls of lemon juice.

Mode.–Scrape the roots gently so as to strip them only of their outside peel; cut them into pieces about 4 inches long and, as they are peeled, throw them into water with which has been mixed a little lemon juice, to prevent their discolouring. Put them into boiling water, with salt, butter, and lemon juice in the above proportion, and let them boil rapidly until tender; try them with a fork, and when it penetrates easily they are done. Drain the salsify, and serve with a good BECHAMEL or MELTED BUTTER.

Time.–30 to 50 minutes.

Note.–This vegetable may be also boiled, sliced, and fried in batter.

BOILED POTATOES.–To obtain this wholesome and delicious vegetable cooked in perfection, it should be boiled and sent to table with the skin on. In Ireland, where perhaps the cooking of potatoes is better understood than in any country, they are always served so. After the potatoes are boiled, they should never be entirely covered up, as the steam, instead of escaping, falls down on them and makes them watery and insipid. In Ireland they are usually served up with the skins on, and a small plate is placed by the side of each guest.

SALSIFY.–This vegetable belongs to the *Compositae* class of flowers, which is the most extensive in the plant kingdom. This family is not only one of the most natural and most uniform in structure, but there is also great similarity in the properties of the plants of which it is composed. Generally speaking, all composite flowers are tonic or stimulant in their medicinal virtues.

SPINACH.–This is a Persian plant, and belongs to the sub-order *Salsolaceae*, or saltworts. It has been cultivated in our gardens about two hundred years, and is the most wholesome of vegetables. It is very easily digested, and is very light and laxative. It is an excellent vegetable, and very beneficial to health. Plainly dressed, it is a resource for the poor; prepared luxuriantly, it is a choice dish for the rich.

— To Boil Spinach —

Ingredients.–4 lbs. of spinach, 1 teaspoonful of salt, 1 oz. of butter, pepper to taste.

Mode.–Pick the spinach carefully, and see that no stalks or weeds are left amongst it; wash it in several waters to prevent it being gritty. Press it into a very large saucepan, with about ½ pint of water, just sufficient to keep the spinach from burning, and the above proportion of salt. Press it down frequently with a wooden spoon, that it may be done equally; when it has boiled for rather more than 10 minutes, or when it is perfectly tender, drain it in a colander, squeeze it quite dry, and chop it finely. Put the spinach into a clean stewpan with the butter and a seasoning of pepper; stir the whole over the fire until quite hot, then put it on a hot dish, and garnish with sippets of toasted bread or leaves of PUFF PASTE.

Time.–10 minutes to boil the spinach, 5 minutes to heat it with the butter. **Sufficient** for 5 or 6 persons.

Spinach garnished with croûtons

— Spinach Dressed with Cream —

Ingredients.–4 lbs. of spinach, 1 teaspoonful of salt, 2 oz. of butter, 8 tablespoonfuls of cream, 1 small teaspoonful of sugar, a little grated nutmeg.

Mode.–Cook and drain the spinach as in the previous recipe; chop it finely, and put it into a stewpan with the butter; stir over a gentle heat and, when the butter has been absorbed, add the remaining ingredients, but not the cream, and simmer for about 5 minutes. Stir in the cream just before serving.

Time.–10 minutes to boil the spinach, 10 minutes to heat it with the other ingredients. **Sufficient** for 5 or 6 persons.

Purée de Pommes de Terre with Fricasséed Fowl, and Spinach dressed with Cream

— *S t e w e d   T o m a t o e s* —

Ingredients.–8 large tomatoes, pepper and salt to taste, 2 oz. of butter, 2 tablespoonfuls of vinegar.

Mode.–Slice the tomatoes into a saucepan, season them with pepper and salt, and place small pieces of butter on them. Cover the lid down closely, and stew from 20 to 25 minutes, or until the tomatoes are perfectly tender; add the vinegar, stir two or three times, and serve with any kind of roast meat.

Time.–20 to 25 minutes. **Sufficient** for 4 persons.

T o   D r e s s   T r u f f l e s   w i t h — *C h a m p a g n e* —

Ingredients.–12 fine black truffles, a few slices of fat bacon, 1 carrot, 1 turnip, 2 onions, a bunch of savoury herbs, including parsley, 1 bayleaf, 2 cloves, 1 blade of pounded mace, 2 glasses of champagne, ½ pint of veal stock.

Mode.–Carefully select the truffles, reject those that have a musty smell, and wash them well with a brush, in cold water only, until perfectly clean. Put the bacon into a stewpan, with the truffles and the remaining ingredients; simmer these gently for 1 hour, and let the whole cool in the stewpan. When to be served, rewarm them, drain them, and arrange them on a white napkin.

Time.–1 hour.

— *M a s h e d   T u r n i p s* —

Ingredients.–10 or 12 large turnips; to each pint of water allow ½ tablespoonful of salt, 2 oz. of butter, cayenne or white pepper.

Mode.–Peel the turnips, quarter them, and put them into boiling water, salted in the above proportion; boil them until tender, then drain them in a colander, and squeeze them as dry as possible by pressing them with the back of a large plate. When quite free from water, rub the turnips with a wooden spoon through the colander, and put them into a saucepan; add the butter, white pepper or cayenne, and, if necessary, a little salt. Keep stirring them over the fire until the butter is well mixed with them, then dish and serve. A little cream or milk added is an improvement.

Time.–15 to 20 minutes to boil the turnips, 10 minutes to heat them through. **Sufficient** for 5 or 6 persons.

— *B o i l e d   I n d i a n   C o r n* —

Ingredients.–4 ears of Indian corn or maize; to every pint of water allow ½ teaspoonful of salt.

Mode.–The outside sheath of the corn being taken off and the waving fibres removed, let the ears be placed in boiling water, salted in the above proportion, where they should remain for about 25 minutes (a longer time may be necessary for larger ears); well drained, they may be sent to table whole, with a piece of toast underneath them. Plain melted butter should be served with them.

Time.–25 to 35 minutes. **Sufficient** for 4 persons.

THE TOMATO, OR LOVE-APPLE.– This vegetable is a native of Mexico and South America, but is also found in the East Indies, where it is supposed to have been introduced by the Spaniards. In this country it is much more cultivated than it formerly was. For ketchup, soups, and sauces it is equally applicable, and the unripe fruit makes one of the best pickles. The tomato is a wholesome fruit and digests easily; its flavour also stimulates the appetite.

THE TURNIP.– This vegetable is the *Brassica rapa* of science. It is said to have been originally introduced from Hanover, and forms an excellent culinary vegetable, much used all over Europe, where it is either eaten alone or mashed and cooked in soups and stews. It does not thrive in a hot climate, for in India, like many more of our garden vegetables, it loses its flavour and becomes comparatively tasteless.

THE COMMON TRUFFLE.–This is the *Tuber cibarium* of science. Truffles grow at a considerable depth under the earth, never appearing on the surface, and are seasonable from November to March. They are found in many parts of France, those of Périgord and Magny being the most esteemed. There are three varieties of the species, the black, the red, and the white. The black has the highest repute, and its consumption is enormous. When the peasantry go to gather truffles, they take a pig with them to scent out the spot where they grow. When that is found, the pig turns up the surface with his snout, and the men then dig until they find the truffles. Good truffles are easily distinguished by their agreeable perfume; they should be light in proportion to their size, and elastic when pressed by the finger. In this country the common truffle is found on the downs of Hampshire, Wiltshire, and Kent, in dry light soils, and more especially in oak and chestnut forests.

— To Dress Cucumbers —

Ingredients.–1 tablespoonful of salad oil, 1 ¼ tablespoonfuls of vinegar, salt and pepper to taste; cucumbers.

Mode.–Pare the cucumbers, cut them equally into very thin slices, put the slices into a dish, sprinkle over salt and pepper, and pour over oil and vinegar in the above proportion; turn the cucumber about, and it is ready to serve. This is a favourite accompaniment to BOILED SALMON, is a nice addition to all descriptions of salads, and makes a pretty garnish to LOBSTER SALAD.

ENDIVE.–This is much used as a salad. It belongs to the family of the *Compositae*, with chicory, common goat's-beard, and others of the same genus. Before the stems of the common goat's beard shoot up, the roots, boiled like asparagus, have the same flavour, and are nearly as nutritious.

Summer Salad with Salad Dressing

Turnip Radishes

Long Radishes

RADISHES.–There are red and white radishes, and the French have also what they call violet and black ones, of which the black are the larger. Radishes are composed of nearly the same constituents as turnips. They are difficult of digestion, and cause flatulency and wind, and are the cause of headaches when eaten to excess. Besides being eaten raw, they are sometimes, but rarely, boiled; and they also serve as a pretty garnish for salads.

— Boiled Salad —

Ingredients.–2 heads of celery, 1 lb. of French beans, lettuce, endive, SALAD DRESSING.

Mode.–Boil the celery and beans separately until tender, and cut the celery into pieces about 2 inches long. Put these into a salad bowl or dish; pour over the salad dressing, and garnish the dish with a little lettuce finely chopped, endive, or a few tufts of boiled cauliflower. This composition, if less agreeable than vegetables in their raw state, is more wholesome, for salads, however they may be compounded, when eaten uncooked prove to some people indigestible. Tarragon, chervil, burnet, or boiled onion may be added to the above salad with advantage, as also slices of cold meat, poultry, or fish.

Sufficient for a salad for 4 or 5 persons.

THE LETTUCE.–
In its young state,
the lettuce forms a
wholesome salad,
containing a bland,
pellucid juice, with
little taste or smell, and
having a cooling and
soothing influence on
the system. This arises
from the large
quantities of water and
mucilage it contains,
and not from any
narcotic principle
which it is supposed to
possess. During the
period of flowering, it
abounds in a peculiar
milky juice, which
flows from the stem
when wounded, and
which has been found
to be possessed of
decided medicinal
properties.

— Potato Salad —

Ingredients.–10 or 12 cold boiled potatoes, 4 tablespoonfuls of tarragon or plain vinegar, 6 tablespoonfuls of salad oil, pepper and salt to taste, 1 teaspoonful of minced parsley.

Mode.–Cut the potatoes into slices about ½ inch in thickness; put these into a salad bowl with oil and vinegar in the above proportion, season with pepper, salt, and a teaspoonful of minced parsley, stir the salad well, that all the ingredients may be thoroughly incorporated, and it is ready to serve. This salad should be made 2 or 3 hours before it is wanted for table. Anchovies, olives, or pickles may be added to this salad, as also slices of cold beef, fowl, or turkey.

Sufficient for 5 or 6 persons.

— Summer Salad —

Ingredients.–3 lettuces, 2 handfuls of mustard-and-cress, 10 young radishes, a few slices of cucumber, SALAD DRESSING.

Mode.–Let the greenstuffs be as fresh as possible for a salad and, if at all tired-looking, let them lie in cold water for an hour or two, which will very much refresh them. Wash and carefully pick them over, and drain them thoroughly by swinging them gently in a clean cloth. Cut the lettuces into small pieces, and the radishes and cucumbers into thin slices; arrange all these ingredients lightly on a dish, with the mustard-and-cress, and pour the dressing under but not over the salad, and do not stir it up until it is to be eaten. It may be garnished with hard-boiled eggs, cut in slices, PICKLED NASTURTIUMS, cut vegetable flowers, and many other things that taste will always suggest to make a pretty and elegant dish. In making a good salad, care must be taken to have the herbs freshly gathered and thoroughly drained before the sauce is added to them. Young spring onions, cut small, are by many persons considered an improvement to salads, but before these are added the cook should always consult the taste of her family or guests. Slices of cold meat or poultry added to a salad make a convenient and quickly-made summer luncheon dish; cold fish, flaked, will also be found exceedingly nice mixed in.

Sufficient for a salad for 5 or 6 persons.

— Winter Salad —

Ingredients.–Endive, mustard-and-cress, boiled beetroot, 3 or 4 hard-boiled eggs, celery, SALAD DRESSING or MAYONNAISE.

Mode.–The above ingredients form the principal constituents of a winter salad, and may be converted into a very pretty dish by nicely contrasting the various colours and tastefully garnishing it. Shred the celery into thin pieces, after having carefully washed it; cleanse the endive and mustard-and-cress free from grit, and arrange these high in the centre of a salad bowl or dish; garnish with the hard-boiled eggs and beetroot, both of which should be cut in slices; and pour into the dish, but not over the salad, either salad dressing or mayonnaise. Never dress a salad long before it is required for table, as, by standing, it loses its freshness and pretty, crisp, and light appearance.

Sufficient for 5 or 6 persons.

SCARCITY OF SALADS IN ENGLAND.–Three centuries ago, very few vegetables were cultivated in England, and an author writing of the period of Henry VIII's reign tells us that neither salad, nor carrots, nor cabbages, nor radishes, nor any other comestibles of a like nature, were grown in any part of the kingdom; they came instead from Holland and Flanders. We further learn that Queen Catharine herself, with all her royalty, could not procure a salad of English growth for her dinner. The king was obliged to mend this sad state of affairs and send to Holland for a gardener in order to cultivate those pot-herbs.

Salad in bowl

Chervil

French beans

CHAPTER 9

Puddings
—and Pastry—

THE HABITS OF A PEOPLE, to a great extent, are formed by the climate in which they live, and by the native or cultivated productions in which their country abounds. Thus we apprehend that the puddings of the ancients would generally have found little favour amongst the insulated inhabitants of Great Britain. Here, from the simple suet dumpling up to the most complicated Christmas production, the grand feature of substantiality is primarily attended to. Variety in the ingredients, we think, is held only of secondary consideration with the great body of the people, provided that the whole is agreeable and of sufficient abundance.

ALTHOUGH FROM PUDDINGS TO PASTRY is but a step, it requires a higher degree of art to make the one than to make the other. Indeed, pastry is one of the most important branches of the culinary science. It unceasingly occupies itself with ministering pleasure to the sight as well as to the taste.

THE FRESHNESS OF ALL INGREDIENTS is of much importance, as one bad article may taint the whole. Flour should be of the best quality, and perfectly dry and sifted before being used; butter should be fresh; lard should be perfectly sweet; suet should be finely chopped, free from skin, and quite sweet; clarified beef dripping answers very well for kitchen pies, puddings, cakes, or for family use, but should be used sparingly; if the freshness of eggs is doubtful, break each one separately in a cup before mixing them together and adding to the article in preparation; the yolks and the whites beaten separately will be found to make puddings and pastries much lighter.

THE ART OF MAKING PASTRY requires much practice, dexterity, and skill. It should be touched as lightly as possible, and made with cool hands in a cool place (a marble slab is better than a board for the purpose). In mixing paste, add the water or other liquids gradually, working the whole together with a knife blade, and then kneading until perfectly smooth. To ensure paste being light, great expedition must be used in the making and baking, for if it

THE ORIENTALS, were, at a very early period, acquainted with the art of manipulating pastry, but they by no means attained to the taste, variety, and splendour of design by which it is characterized amongst the moderns. At first it generally consisted of certain mixtures of flour, oil, and honey, to which it was confined for centuries, even among the southern nations of Europe. At the commencement of the Middle Ages, a change began to take place in the art of mixing it. Eggs, butter, and salt came into repute in the making of paste, which was forthwith used as an enclosure for meat, seasoned with spices. This advance attained, the next step was to enclose cream, fruit, and marmalades, and the next to build pyramids and castles, when the summit of the art of the pastry cook may be supposed to have been achieved.

stand too long before it is put in the oven, it becomes flat and heavy. Tart tins, patty tins, cake moulds, baking sheets, dishes for baked puddings, etc. should all be buttered before the paste is put in. Most pastes or crusts require a moderately hot oven, puff paste in particular requiring a hot oven or it will not rise.

IN THE MAKING OF PUDDINGS, the dry ingredients should be mixed some time before they are wanted, and the liquid portion added just before the pudding is to be boiled or baked. Raisins and dried fruits should be carefully washed and thoroughly dried before use; to plump them, some cooks pour boiling water over them and then dry them in the oven.

The moulds, basins, cups, etc., in which puddings are cooked should be always buttered before the mixture is put in them, and scrupulous attention should be paid to the cleanliness of pudding cloths. As soon as possible after they are taken off a pudding, they should be soaked in water and then well washed, without soap, unless they are very greasy. They should be dried out of doors, then folded up and kept in a dry place. When a cloth is wanted for use, dip it in boiling water and dredge it slightly with flour. To prevent a pudding boiled in a cloth from sticking to the bottom of the saucepan, place a small plate or saucer underneath it.

All boiled puddings should be put into boiling water, which must not be allowed to stop simmering; if necessary, the saucepan should be kept filled up. Great expedition is necessary in sending puddings to table as, by standing, they quickly become heavy.

Raised pie mould, open

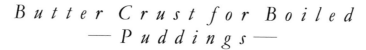

Butter Crust for Boiled — Puddings —

Ingredients.–To every lb. of flour allow 6 oz. of butter, ½ pint of water.

Mode.–With a knife, work the flour to a smooth paste with the water; roll the paste out rather thin; place the butter over it in small pieces; dredge lightly over it some flour, and fold the paste over; repeat the rolling once more, and the paste will be ready for use. It may be enriched by adding another 2 oz. of butter to each lb. of flour, but for ordinary purposes the above quantity will be found quite sufficient.

Common Crust for — Raised Pies —

Ingredients.–To every lb. of flour allow ½ pint of water, 1 ½ oz. of butter, 1 ½ oz. of lard, ½ teaspoonful of salt.

Mode.–Put into a saucepan the water; when it boils, add the butter and lard; when these are melted, make a hole in the middle of the flour, pour in the water gradually, beat well with a wooden spoon, and be particular in not making the paste too soft. When it is well mixed, knead it with the hands until quite stiff, dredging a little flour over the paste and board to prevent them from sticking. When it is well kneaded, put it in a warm place, with a cloth covering it, for a few minutes; it will then be more easily raised into shape.

Boiled pudding moulds

Common Paste for — Family Pies —

Ingredients.–1 ¼ lbs. of flour, ½ lb. of butter, rather more than ½ pint of water.

Mode.–Rub the butter lightly into the flour, and mix it to a smooth paste with the water; roll it out two or three times, and it will be ready for use. This paste may be converted into an excellent short crust for sweet tarts by adding to the flour, after the butter is rubbed in, 2 tablespoonfuls of caster sugar.

— Very Good Puff Paste —

Ingredients.–To every lb. of flour allow 1 lb. of butter, not quite ½ pint of water.

Mode.–Carefully weigh the flour and butter. Sift the flour and proceed in the following manner to make the paste, using a very clean paste board and rolling pin: supposing the quantity to be 1 lb. of flour, work the whole into a smooth paste with not quite ½ pint of water, using a knife to mix it with; the proportion of this latter ingredient must be regulated by the discretion of the cook, for if too much be added, the paste, when baked, will be tough. Roll out the paste until it is of an equal thickness of about 1 inch; cut 4 oz. of the butter into small pieces; place these on the paste, sift over a little flour, fold the paste over, roll out again, and put another 4 oz. of butter pieces on it. Repeat the rolling and buttering until the paste has been rolled out four times, or equal quantities of flour and butter have been used. The next thing to be considered is the oven. Do not put it into the oven until the oven is hot, for the best-prepared puff paste, if not properly baked, will not rise.

Small vol-au-vents of puff paste

Vol-au-vent of puff paste

Patty tins, plain and fluted

Very Good Short Crust —for Fruit Tarts—

Ingredients.–To every lb. of flour allow ¾ lb. of butter, 1 tablespoonful of caster sugar, ⅓ pint of water.

Mode.–Rub the butter into the flour, add the sugar, and mix the whole into a stiff paste with the water. Roll it out two or three times, folding the paste over each time, and it will be ready for use.

—Another Good Short Crust—

Ingredients.–To every lb. of flour allow ½ lb. of butter, the yolks of 2 eggs, 2 oz. of caster sugar, about ¼ pint of milk.

Mode.–Rub the butter into the flour, add the sugar, and mix the whole as lightly as possible to a smooth paste with the yolks of the eggs, well beaten, and the milk. The proportion of the latter ingredient must be judged of by the size of the eggs; if these are large, less will be required, and more if the eggs are smaller.

Suet Crust for Pies — or Puddings—

Ingredients.–To every lb. of flour allow 5 or 6 oz. of finely chopped beef suet, ½ pint of water.

Mode.–Rub the suet well into the flour; work the whole to a smooth paste with the above proportion of water; roll it out, and it is ready for use. This crust is quite rich enough for ordinary purposes, but when a better one is desired, use from ½ to ¾ lb. of suet to every lb. of flour. Some cooks, for rich crusts, pound the suet with a small quantity of butter. It should then be laid on the paste in small pieces, the same as for PUFF PASTE, and will be found exceedingly nice for hot tarts; 5 oz. of suet to every lb. of flour will make a very good crust, and even 4 oz. will answer very well for children, or where the crust is wanted very plain.

—Baked Almond Pudding—
(VERY RICH)

Ingredients.– ¼ lb. of ground almonds, almond essence, 1 glass of sherry, 4 eggs, the rind and juice of ½ lemon, 3 oz. of butter, 1 pint of cream, 2 tablespoonfuls of sugar, PUFF PASTE.

Mode.–Mix the almonds to a smooth paste with a little water and add the butter, which should be melted; beat up the eggs with a few drops of almond essence, grate the lemon rind, and strain the juice; add these, with the cream, sugar, and wine, to the other ingredients, and stir them well together. When well mixed, put it into a pie dish lined with the puff paste, and bake in a moderate oven for ½ hour.

Time.– ½ hour. **Sufficient** for 4 or 5 perons.

Note.–To make the pudding more economically, substitute milk for the cream, but then add rather more than 1 oz. of finely grated white bread.

ALMONDS.– Almonds are cultivated throughout the whole of the south of Europe, Syria, Persia, and Northern Africa. The kernels of the sweet almond are used either in a green or ripe state, and as an article in the dessert. Into cooking, confectionery, perfumery, and medicine they largely enter, and in domestic economy should always be used in preference to bitter almonds. When young and green, they are preserved in sugar, like green apricots. They furnish almond oil, and the matter which is left after the oil is expressed forms the *pâte d'amandes* of perfumers. In medicine the almond is considered a nutritive, laxative, and emollient. In the environs of Alicante, the husks of almonds are ground to a powder, and enter into the composition of common soap.

THE BITTER ALMOND is a variety of the common almond, and is injurious to animal life on account of the great quantity of hydrocyanic acid it contains and is consequently seldom used in domestic economy, except to give flavour to confectionery, and even then it should be used with great caution. A single drop of the essential oil of bitter almonds is sufficient to destroy a bird, and four drops have caused the death of a middle-sized dog.

*Small Almond
Puddings*

— S m a l l   A l m o n d   P u d d i n g s —

Ingredients.– ½ lb. of ground almonds, almond essence, ¼ lb. of butter, 4 eggs, 2 tablespoonfuls of caster sugar, 2 tablespoonfuls of cream, 1 tablespoonful of brandy.

Mode.–Mix the almonds to a smooth paste with a spoonful of water; warm the butter, mix the almonds with this, and add the other ingredients, leaving out the whites of 2 eggs, and be particular that these are well beaten. Mix well, butter some small moulds, half fill them, and bake the puddings in a moderate oven for 20 minutes to ½ hour. Turn them out on a dish, and serve with SWEET SAUCE.

Time.–20 minutes to ½ hour. **Sufficient** for 4 or 5 persons.

— B a k e d   A p r i c o t   P u d d i n g —

Ingredients.–12 large apricots, ¾ pint of breadcrumbs, 1 pint of milk, 3 oz. of sugar, the yolks of 4 eggs, 1 glass of sherry, ¼ lb. of SHORT CRUST.

Mode.–Make the milk boiling hot, and pour it on to the breadcrumbs; when half cold, add the sugar, the well whisked yolks of the eggs, and the sherry. Divide the apricots in half, scald them until they are soft, and break them up with a spoon, adding a few of the kernels, which should be well pounded in a mortar; then mix the fruit and other ingredients together, put a border of short crust round the dish, fill it with the pudding mixture and bake in a moderate oven.

Time.– ½ to ¾ hour. **Sufficient** for 4 or 5 persons.

Bachelor's
Pudding

— A Bachelor's Pudding —

Ingredients.–¼ lb. of fresh breadcrumbs, ¼ lb. of currants, ¼ lb. of finely grated apple, 2 oz. of sugar, 3 eggs, a few drops of essence of lemon, a little grated nutmeg.

Mode.–Mix together the currants, the breadcrumbs, and sugar; whisk the eggs, beat these up with the remaining ingredients and, when all is thoroughly mixed, put into a buttered basin, tie down with a cloth, and boil for 3 hours.

Time.–3 hours. **Sufficient** for 4 or 5 persons.

Baked Batter Pudding, — with Dried or Fresh Fruit —

Ingredients.–1½ pints of milk, 4 tablespoonfuls of flour, 3 eggs, 2 oz. of finely shredded suet, ¼ lb. of currants, a pinch of salt.

Mode.–Mix the milk, flour, and eggs to a smooth batter; add a little salt, the suet, and the currants; put the mixture into a buttered pie dish, and bake in a moderate oven for 1 ¼ hours. When fresh fruits are in season, this pudding is exceedingly nice with damsons, plums, redcurrants, gooseberries, or apples; when made with these, the pudding must be thickly sprinkled over with sifted sugar. Boiled batter pudding, with fruit, is made in the same manner, by putting the fruit into a buttered basin, and filling it up with batter made in the above proportion, but omitting the suet. It must be sent quickly to table, and covered plentifully with sifted sugar.

Time.–Baked, with fresh fruit, 1 ¼ to 1 ½ hours; boiled, 1 ½ to 1 ¾ hours; smaller puddings, ¾ or 1 hour. **Sufficient** for 7 or 8 persons.

Black- or Redcurrant — Pudding —

Ingredients.–2 lbs. of red- or blackcurrants, measured with the stalks, ¼ lb. of moist brown sugar, BUTTER CRUST or SUET CRUST.

Mode.–Make, with ¾ lb. of flour, either a butter crust or a suet crust; butter a basin, and line it with part of the crust; put in the currants, which should be stripped from the stalks, and sprinkle the sugar over them; put the cover of the pudding on; make the edges very secure, so that the juice does not escape; tie it down with a floured cloth, put it into boiling water, and boil for 2 ½ to 3 hours. Boiled in a cloth alone, without a basin, allow ½ hour less. We have allowed rather a large proportion of sugar, but we find fruit puddings are so much more juicy and palatable when well sweetened. A few raspberries added to a redcurrant pudding are a very nice addition; about ½ lb. would be sufficient for the above quantity of fruit. Gooseberries also make a good pudding. Fruit puddings are very delicious if, when they are turned out of the basin, the crust is browned in a very hot oven for a few minutes to colour it and crisp the surface.

Time.–2 ½ to 3 hours; without a basin, 2 to 2 ½ hours. **Sufficient** for 6 or 7 persons.

Baked Bread-and-Butter — Pudding —

Ingredients.–9 thin slices of bread-and-butter, 1 ½ pints of milk, 4 eggs, sugar to taste, ¼ lb. of currants, vanilla flavouring, grated lemon peel or nutmeg.

Mode.–Put the slices of bread-and-butter into a pie dish, with currants between each layer and on the top. Sweeten and flavour the milk, either by infusing a little lemon peel in it or adding a few drops of essence of vanilla; well whisk the eggs, and stir these to the milk. Strain this over the bread-and-butter, and bake in a moderate oven for 1 hour, or rather longer. This pudding may be enriched by adding cream, candied peel, or more eggs than stated above. It should not be turned out, but sent to table in the pie dish, and is better for being made about 2 hours before it is baked.

Time.–1 hour, or rather longer. **Sufficient** for 6 or 7 persons.

CURRANTS.–The utility of currants, red, black, or white, has long been established in domestic economy. The juice of the red species, if boiled with an equal weight of loaf sugar, forms an agreeable jelly, much employed in sauces, and very valuable in the cure of sore throats and colds. The juice of currants is also a valuable remedy in obstructions of the bowels. White and flesh-coloured currants have the same qualities as the red species. The black variety is mostly used for culinary and medicinal purposes, especially in the form of jelly for quinsies. The leaves of the blackcurrant make a pleasant tea.

Cabinet pudding

Cabinet or Chancellor's — Pudding —

Ingredients.–1 ½ oz. of candied peel, ¼ lb. of currants, 4 dozen sultanas, sponge fingers or slices of sponge cake, 4 eggs, 1 pint of milk, grated lemon rind, grated nutmeg to taste, 3 tablespoonfuls of caster sugar, butter.

Mode.–Melt some butter, and with it grease the mould or basin in which the pudding is to be boiled, taking care that it is buttered in every part. Cut the peel into thin slices, and place these in a fanciful design at the bottom of the mould, and fill in the spaces between with currants and sultanas; then add a few sponge fingers or slices of sponge cake; dot melted butter on these, and between each layer sprinkle a few currants. Proceed in this manner until the mould is nearly full; then flavour the milk with the nutmeg and grated lemon rind, add the sugar, and stir it into the eggs, which should be well beaten. Beat this mixture for a few minutes, then strain it into the buttered mould, which should be quite full; tie a piece of buttered paper over it, and let it stand for 2 hours; then tie it down with a cloth, put it into boiling water, and let it boil slowly for 1 hour. In taking it up, let it stand for a minute or two before the cloth is removed; then quickly turn it out of the mould and serve with SWEET SAUCE.

Time.–1 hour. **Sufficient** for 5 or 6 persons.

— Canary Pudding —

Ingredients.–The weight of 3 eggs in caster sugar, the weight of 3 eggs in butter, the weight of 2 eggs in flour, the rind of 1 small lemon, 3 eggs.

Mode.–Melt the butter to a liquid state, but do not allow it to oil; stir into this the sugar and finely minced lemon peel, and gradually dredge in the flour, keeping the mixture well stirred; whisk the eggs, add these to the pudding, beat all the ingredients until thoroughly blended, and put them into a buttered mould or basin covered with buttered paper and a cloth; boil for 2 hours, and serve with SWEET SAUCE.

Time.–2 hours. **Sufficient** for 4 or 5 persons.

— Carrot Pudding —

Ingredients.–½ lb. of fresh breadcrumbs, ¼ lb. of suet, ¼ lb. of raisins, ¾ lb. of fresh boiled carrot, ¼ lb. of currants, 3 oz. of caster sugar, 3 eggs, milk, grated nutmeg.

Mode.–Boil the carrots until tender enough to mash to a pulp; add the other ingredients, and moisten with sufficient milk to make the pudding of the consistency of thick batter. If to be boiled, put the mixture into a buttered basin, tie it down with a cloth, and boil for 2 ½ hours; if to be baked, put it into a pie dish and bake in a moderate oven for nearly 1 hour; turn it out, strew sifted sugar over it, and serve.

Time.–2 ½ hours to boil, 1 hour to bake. **Sufficient** for 5 or 6 persons.

Z ANTE CURRANTS.–The dried fruit which goes by the name of currants in grocers' shops is not a currant really, but a small kind of grape, chiefly cultivated in the Ionian Islands, Corfu, Zante, etc. When gathered and dried by the sun and air, on mats, they are heaped together and left to cake, until ready for shipping. They are then dug out by iron crowbars, trodden into casks, and exported. In cakes and puddings this delicious little grape is most extensively used; in fact, we could not make a *plum* pudding without it.

*Cabinet or
Chancellor's
Pudding*

— Christmas Plum Pudding —
(VERY GOOD)

Ingredients.–1 ½ lbs. of raisins, ½ lb. of currants, ½ lb. of mixed peel cut into thin slices, ¾ lb. of fresh breadcrumbs, ¾ lb. of finely minced suet, 8 eggs, 1 wineglassful of brandy.

Mode.–When all the dry ingredients are prepared, mix them well together, then moisten the mixture with the eggs, which should be well beaten, and the brandy; stir well, so that everything may be very thoroughly blended, and press the pudding into a buttered mould or basin, filling it well; tie it down tightly with a floured cloth, and boil for 5 or 6 hours. If boiled in a cloth without a mould, it will require the same time for cooking. Turn out, and serve with BRANDY SAUCE. On Christmas Day a sprig of holly is usually placed in the middle of the pudding, and about a wineglassful of hot brandy poured round it, which, at the moment of serving, is lighted, and the pudding thus brought to table encircled in flame.

Time.–5 or 6 hours. **Sufficient** for 9 or 10 persons.

*Christmas plum
pudding in a
mould*

A Plain Christmas —Pudding for Children—

Ingredients.–1 lb. of flour, 1 lb. of fresh breadcrumbs, ¾ lb. of raisins, ¾ lb. of currants, ¾ lb. of suet, 3 or 4 eggs, milk, 2 oz. of candied peel, 1 teaspoonful of powdered allspice, ½ saltspoonful of salt.

Mode.–Let the suet be finely chopped, the raisins and the currants well washed, picked, and dried. Mix these with the other dry ingredients, and stir all well together; beat and strain the eggs and stir them into the pudding, adding just sufficient milk to make it mix properly. Tie it up in a well-floured cloth, put it into boiling water, and boil for at least 5 hours. Serve with a sprig of holly placed on top, and a little sugar sprinkled over it.

Time.–5 hours. **Sufficient** for 9 or 10 children.

— Currant Dumplings —

Ingredients.–1 lb. of flour, 6 oz. of suet, ½ lb. of currants, rather more than ½ pint of water.

Mode.–Mix the suet with the flour, and add the currants; mix the whole to a light paste with the water (if wanted very nice, use milk), divide it into 7 or 8 dumplings, tie them in floured cloths, and boil for 1¼ hours. They may also be boiled without a cloth; they should then be made into round balls and dropped directly into boiling water, and should be moved about at first, to prevent them from sticking to the bottom of the saucepan. Serve with a cut lemon, cold butter, and a sifting of sugar.

Time.–In a cloth, 1¼ hours; without a cloth, ¾ hour. **Sufficient** for 6 or 7 persons.

Currant Dumplings and Golden Pudding with Wine Sauce, and Fig Pudding

— Baked Custard Pudding —

Ingredients.–1½ pints of milk, the rind of ¼ lemon, ¼ lb. of caster sugar, 5 eggs.

Mode.–Put the milk into a saucepan with the sugar and lemon rind, and let this infuse for about ½ hour, or until the milk is well flavoured; whisk the eggs, yolks and whites; pour the milk on to them, stirring all the while; then have ready a pie dish, lined at the edge with paste ready baked; strain the custard into the dish, grate a little nutmeg over the top, and bake in a slow oven for about ¾ hour. The flavour of this pudding may be varied by substituting a few drops of almond essence for the lemon rind; and it may be very much enriched by using half cream and half milk, and two or three more eggs.

Time.–¾ hour, or a little longer. **Sufficient** for 5 or 6 persons.

Note.–This pudding is usually served cold with fruit tarts.

— Fig Pudding —

Ingredients.–2 lbs. of dried figs, 1 lb. of finely chopped suet, ½ lb. of flour, ½ lb. of fresh breadcrumbs, 2 eggs, milk.

Mode.–Cut the figs into small pieces; mix well together with the suet and breadcrumbs, add the flour, the eggs, which should be well beaten, and sufficient milk to form the whole into a stiff paste; butter a mould or basin, press the pudding into it very closely, tie it down with a cloth, and boil for at least 3 hours. Turn it out of the mould, and serve with plain melted butter, WINE SAUCE, or cream.

Time.–3 hours, or longer. **Sufficient** for 7 or 8 persons.

— Golden Pudding —

Ingredients.– ¼ lb. of fresh breadcrumbs, ¼ lb. of suet, ¼ lb. of orange marmalade, ¼ lb. of sugar, 4 eggs.

Mode.–Put the breadcrumbs into a basin, and mix with them the suet, which should be finely minced, the marmalade, and the sugar; stir all these ingredients together, beat the eggs to a froth, moisten the pudding with these, and when well mixed, put it into a mould or buttered basin; tie down with a cloth, and boil for 2 hours. When turned out, strew a little sifted sugar over the top, and serve.

Time.–2 hours. **Sufficient** for 5 or 6 persons.

— Baked Lemon Pudding —

Ingredients.–10 oz. of fresh breadcrumbs, 2 pints of milk, 2 oz. of butter, 1 lemon, ¼ lb. of caster sugar, 6 eggs, 1 tablespoonful of brandy.

Mode.–Bring the milk to the boiling point, stir in the butter, and pour these hot over the breadcrumbs; add the sugar and the very finely-minced peel of the lemon; beat the eggs and stir these in, with the brandy, to the other ingredients; put a ring of PUFF PASTE or SHORT CRUST round the dish, and bake in a moderate oven for ¾ hour.

Time.–¾ hour. **Sufficient** for 6 or 7 persons.

LEMON.–The lemon is a variety of the citron. The juice of this fruit makes one of our most popular and refreshing beverages, lemonade, which is gently stimulating and cooling, and soon quenches the thirst. The fresh rind of the lemon is a gentle tonic and, when dried and grated, is used in flavouring a variety of culinary preparations. Lemons appear in company with the orange in most orange-growing countries.

ORANGE (*Citrus aurantium*).–The principal varieties are the sweet or China orange, and the bitter or Seville orange; the Maltese is also worthy of notice, from its red, blood-like pulp. The orange is extensively cultivated in the south of Europe, and in Devonshire, on walls with a south aspect, it bears an abundance of fruit. So great is the increase in the demand for the orange, and so ample the supply, that it promises to rival the apple in its popularity. The orange blossom is proverbially chosen for the bridal wreath and, from the same flower, an essential oil is extracted hardly less esteemed than the celebrated attar of roses.

— Baked Orange Pudding —

Ingredients.–6 oz. of stale sponge cake or bruised RATAFIAS, 6 oranges, 1 pint of milk, 6 eggs, ½ lb. of caster sugar.

Mode.–Bruise the sponge cake or ratafias into fine crumbs, and pour upon them the milk, which should be boiled with the rind of 2 of the oranges, to absorb the flavour; add the sugar and the juice of all the oranges; beat up the eggs, stir them in, sweeten to taste, and put the mixture into a pie dish previously lined with PUFF PASTE. Bake in a moderate oven for rather more than ½ hour; turn it out of the dish, strew sifted sugar over, and serve.

Time.–Rather more than ½ hour. **Sufficient** for 3 or 4 persons.

— Paradise Pudding —

Ingredients.–3 eggs, 3 apples, ¼ lb. of fresh breadcrumbs, 3 oz. of sugar, 3 oz. of currants, salt and grated nutmeg to taste, the grated rind of ½ lemon, ½ wineglassful of brandy.

Mode.–Peel, core, and mince the apples into small pieces, and mix them with the other dry ingredients; beat up the eggs, moisten the mixture with these, and beat it well; stir in the brandy, and put the pudding into a buttered mould or basin; tie down with a cloth, boil for 1 ½ hours, and serve with SWEET SAUCE.

Time.–1 ½ hours. **Sufficient** for 4 or 5 persons.

An Excellent Plum — Pudding —
(MADE WITHOUT EGGS)

Ingredients.–½ lb. of flour, 6 oz. of raisins, 6 oz. of currants, ¼ lb. of finely chopped suet, ¼ lb. of brown sugar, ¼ lb. of mashed carrot, ¼ lb. of mashed potato, 1 tablespoonful of treacle, 1 oz. of candied lemon peel, 1 oz. of candied citron peel.

Mode.–Mix the flour, dried fruit, suet, and sugar well together; have ready the above proportions of mashed carrot and potato, and stir them into the other ingredients; add the treacle, and lemon and citron peel, but put *no liquid* in the mixture, or it will be spoiled. Tie it loosely in a cloth or, if put in a basin, do not quite fill it, as the pudding should have room to swell. Boil for 4 hours. Serve with BRANDY SAUCE. This pudding is better for being mixed overnight.

Time.–4 hours. **Sufficient** for 6 or 7 persons.

Plum Pudding of Fresh Fruit

Ingredients.–¾ lb. of SUET CRUST, 1 ½ lbs. of plums, ¼ lb. of moist brown sugar.

Mode.–Line a pudding basin with suet crust rolled out to the thickness of about ½ inch; fill the basin with the stoned and washed fruit, put in the sugar, and cover with a round of crust. Fold the edges over and pinch them together, to prevent the juice escaping. Tie over a floured cloth, put the pudding into boiling water, and boil from 2 to 2 ½ hours. Turn it out of the basin, and serve quickly.

Time.–2 to 2 ½ hours. **Sufficient** for 6 or 7 persons.

PLUMS.–Almost all the varieties of the cultivated plum are agreeable and refreshing; it is not a nourishing fruit, and if indulged in to excess, when unripe, is almost certain to cause diarrhœa and colic. Weak and delicate persons had better abstain from plums altogether. The objections raised against raw plums do not apply to the cooked fruit, which even the invalid may eat in moderation.

— Baked Rice Pudding —

Ingredients.–1 small teacupful of rice, 4 eggs, 1 pint of milk,
2 oz. of butter, ¼ lb. of currants, 2 tablespoonfuls of brandy,
nutmeg, ¼ lb. of sugar, the rind of ½ lemon, PUFF PASTE.

Mode.–Put the lemon rind into a stewpan with the milk, and let it
infuse till the milk is well flavoured with the lemon; in the meantime,
boil the rice in water until tender, with a very small quantity of salt,
and when done let it be thoroughly drained. Beat the eggs, stir into
them the milk, which should be strained of the lemon rind, and add
the butter, currants, and remaining ingredients; add the rice, and mix
all well together. Line the edges of the dish with puff paste, put in
the pudding, and bake for about ¾ hour in a slow oven.

Time.–¾ hour. **Sufficient** for 5 or 6 persons.

— French Rice Pudding —

Ingredients.–To every ¼ lb. of rice allow 2 pints of milk, the
rind of 1 lemon, a pinch of salt, sugar to taste, ¼ lb. of butter,
6 eggs, fresh breadcrumbs.

Mode.–Put the milk into a stewpan with the lemon rind, and let it
infuse for ½ hour, or until the former is well flavoured; then take out
the peel. Have ready the rice, washed, picked, and drained; put it
into the milk, and let it gradually swell over a very low heat. Stir in
the butter, salt, and sugar, add the yolks of the eggs, and then the
whites, both of which should be well beaten and added separately.
Butter a mould, strew in some fine breadcrumbs, and let them be
spread equally over it; then carefully pour in the rice, and bake the
pudding in a slow oven for 1 hour. Turn it out of the mould, and
garnish with preserved cherries, or any bright-coloured jelly or jam.

Time.–¾ to 1 hour for the rice to swell, then 1 hour in a slow
oven. **Sufficient** for 5 or 6 persons.

RICE, with proper
management in
cooking it, forms a
very valuable and
cheap addition to our
farinaceous food and,
in years of scarcity, has
been found eminently
useful in lessening the
consumption of flour.
When boiled, it should
be so managed that the
grains, though soft,
should be as little
broken and as dry as
possible. The water in
which it is cooked
should only simmer,
and not boil hard.

— R o l y - P o l y   J a m   P u d d i n g —

Ingredients.–¾ lb. of SUET CRUST, ¾ lb. of any kind of jam.

Mode.–Make a nice light suet crust and roll it out to the thickness of about ½ inch. Spread the jam equally over it, leaving a small margin of paste without any, where the pudding joins. Roll it up, fasten the ends securely, and tie it in a floured cloth; put the pudding into boiling water, and boil for 2 hours. Mincemeat or marmalade may be substituted for the jam, and makes excellent puddings.

Time.–2 hours. **Sufficient** for 5 or 6 persons.

Roly-Poly Jam Pudding

— B r a n d y   S a u c e   f o r   P u d d i n g s —

Ingredients.–½ pint of MELTED BUTTER, 3 heaped teaspoonfuls of sugar, 3 tablespoonfuls of brandy.

Mode.–Make ½ pint of melted butter, omitting the salt, then stir in the sugar and brandy in the above proportion, and bring the sauce to the point of boiling. Serve in a boat or tureen separately and, if liked, pour a little of it over the pudding. To convert this into a punch sauce, add to the brandy a small wineglassful of rum, and the juice and grated rind of ½ lemon. Liqueurs such as Maraschino or Curaçao, substituted for the brandy, also make excellent sauces.

Time.–Altogether, 15 minutes.

Cherry Sauce for Sweet — Puddings —

Ingredients.–1 lb. of fresh black cherries, 1 tablespoonful of flour, 1 oz. of butter, ½ pint of water, 1 wineglassful of port, a little grated lemon rind, a pinch of ground cloves, 2 tablespoonfuls of lemon juice, sugar to taste.

Mode.–Stone the cherries and pound the kernels in a mortar to a smooth paste; put the butter and flour into a saucepan and stir them over the fire until a pale brown; then add the cherries, the pounded kernels, the port, and the water. Simmer these gently for ¼ hour, or until the cherries are quite cooked, and rub the whole through a sieve; add the remaining ingredients, let the sauce boil for another 5 minutes, and serve. This is a delicious sauce to serve with boiled batter pudding.

Time.–20 minutes to ½ hour.

— Custard Sauce —

Ingredients.–1 pint of milk, 2 eggs, 3 oz. of caster sugar, nutmeg, 1 tablespoonful of brandy.

Mode.–Put the milk in a very clean saucepan, and let it boil. Beat the eggs, stir to them the milk and sugar, and put the mixture into a pudding basin. Place the basin in a saucepan of boiling water; keep stirring well until the mixture thickens, but do not allow it to boil, or it will curdle. Serve the sauce in a tureen, stir in the brandy, and grate a little nutmeg over the top. This sauce may be made very much nicer by using cream instead of milk, but the above recipe will be found quite good enough for ordinary purposes.

Time.–Altogether, about 25 minutes.

— Plum Pudding Sauce —

Ingredients.–1 wineglassful of brandy, 2 oz. of butter, 1 glass of Madeira, caster sugar to taste.

Mode.–Put the sugar in a basin, with part of the brandy and the butter; let it stand by the side of the fire until it is warm and the sugar and butter are dissolved; then add the rest of the brandy, with the Madeira. Either pour it over the pudding, or serve in a tureen. This is a very rich and excellent sauce.

Time.–About 10 minutes to dissolve the sugar and butter.

— Sweet Sauce for Puddings —

Ingredients.–½ pint of MELTED BUTTER made with milk, 4 heaped teaspoonfuls of caster sugar, flavouring of grated lemon rind, or nutmeg, or cinnamon.

Mode.–Make ½ pint of melted butter, omitting the salt; stir in the sugar, add a little grated lemon rind, nutmeg, or powdered cinnamon, and serve. Previously to making the melted butter, the milk can be flavoured with essence of almonds. This simple sauce may be served for children with rice, batter, or bread pudding.

Time.–Altogether, 15 minutes.

Ice spattle

An Excellent Wine Sauce —for Puddings—

Ingredients.–The yolks of 4 eggs, 1 teaspoonful of flour, 2 oz. of caster sugar, 2 oz. of butter, a pinch of salt, ½ pint of sherry or Madeira.

Mode.–Put the butter and flour into a saucepan, and stir them over the heat until the mixture thickens; then add the sugar, salt, and sherry, and mix well together. Separate the yolks from the whites of the eggs; beat up the former, and stir them briskly into the sauce; let it remain on the heat until it is on the point of simmering, but do not allow it to boil, or it will instantly curdle.

Time.–5 to 7 minutes to thicken the butter; about 5 minutes to cook the sauce.

—Iced Pudding—
(PARISIAN RECIPE)

Ingredients.–¾ lb. of ground almonds, a few drops of almond essence, ¾ lb. of caster sugar, 8 eggs, 1½ pints of milk.

Mode.–Add to the ground almonds the well beaten eggs, milk, sugar, and almond essence; stir these ingredients over the heat until they thicken, but do not allow them to boil; then strain the mixture into a buttered mould and freeze. When required for table, turn it out on a dish, and garnish it with a compote of any fruit that may be preferred, pouring a little over the top of the pudding. This pudding may also be flavoured with Curaçao or Maraschino liqueur.

Time.–2 hours to freeze the mixture. **Sufficient** to fill a 3-pint mould.

—Iced Apple Pudding—
(A FRENCH RECIPE, AFTER CAREME)

Ingredients.–2 dozen dessert apples, a small pot of apricot jam, ½ lb. of caster sugar, 1 Seville orange, 1 teacupful of bottled cherries. ¼ lb. of raisins, 1 oz. of candied citron peel, 2 oz. of almonds, ¼ pint of Curaçao liqueur, ¼ pint of Maraschino liqueur, 1 pint of cream.

Mode.–Peel, core, and cut the apples into quarters, and simmer them gently, with the rind of the orange, until soft; then take out the rind and add the apricot jam and the sugar; work all these ingredients through a sieve, and put them into a bowl, which freeze for 15 minutes. Simmer the raisins in a little sugar and water for a few minutes, then add them, with the sliced citron peel, the chopped almonds, and the cherries drained from their syrup, to the apple and jam mixture; freeze again for 15 minutes; stir in the liqueurs and the cream, well whipped, and freeze for ½ hour; then press the mixture into an oiled ice cream mould and freeze until required for the table. To serve, wrap a hot cloth around the mould to loosen the pudding from the top and sides, and turn out on to a napkin.

Time.–Altogether, 2 to 2½ hours to freeze. **Sufficient** to fill a 3-pint mould.

M ETHOD OF FREEZING.–Put into the outer pail some pounded ice, upon which strew some saltpetre; then fix the pewter freezing-pot upon this, and surround it entirely with ice and saltpetre. Wipe the cover and edges of the pot, pour in the preparation, and close the lid; a quarter of an hour after, begin turning the freezing pot from right to left, and when the mixture begins to be firm round the sides, stir it about with the spattle, that the preparation may be equally congealed. Close the lid again, keep working from right to left and, from time to time, remove the mixture from the sides that it may be smooth; when perfectly frozen, it is ready to put in the mould; the mould should then be placed in the ice again, where it should remain until wanted for table.

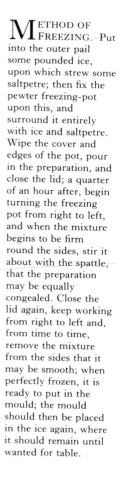

Iced-pudding mould

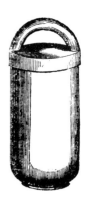

Ice-freezing pail

— *Nesselrode Pudding* —
(A FASHIONABLE ICED PUDDING – CAREME'S RECIPE)

Ingredients.–40 chestnuts, ¾ lb. of caster sugar, essence of vanilla, 1 pint of cream, the yolks of 12 eggs, 1 glass of Maraschino liqueur, 1 oz. of candied citron peel, 2 oz. of currants, 2 oz. of raisins, ½ pint of cream whipped up with the whites of 3 eggs.

Mode.–Blanch the chestnuts in boiling water, remove the husks and skins, and pound them in a mortar until perfectly smooth, adding a few spoonfuls of water and a little sugar; then rub them through a fine sieve. Gently heat together ¾ lb. of caster sugar, 1 pint of cream, the 12 egg yolks, and the essence of vanilla, add the chestnut pulp, and set the mixture over a low heat, stirring it continuously; just as it begins to boil, take it off the heat and pass through a sieve. Allow the mixture to cool, add the liqueur, the citron peel cut into thin slices, the currants and raisins (these should be soaked the day previously in Maraschino and vanilla-flavoured sugar), and the ½ pint of cream, whipped up with the frothed egg whites. Mix all thoroughly together, put it into a basin, and freeze, stirring every 20 minutes so that the pudding congeals smoothly; when it is thick and smooth, press it into a shaped mould and refreeze until wanted. Turn the pudding out to serve.

Time.–Altogether, 2 to 2½ hours to freeze. **Sufficient** to fill a 3-pint mould.

QUINCES.—The environs of Corinth originally produced the most beautiful quinces, but the plant was subsequently introduced into Gaul with the most perfect success. The ancients preserved the fruit by placing it, with its branches and leaves, in a vessel filled with honey or sweet wine, which was reduced to half the quantity by ebullition. Quinces may be profitably cultivated in this country with other fruit trees, and may be planted in espaliers or as standards. A very fine-flavoured marmalade may be prepared from quinces, and a small portion of quince in apple pie much improves its flavour. The French use quinces for flavouring many sauces. This fruit has the remarkable peculiarity of exhaling an agreeable odour, taken singly; but when in any quantity, or when they are stowed away in a drawer or close room, the pleasant aroma becomes an intolerable stench, although the fruit may be perfectly sound; it is therefore desirable, as but a few quinces are required for keeping, that they should be kept in a high and dry loft, and out of the way of the rooms used by the family.

—Baked Apple Dumplings—
(A PLAIN FAMILY DISH)

Ingredients.—6 apples, ¾ lb. of SUET CRUST, sugar to taste.

Mode.—Peel and take out the cores of the apples without dividing them. Roll the apples in the suet crust, previously sweetening them with brown sugar, and taking care to join the paste nicely. When they are formed into round balls, put them on a tin and bake them in a moderate oven for about ½ hour, or longer should the apples be very large; arrange them pyramidically on a dish, and sift over them some caster sugar. These may be made richer by using PUFF PASTE instead of suet crust.

Time.—½ to ¾ hour, no longer. **Sufficient** for 4 persons.

—Apple Tart or Pie—

Ingredients.—PUFF PASTE, 2 lbs. of apples; to every lb. of unpared apples allow 2 oz. of sugar, ½ teaspoonful of finely minced lemon peel, 1 tablespoonful of lemon juice, a little water, 1 egg white.

Mode.—Make ½ lb. of puff paste, place a border of it round the edge of a pie dish, and fill the dish with apples pared, cored, and cut into slices; sweeten with sugar, add the lemon peel and juice, and 2 or 3 tablespoonfuls of water; cover with a lid of paste, and bake in a hot oven for ½ to ¾ hour, or rather longer should the pie be very large. When it is three-quarters done, take it out of the oven, brush it over with the whisked egg white, then sprinkle upon it some sifted sugar. Put the pie back into the oven, and finish baking, and be particularly careful that it does not catch or burn, which it is very liable to do after the crust is iced. If made with a plain crust, the icing may be omitted.

Time.—½ hour before the crust is iced; 10 to 15 minutes afterwards. **Sufficient** for a tart for 6 persons.

Note.—Many things are suggested for the flavouring of apple pie; some say 2 or 3 tablespoonfuls of beer, others the same quantity of sherry, which very much improve the taste; whilst the old-fashioned addition of a few cloves is, by many persons, preferred to anything else, as also a few slices of quince.

—Bakewell Pudding—
(VERY RICH)

Ingredients.—¼ lb. of PUFF PASTE, 5 eggs, 6 oz. of caster sugar, ¼ lb. of butter, 1 oz. of ground almonds, jam.

Mode.—Cover a dish with the paste, rolled thin, and put over this a layer of any kind of jam, ½ inch thick; put the yolks of the eggs into a basin with the white of one, and beat these well; add the sugar, the butter, which should be melted, and the almonds; beat all together until well mixed, then pour it into the dish over the jam, and bake for 1 hour in a moderate oven.

Time.—1 hour. **Sufficient** for 4 or 5 persons.

MANY PRETTY DISHES OF PASTRY, such as puits d'amour or puff paste rings, pastry sandwiches, and fanchonnettes or custard tartlets, may be made by stamping puff paste out with fancy cutters, and filling the pieces, when baked, with jelly or preserve, but our space will not allow us to give a separate recipe for each of them. As they are all made from one paste, and only the shape and garnishing varies, perhaps it is not necessary, and by exercising a little ingenuity, variety may always be obtained. Half-moons, leaves, diamonds, stars, shamrocks, rings, etc., are the most appropriate shapes for fancy pastry.

— M i n c e P i e s —

Ingredients.– ½ lb. of good PUFF PASTE, MINCEMEAT, the white of 1 egg, a little caster sugar.

Mode.–Make some puff paste, roll it out to the thickness of about ¼ inch, and line some good-sized patty tins with it; fill them with mincemeat, cover with the paste, and cut it off all round close to the edge of the tin. Put the pies into a brisk oven, to draw the paste up, and bake for 25 minutes, or longer should the pies be very large; brush them over with the white of an egg, beaten to a stiff froth; sprinkle over a little sugar, and put them into the oven for a minute or two, to dry the egg; dish the pies on a white doyley, and serve hot.

Time.–25 to 30 minutes; 10 minutes to re-warm them. **Sufficient** for 4 good-sized pies.

— R h u b a r b T a r t —

Ingredients.– ½ lb. of PUFF PASTE, 5 large sticks of rhubarb, ¼ lb. of sugar.

Mode.–Make the puff paste, line the edges of a deep pie dish with it, and wash, wipe, and cut the rhubarb into pieces about 1 inch long. Should the rhubarb be old and tough, string it, that is to say pare off the outside skin. Pile the fruit high in the dish, as it shrinks very much in the cooking; put in the sugar, cover with a lid of paste, ornament the edges, and bake in a brisk oven for ½ to ¾ hour. If wanted very nice, when the tart is nearly baked, brush it over with the white of an egg beaten to a stiff froth, then sprinkle on it some sifted sugar, and put it in the oven to set the glaze. A small quantity of lemon juice, and a little of the peel minced, are by many persons considered an improvement to the flavour of rhubarb tart.

Time.– ½ to ¾ hour. **Sufficient** for 4 or 5 persons.

V o l - a u - v e n t o f F r e s h — S t r a w b e r r i e s —

Ingredients.–1 lb. of PUFF PASTE, 1 lb. of freshly gathered strawberries, sugar to taste, WHIPPED CREAM.

Mode.–Make a vol-au-vent case by the following method: roll out the puff paste to a thickness of 1 inch; using a fluted cutter, press out a round of paste about 6 inches across; with a sharp knife, make a slight incision in the paste all round the top, about 1 inch from the edge, which, when baked, will form the lid; put the vol-au-vent into a hot oven for about ½ hour; when nearly done, brush the paste over with the white of an egg, then sprinkle on it some caster sugar, and put it back in the oven to set the glaze; when of a nice golden colour, without being scorched, take it out of the oven, instantly remove the lid where it was marked, and detach all the soft crumb from the centre, when it will be ready to fill. At the moment of serving, fill it with the strawberries, broken up with sufficient sugar to sweeten them nicely. Place a few spoonfuls of whipped cream on top, and send to table.

Time.– ½ hour to 40 minutes to bake the vol-au-vent.

Open tart mould

OPEN TARTS of puff paste should be cooked before being filled with fruit or preserve; a few stars or leaves, previously cut out of the paste and baked, much improve the appearance of a tart.

RHUBARB.–This is one of the most useful of all garden productions that are put into pies and puddings. It was comparatively little known till within the last 20 or 30 years, but it is now cultivated in almost every British garden. The part used is the footstalks of the leaves. Rhubarb comes in season when apples are going out. The common rhubarb is a native of Asia, and the scarlet variety has the finest flavour. Turkey rhubarb, the well-known medicinal drug, is the root of a very elegant plant (*Rheum palmatum*), coming to greatest perfection in Tartary.

— Sussex or Hard Dumplings —

Ingredients.–1 lb. of flour, ½ pint of water, ½ saltspoonful of salt.

Mode.–Mix the flour and water together to a smooth paste, previously adding a small quantity of salt. Form this into small round dumplings; drop them into boiling water, and boil from ½ to ¾ hour. They may be served with roast or boiled meat; in the latter case they may be cooked with the meat, but should not be dropped into the water until it is quite boiling.

Time.– ½ to ¾ hours. **Sufficient** for 10 or 12 dumplings.

— Pease Pudding —

Ingredients.–1 ½ lbs. of split peas, 2 oz. of butter, 2 eggs, pepper and salt to taste.

Mode.–Put the peas to soak overnight, and float off any that are wormeaten or discoloured. Tie them loosely in a clean cloth, leaving a little room for them to swell, and put them on to boil in cold water, allowing 2 ½ hours after the water has simmered up. When the peas are tender, take them up and drain; rub them through a colander with a wooden spoon, add the butter, eggs, pepper, and salt, beat all well together for a few minutes, until the ingredients are well incorporated, then tie the mixture tightly in a floured cloth; boil the pudding for another hour, turn it out, and serve very hot.

Time.–2 ½ hours to boil the peas, tied loosely in the cloth; 1 hour for the pudding. **Sufficient** for 7 or 8 persons.

Pease Pudding

TO SERVE SUET PUDDING.– When there is a joint roasting or baking, suet pudding may be boiled in a long shape, and then cut into slices a few minutes before dinner is served; these slices should be laid in the dripping pan for a minute or two, and then browned before the fire. Most children like this accompaniment to roast meat. Where there is a large family of children, and the means of keeping them are limited, it is a most economical plan to serve up the pudding before the meat, as, in this case, consumption of the latter article will be much smaller than it otherwise would be.

Suet Pudding to serve —with Roast Meat—

Ingredients.–1 lb. of flour, 6 oz. of finely chopped suet, ½ saltspoonful of salt, ½ saltspoonful of pepper, ½ pint of milk or water.

Mode.–Chop the suet very finely, mix it well with the flour, add the salt and pepper (this latter ingredient may be omitted if the flavour is not liked), and make the whole into a smooth paste with the above proportion of milk or water. Tie the mixture in a floured cloth, or put it into a buttered basin and tie a cloth over the top, and boil for 2½ to 3 hours.

Time.–2½ to 3 hours. **Sufficient** for 5 or 6 persons.

—Yorkshire Pudding—

Ingredients.–1½ pints of milk, 6 large tablespoonfuls of flour, 3 eggs, 1 saltspoonful of salt.

Mode.–Put the flour into a basin with the salt, and gradually stir in enough milk to make a stiff batter. When this is perfectly smooth, and all the lumps are well rubbed down, add the remainder of the milk and the eggs, which should be well beaten. Beat the mixture for a few minutes, and pour it into a shallow tin, which has been previously well rubbed with beef dripping. Put the pudding into the oven, and bake it for 1 hour; then, for another ½ hour, place it under the meat, to catch a little of the gravy that flows from it. Cut the pudding into small square pieces, put them on a hot dish, and serve.

Time.–1½ hours. **Sufficient** for 5 or 6 persons.

Raised Pie of Poultry or Game

Ingredients.–To every lb. of flour allow ½ lb. of butter, ½ pint of water, the yolks of 2 eggs, ½ teaspoonful of salt (these are for the crust); 1 large fowl or a brace of pheasants, a few slices of lean veal, a few slices of cooked ham, FORCEMEAT, seasoning of mace, allspice, pepper and salt, gravy made from poultry trimmings.

Mode.–Make a stiff crust with the above proportion of butter, flour, water, and eggs, and work it up very smoothly; butter a raised pie mould, and line it with the paste. Bone the fowl, or whatever bird is intended to be used, and season the meat with pounded mace, allspice, pepper, and salt; put a layer of this into the mould, then spread over it a layer of forcemeat, then a layer of seasoned veal, and then one of ham, and then another layer of poultry meat, and so on; fill up all the cavities with slices of seasoned veal and ham and forcemeat; wet the edges of the pie, put on the cover, pinch the edges together, decorate it with leaves, and make a hole in the top; brush it over with a little egg yolk, and bake in a moderate oven for 4 hours, covering the top with paper as soon as it is brown. In the meantime, make a good strong stock from the bones; when the pie is cold, pour it through a funnel into the hole in the top; cover this hole with a small leaf, and the pie, when cold, will be ready for use. Let it be remembered that the stock must be considerably reduced before it is poured into the pie, as, when cold, it should form a firm jelly.

Time.–A large pie, 4 hours.

Raised pie

CHAPTER 10

Creams

Jellies, Soufflés, Omelettes,
— and Sweet Dishes —

CREAMS variously flavoured, depend for their smooth and unctuous consistency on the yellowish-white, opaque fluid which separates itself from new milk, and for their firmness on the addition of isinglass or gelatine; when put into oiled moulds, or moulded with sponge fingers, as in Charlotte Russe, they are generally turned out to send to table and have a very pretty effect. The flavourings most popularly esteemed are lemon, ginger, vanilla, chocolate, noyeau, and those of various soft fruits, mixed in as juice or pulp.

JELLIES are made from the sweetened and clarified juices of various fruits in which a small quantity of gelatine has been dissolved, rather more gelatine being needed when jellies are required to be moulded with fruit in them. Pieces of fruit held in suspension in brilliant clear jelly of one or more colours, the whole ornamented with whipped cream, make a most pleasant impression in the dessert. Gelatine is made from animal bodies, such as calf's feet, and isinglass, which may be substituted for it, of the swim bladders of certain fish, chiefly the sturgeon. The whites of eggs, put into liquid that is muddy from substances suspended in it, will, when the liquid is boiled, coagulate in a flocculent manner, entangling with it the impurities, and rise with them to the surface as scum. In this manner the liquids used in making jellies may be perfectly clarified.

SOUFFLES, OMELETTES, AND MERINGUES, in which eggs form the principal ingredient, demand, for their successful manufacture, an experienced hand. In the making of omelettes the frying-pan must have a lively heat to seize the eggs when they are first put in, and then a gentler heat to cook them through; great expedition is necessary in bringing soufflés to table, as with delay they quickly fall and lose their puffy appearance; with meringues, the coolest possible oven will not be found too gentle, as the operation wrought on egg whites and sugar stiffly whisked together is that of drying rather than cooking. Entremets based on eggs are healthy, nourishing, and pleasant to the taste, and may be eaten with safety by persons of the most delicate stomachs.

THE PRINCIPAL KINDS OF CREAM now used are the Devonshire and Dutch clotted creams, the Costorphin cream, and the Scotch sour cream. The Devonshire cream is produced by nearly boiling the milk in shallow tin vessels over a charcoal fire, and keeping it in that state until the whole of the cream is thrown up; it is used for eating with fruits and tarts. The cream from Costorphin, a village near Edinburgh, is accelerated in its separation from three or four days old milk by a certain degree of heat. The Dutch clotted cream, a coagulated mass in which a spoon will stand upright, is manufactured from fresh-drawn milk, which is put into a pan and stirred with a spoon two or three times a day to prevent the cream from separating from the milk. The Scotch "sour cream" is a misnomer, for it is a material produced from skimmed milk.

— Whipped Cream —
(FOR PUTTING ON TRIFLES, SERVING IN GLASSES, ETC.)

Ingredients.–To every pint of cream allow 3 oz. of caster sugar, 1 glass of sherry or sweet white wine, the rind of ½ lemon, the white of 1 egg.

Mode.–Pound the sugar with the lemon rind in a mortar so that the sugar absorbs the lemon flavour, then discard the rind; beat up the white of the egg until quite stiff; put the cream into a large bowl, with the flavoured sugar, wine, and beaten egg white, and whisk it to a froth. A plain whipped cream may be served on a glass dish, garnished with strips of angelica, or pastry leaves, or pieces of bright-coloured jelly; it makes a very pretty addition to the supper table.

— Apricot Cream —

Ingredients.–12 to 16 ripe apricots, ½ lb. of sugar, 1½ pints of milk, the yolks of 8 eggs, 1 oz. of gelatine.

Mode.–Divide the apricots, take out the stones, and boil them in a syrup made with ¼ lb. of sugar and ¼ pint of water, until they form a thin marmalade, which rub through a sieve. Boil the milk with the other ¼ lb. of sugar, let it cool a little, then mix with it the yolks of the eggs which have been previously well beaten; put this mixture into a jug, place this jug in boiling water, and stir it one way over the heat until it thickens, but on no account let it boil. Strain through a sieve, add the gelatine, previously dissolved in a small quantity of water, and keep stirring it till nearly cold; then mix with the apricots, stir well, put it into an oiled mould, and put in a very cool place. It should turn out without any difficulty.

Time.–From 20 to 30 minutes to boil the apricots. **Sufficient** to fill a 2-pint mould.

— Charlotte Russe —

Ingredients.–About 18 SAVOY BISCUITS or sponge fingers, the white of 1 egg, ¾ pint of cream, flavouring of vanilla, or liqueurs, or sherry, 1 tablespoonful of caster sugar, ½ oz. of gelatine.

Mode.–Procure about 18 Savoy biscuits or sponge fingers, and brush the edges of them with the white of an egg; line the bottom of a plain mould with them, placing them like a star or rosette; then stand them upright all round the edge of the mould, carefully putting them so close together that the white of the egg connects them firmly. Place this case in the oven for about 5 minutes, just to dry the egg. Whisk the cream to a stiff froth with the sugar, flavouring, and gelatine dissolved in 2 tablespoonfuls of warm water; fill the mould with this mixture, cover with a slice of sponge cake cut in the shape of the mould, and put it in ice until wanted for table. Turn it out on a dish to serve.

Time.–5 minutes to set the case in the oven.

Note.–Great care and attention are required in the turning out of this dish, that the cream does not burst the case; it is important to cut the biscuits level with the top of the cream so that, when turned out, there may be something firm for the cream to rest upon.

Charlotte Russe

A moulded cream

Charlotte Russe and Chocolate Cream

— Chocolate Cream —

Ingredients.–3 oz. of grated chocolate, ¼ lb. of caster sugar, 1 ½ pints of cream, 1 oz. of gelatine, the yolks of 6 eggs.

Mode.–Beat the yolks of the eggs well; put them into a basin with the grated chocolate, the sugar, and 1 pint of the cream; stir these ingredients well together, then set the basin in a saucepan of boiling water; stir one way until the mixture thickens, but do not allow it to boil, or it will curdle. Strain the cream through a sieve into another basin; stir in the gelatine, previously dissolved in ¼ pint of warm water and the other ½ pint of cream, which should be well whipped; mix all well together, pour it into an oiled mould, and set it on ice until wanted for table.

Time.–About 10 minutes to stir the mixture over the heat.
Sufficient for 6 persons.

— To make Gooseberry Fool —

Ingredients.–1 ¼ lbs. of ripe gooseberries; to every pint of fruit pulp add 1 pint of milk, or ½ pint of cream and ½ pint of milk, sugar to taste.

Mode.–Cut the tops and tails off the gooseberries; put them into a jar, with 2 tablespoonfuls of water and a little sugar; set this jar in a saucepan of boiling water, and let it boil until the fruit is soft enough to mash. When done, beat it to a pulp, work the pulp through a colander, and stir into every pint the above proportion of milk, or equal quantities of milk and cream. Ascertain if the mixture is sweet enough, and put in plenty of sugar, or it will not be eatable; serve in a glass dish, or in small glasses. This, although a very old-fashioned and homely dish, is very delicious when well made.

Time.–¾ to 1 hour. **Sufficient** for 5 or 6 persons.

— Swiss Cream —

Ingredients.–6 to 8 macaroons or 6 sponge fingers, sherry, 1 pint of cream, 5 oz. of caster sugar, 2 large tablespoonfuls of arrowroot, the rind of 1 lemon, the juice of ½ lemon, 3 tablespoonfuls of milk.

Mode.–Lay the macaroons or sponge fingers in a glass dish, and pour over them as much sherry as will cover them, or sufficient to soak them well. Put the cream into a saucepan, with the sugar and lemon rind, and warm over a very low heat until the cream is well flavoured, when take out the lemon rind. Mix the arrowroot smoothly with the cold milk, add it to the cream, and let it simmer gently for about 3 minutes, keeping it well stirred. Take it off the heat, stir till nearly cold, when add the lemon juice, and pour the whole over the macaroons or sponge fingers. Garnish the cream with strips of angelica or candied citron, or bright-coloured jelly or preserve.

Time.–About ½ hour to infuse the lemon rind; 5 minutes to simmer the cream. **Sufficient** for 5 or 6 persons.

— Blancmange —

Ingredients.–1 pint of milk, 1¼ oz. of gelatine, the rind of ½ lemon, ¼ lb. of sugar, a few drops of almond essence, 1 oz. of ground almonds, 1 pint of cream.

Mode.–Put the milk into a saucepan, with the gelatine, lemon rind, almond essence, and sugar, and warm through until the milk is well flavoured; add the ground almonds, and let the milk just boil up; strain it through a fine sieve or muslin into a bowl, add the cream, and stir the mixture occasionally until nearly cold. Let it stand for a few minutes, then pour it into a mould, which should be previously oiled with the purest salad oil, or dipped in cold water. There will be a sediment at the bottom of the bowl, which must not be poured into the mould as, when turned out, it would very much disfigure the appearance of the blancmange. The flavour may also be very much varied by adding bayleaves or essence of vanilla, instead of the lemon rind and almonds. In turning it out, just loosen the edges of the blancmange from the mould, place a dish on it, and turn it quickly over.

Time.–About 1½ hours to steep the lemon rind and almonds in the milk. **Sufficient** to fill a 2-pint mould.

Blancmange moulds

— Liqueur Jelly —

Ingredients.–1 lb. of sugar, 1½ oz. of gelatine, 1½ pints of water, the juice of 2 lemons, ¼ pint of liqueur.

Mode.–Put the sugar, with 1 pint of the water, into a saucepan, and heat gently; dissolve the gelatine in the the other ½ pint of water; strain the lemon juice and add it, with the gelatine, to the syrup; put in the liqueur and bring the whole to the boiling point. Take the saucepan off the heat, then pour the jelly into a mould, and set the mould in ice until required for table. Dip the mould in hot water, wipe the outside, loosen the jelly by passing a knife round the edges, and turn it out carefully on a dish. NOYEAU, Maraschino, Curaçao, brandy, or any kind of liqueur answers for this jelly.

Time.–10 minutes to boil the sugar and water. **Sufficient** to fill a 2-pint mould.

Jelly mould

Jelly bag

Jelly moulded with Fresh Fruit, and Swiss Cream

Jelly moulded with cherries

Open jelly with whipped cream

Oval jelly mould

Open mould

Jelly Moulded with — Fresh Fruit —

Ingredients.–Rather more than 1½ pints of jelly, made with equal quanties of water and clarified fruit syrup, with 1½ oz. of gelatine dissolved in it, a few nice strawberries, or red- or whitecurrants, or raspberries, or any fresh fruit that may be in season.

Mode.–Have ready the above proportion of jelly, which must be very clear and rather sweet, the raw fruit requiring an additional quantity of sugar. Select ripe, nice-looking fruits; pick off the stalks, wash them, and dry them with a soft cloth. Begin by putting a little jelly at the bottom of the mould, and allowing it to set; then arrange the fruit round the sides of the mould, recollecting that it will be the other way up when turned out, then carefully pour in some more jelly to make the fruit adhere and, when that layer is set, put in another row of fruit and jelly until the mould is full. When required for table, wring a cloth in boiling water, wrap it round the mould for a minute, and turn the jelly carefully out. Peaches, apricots, plums, apples, etc., are better for being boiled with a little sugar before they are laid in the jelly; strawberries, raspberries, grapes, cherries, and currants are put in raw. In winter, when fresh fruits are not obtainable, a very pretty jelly may be made with preserved or brandied fruits; these, in a bright and clear jelly, have a very pretty effect; of course, unless the jelly be very clear, the beauty of the dish will be spoiled.

Time.–2 hours to set each layer of jelly. **Sufficient** for 6 persons.

Apple jelly stuck with almonds

— To make a Soufflé —

Ingredients.–3 heaped tablespoonfuls of potato flour, or rice flour, or arrowroot, 1 pint of milk, 5 eggs, a piece of butter the size of a walnut, sifted sugar to taste, a pinch of salt, flavouring.

Mode.–Mix the potato flour, or whichever one of the above ingredients is used, with a little of the milk; put it into a saucepan, with the remainder of the milk, the butter, salt, and sufficient sugar to sweeten the whole nicely. Stir these ingredients over the heat until the mixture thickens; then take it off the heat, and let it cool a little. Separate the whites from the yolks of the eggs, beat the latter, and stir them into the soufflé batter. Now whisk the whites of the eggs to the firmest possible froth, for on this depends the excellence of the dish; stir them into the other ingredients, and add a few drops of essence of any flavouring that may be preferred, such as vanilla, lemon, orange, ginger, etc. Pour the mixture into a buttered soufflé dish, put it immediately into a moderately hot oven, and bake for about ½ hour; then take it out, strew it with sifted sugar, and send it instantly to table. The secret of making a soufflé well is to have the eggs well whisked, but particularly the whites, the oven not too hot, and to send it to table the moment it comes from the oven. If the soufflé is allowed to stand before being sent to table, its appearance and goodness will be entirely spoiled.

Time.–About ½ hour in the oven. **Sufficient** for 3 or 4 persons.

— Meringues —

Ingredients.– ½ lb. of caster sugar, the whites of 4 eggs.

Mode.–Whisk the whites of the eggs to a stiff froth and, with a metal spoon, lightly stir in 1 tablespoonful of the sugar; gradually mix in the rest of the sugar, whisking each time more sugar is added. Lightly oil a sheet of paper and place it on a flat baking tray; onto this drop a tablespoonful at a time of the meringue mixture, taking care to let all the meringues be of the same size and about 2 inches apart from each other. Strew over them some sifted sugar, and bake in the bottom of a very cool oven for 1 ½ to 2 hours. As soon as they begin to colour, remove them from the oven. When cool, detach them from the paper, and fill them with whipped cream, flavoured with liqueur or vanilla and sweetened with caster sugar, or join them together in pairs with the same cream mixture. Pile them high in the dish to send to table. To vary their appearance, a colouring of cochineal may be added to the egg whites, or finely chopped almonds or currants may be strewn over the meringues as they go into the oven, or they may be garnished, when cooked, with any bright-coloured preserve. Great expedition is necessary in making this sweet dish, as, if the meringues are not put into the oven as soon as the sugar and eggs are mixed, the former melts, and the mixture runs and does not keep its shape. The sweeter the meringues are made, the crisper they will be; but, if there is not sufficient sugar mixed with them, they will most likely be tough. If kept well sealed in a dry place, they will remain good for a month to six weeks.

Time.–Altogether, about 2 hours. **Sufficient** to make 2 dozen small meringues.

Meringues

Meringues with Cream

— To make a Plain Omelette —

Ingredients.–6 eggs, 1 saltspoonful of salt, ½ saltspoonful of pepper, ¼ lb. of butter.

Mode.–Break the eggs into a basin, omitting the whites of 3, and beat them up with the salt and pepper until extremely light; then add 2 oz. of the butter broken into small pieces, and stir this into the mixture. Put the other 2 oz. of butter into a frying-pan, make it quite hot and, as soon as it begins to bubble, whisk the eggs very briskly for a minute or two and pour them into the pan; stir the omelette with a spoon one way until the mixture thickens and becomes firm, and when the whole is set, fold the edges over, so that the omelette assumes an oval form; when it is nicely brown on one side, and quite firm, it is done. To take off the rawness on the upper side, hold the pan under a hot grill for a minute or two. Serve very expeditiously on a hot dish, and never cook it until it is just wanted. The flavour may be very much enhanced by adding minced parsley, minced onion or shallot, or grated cheese, allowing 1 tablespoonful of the former, and half the quantity of the latter, to the above proportion of eggs. Shrimps or oysters may also be added. In making an omelette, be particularly careful that it is not too thin; to avoid this, do not make it in too large a frying-pan, as the mixture would then spread too much and taste of the outside. It should also not be greasy, burnt, or too much done, and should be cooked over a gentle fire, that the whole of the substance may be heated without drying up the outside.

Time.–With 6 eggs, in a large frying-pan, 4 to 6 minutes.
Sufficient for 3 or 4 persons.

Omelette aux Confitures, —or Jam Omelette—

Ingredients.–6 eggs, ¼ lb. of butter, 2 oz. of caster sugar, 3 tablespoonfuls of apricot, strawberry, or any jam that may be preferred.

Mode.–Make the omelette by the recipe on page 153, adding caster sugar but omitting the salt and pepper; instead of doubling it over, leave it flat in the pan. When quite firm, and nicely brown on one side, turn it carefully on to a hot dish, spread over the middle of it the jam, and fold the omelette over on each side; sprinkle sifted sugar over and serve very quickly. A pretty dish of small omelettes may be made by dividing the batter into 3 or 4 portions and frying them separately; they should then be spread each one with a different kind of preserve, and the omelettes rolled over. Always sprinkle sweet omelettes with sifted sugar before sending them to table.

Time.–4 to 6 minutes. **Sufficient** for 3 or 4 persons.

—Omelette Soufflée—

Ingredients.–6 eggs, 5 oz. of caster sugar, flavouring of vanilla, or orange-flower water, or lemon rind, 3 oz. of butter, 1 dessertspoonful of rice flour.

Mode.–Separate the yolks from the whites of the eggs, add to the former the sugar, the rice flour, and whichever of the above flavourings may be preferred, and stir these ingredients well together. Whisk the whites of the eggs, mix them lightly with the batter, and put the butter into a small frying-pan. As soon as it begins to bubble, pour the batter into it and set the pan over a moderate heat; when the omelette is set, turn the edges over to make it an oval shape, and slip it on to a silver dish, which has been previously well buttered. Put it in the oven, and bake for 12 to 15 minutes; sprinkle sugar over it, and *serve immediately*.

Time.–About 4 minutes in the frying-pan; 12 to 15 minutes in the oven. **Sufficient** for 3 or 4 persons.

A Very Simple Apple —Charlotte—

Ingredients.–9 slices of bread-and-butter, about 6 good-sized apples, 1 tablespoonful of minced lemon peel, 2 tablespoonfuls of lemon juice, sugar to taste.

Mode.–Butter a pie dish, and place a layer of bread-and-butter, without the crusts, at the bottom, then a layer of apples, pared, cored, and cut into thin slices; sprinkle over these a portion of the lemon peel and juice and sweeten with sugar. Put in another layer of bread-and-butter, and then one of apples, proceeding in this manner until the dish is full; then cover it up with the peel of the apples to preserve the top from browning or burning; bake in a moderately hot oven for rather more than ¾ hour; remove the apple peel, turn the charlotte out on to a dish, sprinkle sifted sugar over, and serve.

Time.–¾ hour. **Sufficient** for 5 or 6 persons.

Omelettes aux Confitures, or Jam Omelettes

Iced Apples, or Apple — Hedgehog —

Ingredients.–12 middling-sized cooking apples, ½ lb. of sugar, ½ pint of water, the rind of ½ lemon minced very fine, the whites of 2 eggs, 3 tablespoonfuls of caster sugar, a few whole blanched almonds.

Mode.–Peel and core 6 of the apples without dividing them, and stew them very gently with the sugar and water till tender, then lift them carefully on to a dish. Have ready the remainder of the apples peeled, cored, and cut into thin slices; put them into the cooking syrup with the lemon peel, and boil gently until they are reduced to a mashed consistency; they must be kept stirred to prevent them from burning. Cover the bottom of a dish with some of the mashed apples, and place 4 of the stewed apples on top of them; inside and between each place more mashed apples; then put the other 2 whole apples on top, and fill up the cavities as before, forming the whole into a raised oval shape. Whip the whites of the eggs to a stiff froth, mix with them the caster sugar, and cover the apples very smoothly all over with the mixture; cut each almond into 4 or 5 strips and place these strips at equal distances over the icing, sticking up; strew over a little more sugar, and place the dish in a very cool oven, to colour the almonds and to warm the apples through.

Time.–20 minutes to ½ hour to stew the apples; 15 minutes in the oven. **Sufficient** for 6 persons.

A Pretty Dish of Apples
— and Rice —

Ingredients.–6 oz. of rice, 2 pints of milk, the rind of ½ lemon, sugar to taste, 8 apples, ¼ lb. of sugar, ¼ pint of water, ½ pint of BOILED CUSTARD.

Mode.–Flavour the milk with the lemon rind, by boiling them together for a few minutes, then take out the peel and put in the rice, with sufficient sugar to sweeten it nicely, and boil gently until the rice is quite soft; then let it cool. In the meantime peel, quarter, and core the apples, and boil them until tender in a syrup made with sugar and water in the above proportion; when soft, lift them out on a sieve to drain. Now put a middling-sized bowl in the centre of a dish; lay the rice all round till the middle of the bowl is reached; remove the bowl and smooth the rice with the back of a spoon; stick the apples into it in rows, one row sloping to the right and the next to the left. Set it in the oven to colour the apples; then, when required for table, garnish the rice with preserved fruits, and pour in the middle sufficient custard to be level with the top of the rice, and serve hot.

Time.–20 minutes to ½ hour to stew the apples; ¾ hour to simmer the rice; ¼ hour to bake. **Sufficient** for 5 or 6 persons.

— Apple Snow —
(A PRETTY SUPPER DISH)

Ingredients.–10 good-sized apples, the whites of 10 eggs, the rind of 1 lemon, ½ lb. of caster sugar.

Mode.–Peel, core, and cut the apples into quarters, and put them into a saucepan with the lemon peel and sufficient water to prevent them from burning–rather less than ½ pint. When they are tender, take out the peel, beat them to a pulp, let them cool, and stir them into the whites of the eggs, which should be previously beaten to a strong froth. Add the sugar, and continue the whisking until the mixture becomes quite stiff, then heap it on a glass dish or serve it in small glasses. This dish may be garnished with preserved barberries or strips of bright-coloured jelly; and a dish of custard should be served with it or a jug of cream.

Time.– ½ hour to 40 minutes to stew the apples. **Sufficient** for 6 or 7 persons.

— Boiled Custard —

Ingredients.–1 pint of milk, 5 eggs, 3 oz. of sugar, the rind of ½ lemon, or a few drops of essence of vanilla, 1 tablespoonful of brandy.

Mode.–Put the milk into a saucepan, with the sugar and whichever of the above flavourings may be preferred (lemon rind flavours custards most deliciously), and let the milk steep over a very low heat until it is well flavoured. Bring it to the point of boiling, then strain it into a basin; whisk the eggs well and, when the milk has cooled a little, stir in the eggs and strain the mixture into a basin. Place this in a saucepan of boiling water, and keep stirring the custard one way until it thickens, but on no account allow it to reach boiling point or it will instantly curdle and be full of lumps. Take it off the fire, stir

PALE SHERRIES are made from the same grapes as brown. The latter are coloured by an addition of some cheap must or wine which has been boiled till it has acquired a deep brown tint. Pale sherries were, some time ago, preferred in England, being supposed most pure, but the brown are now preferred by many people. The inferior sherries exported to England are often mixed with a cheap and light wine called Moguer, and are strengthened in the making by brandy; but too frequently they are adulterated by the London dealers.

Iced Apples, or Apple Hedgehog, and Boiled Custard in glasses

in the brandy and, when this is well mixed in, pour the custard into glasses, which should be rather more than three-quarters full; grate a little nutmeg over the top, and they are ready for table. To make custards look and eat better, ducks' eggs should be used, when obtainable; they add very much to the flavour and richness, and so many are not required as of ordinary eggs, 4 ducks' eggs to 1 pint of milk making a delicious custard. When desired extremely rich and good, cream should be substituted for the milk, and double the quantity of eggs used, omitting the whites.

Time.– ½ hour to infuse the lemon rind; about 10 minutes to thicken the custard. **Sufficient** to fill 8 dessert glasses.

— D u t c h   F l u m m e r y —

Ingredients.–1 ½ oz. of gelatine, the rind and juice of 1 lemon, 1 pint of water, 4 eggs, 1 pint of sherry, Madeira, or raisin wine, caster sugar to taste.

Mode.–Put the water, gelatine, and lemon rind into a saucepan, and heat gently until the gelatine is dissolved; strain this into a basin, stir in the eggs, which should be well beaten, the lemon juice, which should be strained, and the sherry; sweeten to taste with sugar, mix all well together, pour it into a basin, set this basin in a saucepan of boiling water over the heat, and keep stirring it one way until it thickens, but take care that it does not boil. Strain it into a mould that has been oiled, and put it in a cool place to set. A tablespoonful of brandy stirred in just before it is poured into the mould improves this dish, which is better if made the day before it is required.

Time.– ¼ hour to dissolve the gelatine; about ¼ hour to thicken the mixture. **Sufficient** to fill a 2-pint mould.

— Apple Fritters —

Ingredients.–For the batter, ½ lb. of flour, ½ oz. of butter, ½ saltspoonful of salt, 2 eggs, milk; 4 large apples, hot oil or lard, a little sugar.

Mode.–Break the eggs, separate the whites from the yolks, and beat them separately. Put the flour into a basin and stir in the butter, which should be melted to a cream; add the salt, and moisten with sufficient warm milk to make it of a consistency that will drop from the spoon. Stir this well, rub down any lumps that may be seen, and add the well whisked whites of the eggs; beat up the batter for a few minutes, and it is ready for use. Now peel and cut the apples into rather thick whole slices, without dividing them, and stamp out the middle of each slice, where the core is, with a cutter. Put the slices into the batter; have ready a pan of hot oil or lard; take out the pieces of apple one by one, put them into the hot fat, and fry a nice brown, turning them when required. When done, lay them on absorbent paper in a warm oven; then dish on a white doyley, piled one above the other; strew over them some sugar, and serve very hot.

Time.–About 10 minutes to fry them; 5 minutes to drain them. **Sufficient** for 4 or 5 persons.

— Pineapple Fritters —

Ingredients.–A small pineapple, a small wineglassful of brandy or liqueur, 2 oz. of caster sugar, batter as for APPLE FRITTERS, hot oil or lard.

Mode.–This elegant dish, although it may appear extravagant, is really not so if made when pineapples are plentiful. Peel the pine with as little waste as possible, cut it into rather thin slices, and soak these slices in the above proportion of brandy or liqueur and sugar for 4 hours; then make a batter the same as for apple fritters, but substituting cream for the milk and using a smaller quantity of flour; when this is ready, dip in the slices of pineapple, and fry them in hot oil or lard for 5 to 8 minutes; turn them when sufficiently brown on one side; when done, drain them in the oven on absorbent paper, dish them on a white doyley, strew with sugar, and serve quickly.

Time.–5 to 8 minutes. **Sufficient** for 3 or 4 persons.

— A Sweet Dish of Macaroni —

Ingredients.–¼ lb. of macaroni, 1 ½ pints of milk, the rind of ½ lemon, 3 oz. of sugar, ¾ pint of BOILED CUSTARD.

Mode.–Put the milk into a saucepan, with the lemon peel and sugar; bring it to boiling point, drop in the macaroni, and let it gradually swell over a low heat, but do not allow it to break. Though tender, the macaroni should be firm. Should the milk dry away before the macaroni is sufficiently swelled, add a little more. Have ready the custard, place the hot macaroni in a dish, and pour the custard over it; garnish with grated nutmeg and slices of citron.

Time.–40 to 50 minutes to swell the macaroni. **Sufficient** for 4 or 5 persons.

PINEAPPLE.–The pineapple has not been known in Europe above two hundred years, and has not been cultivated in England much above a century. It is said to have been first cultivated here by Sir Matthew Decker of Richmond. In Kensington Palace there is a picture in which Charles II is represented as receiving a pineapple from his gardener Rose, who is presenting it on his knees.

THE CITRON belongs to the same species as the lemon, being considered only as a variety, the distinction between them not being very great. It is larger, and is less succulent, but more acid; with a little artificial heat, the citron comes to as great perfection in England as in Spain and Italy. The fruit is oblong, and about 5 or 6 inches in length. The tree is thorny. The juice forms an excellent lemonade with sugar and water; its uses in punch, negus, and in medicine, are well known. The rind is very thick and, when candied with sugar, forms an excellent sweetmeat. There are several varieties cultivated in England, one of which is termed the Forbidden Fruit.

— To make Pancakes —

Ingredients.–Eggs, flour, milk; to every egg allow 1 oz. of flour, about ¼ pint of milk, a pinch of salt.

Mode.–Ascertain that the eggs are fresh; break each one separately in a cup, whisk them well, put them into a basin with the flour, salt, and a few drops of milk, and beat the whole to a perfectly smooth batter; then add by degrees the remainder of the milk. The proportion of this latter ingredient must be regulated by the size of the eggs, etc., but the batter, when ready for frying, should be of the consistency of thick cream. Place a small frying-pan on the heat to get hot; let it be delicately clean, or the pancakes will stick, and when quite hot put into it a small piece of butter, allowing about ½ oz. to each pancake; when it is melted, pour in the batter, about ½ teacupful to a pan 5 inches in diameter, and fry it for about 4 minutes, or until it is nicely brown on one side. By only pouring in a small quantity of batter and so making the pancakes thin, the necessity of turning them (an operation rather difficult to unskilful cooks) is obviated. When the pancake is done, sprinkle over it some fine sugar, roll it up in the pan, take it out with a large slice, and place it on a dish in the oven. Proceed in this manner until sufficient are cooked for a dish; then send them quickly to table, and continue to send in a further quantity, as pancakes are never good unless eaten almost immediately they come from the frying-pan. Send sifted sugar and a cut lemon to table with them. To render the pancakes very light, the yolks and whites of the eggs should be beaten separately, and the whites added to the batter just before frying.

Time.–4 to 5 minutes for a pancake that does not require turning; 6 to 8 minutes for a thicker one. **Sufficient**, if 3 eggs are used, with the other ingredients in correct proportion, for 3 persons.

Pancakes

Pineapple Fritters and a Sweet Dish of Macaroni

— Richer Pancakes —

Ingredients.–6 eggs, 1 pint of cream, ¼ lb. of caster sugar, 1 glass of sherry, ½ teaspoonful of grated nutmeg, flour.

Mode.–Ascertain that the eggs are extremely fresh, beat them well, strain them and mix with them the cream, sugar, sherry, nutmeg, and as much flour as will make the batter nearly as thick as that for ordinary pancakes. Make the frying-pan hot, wipe it with a little butter, pour in sufficient batter to make a thin pancake, and fry it for about 5 minutes. Dish the pancakes piled one above the other, strewing sifted sugar between each, and serve.

Time.–About 5 minutes. **Sufficient** to make about 12 pancakes.

Pears à l' Allemande

— Pears à l' Allemande —

Ingredients.–6 to 8 pears, water, sugar, 2 oz. of butter, the yolk of 1 egg, ½ oz. of gelatine.

Mode.–Peel and cut the pears into any form that may be preferred, and steep them in cold water to prevent them turning brown; put them into a saucepan with sufficient cold water to cover them, and simmer them, with the butter and enough sugar to sweeten them nicely, until tender; then brush them over with the yolk of an egg, sprinkle them with sifted sugar, and arrange them on a dish. Dissolve the gelatine in the cooking syrup, boil it up quickly for about 5 minutes, strain it over the pears, and let it remain until set. The syrup may be coloured with a little cochineal, which would very much improve the appearance of the dish.

Time.–From 20 minutes to ½ hour to stew the pears; 5 minutes to boil the syrup. **Sufficient** for 6 persons.

— Tipsy Cake —

Tipsy cake

Ingredients.–1 moulded sponge cake, sufficient sweet wine or sherry to soak it, 6 tablespoonfuls of brandy, 2 oz. of whole blanched almonds, 1 pint of rich BOILED CUSTARD.

Mode.–Procure a sponge cake that is three or four days old; cut the bottom of the cake level to make it stand firm in the dish; make a small hole in the centre, and pour in and over the cake sufficient sweet wine or sherry, mixed with the above proportion of brandy, to soak it nicely. When the cake is well soaked, blanch and cut the almonds into strips, stick them all over the cake, and pour round it a good custard, made with 8 eggs instead of 5 to each pint of milk.

Time.–About 2 hours to soak the sponge. **Sufficient** for 5 or 6 persons.

— To make a Trifle —

Ingredients.–For the topping, 1 pint of cream, 3 oz. of caster sugar, the whites of 2 eggs, a small glass of sherry or raisin wine; for the trifle, 1 pint of rich BOILED CUSTARD, made with 8 eggs to 1 pint of milk, 6 sponge fingers or 6 slices of sponge cake, 12 macaroons, 2 dozen ratafias, 2 oz. of whole almonds, the grated rind of 1 lemon, a layer of raspberry or strawberry jam, ½ pint of sherry or sweet wine, 6 tablespoonfuls of brandy.

Mode.–The topping for this trifle should be made the day before it is required, as the flavour is better, and it is much more solid than when prepared the same day. Put into a large bowl the sugar, the whites of the eggs, which should be beaten to a stiff froth, a glass of sherry or sweet wine, and the cream. Whisk these ingredients well in a cool place and, when well frothed, put away in a cool place. The next day, place the sponge fingers, macaroons, and ratafias at the bottom of a trifle dish; pour over them ½ pint of sherry or sweet wine, mixed with 6 tablespoonfuls of brandy; should this proportion of wine not be found quite sufficient, add a little more, as the cakes should be well soaked. Over the cakes put the grated lemon rind, the almonds, blanched and cut into strips, and a layer of raspberry or strawberry jam. Make a rich custard, using 8 instead of 5 eggs to 1 pint of milk, and let this cool a little; then pour it over the cakes, etc. The topping being made the day previously, there remains nothing to do now but heap it on top of the trifle.

Sufficient for 7 or 8 persons.

— Victoria Sandwiches —

Ingredients.–4 eggs, their weight in caster sugar, in butter, and in flour, a pinch of salt, a layer of any kind of jam or marmalade.

Mode.–Beat the butter to a cream, add the flour, salt, and sugar, stir these ingredients well together, and add the eggs, which should be previously whisked stiff. When the mixture has been well beaten for about 10 minutes, butter a sponge tin, pour in the batter, and bake in a moderate oven for 20 minutes. Let it cool, cut it in two, and spread one half of the cake with a layer of nice preserve; press the other half on top, and then cut it into long finger pieces; pile them in cross-bars on a glass dish, and serve.

Time.–20 minutes. **Sufficient** for 5 or 6 persons.

Trifle

CHAPTER 11

Preserves
Confectionery, Ices,
— and Dessert Dishes —

THE DESSERT IS, with moderns, not so profuse as it was with the ancients, nor does it hold the same relationship to the dinner. However, as late as the reigns of our two last Georges, fabulous sums were often expended upon fanciful desserts. The dessert certainly repays, in its general effect, the expenditure upon it of much pains; and it may be said that if there be any poetry at all in meals, or the process of feeding, there is poetry in the dessert.

FRUITS INTENDED FOR PRESERVATION should be gathered in the morning, in dry weather, with the morning sun upon them if possible; they will then have their fullest flavour, and keep in good condition longer than when gathered at any other time. In proportioning the amount of sugar in which fruits are preserved there is a great nicety. The principal thing to be acquainted with is the fact that, in proportion as the syrup is longer boiled, its water will become evaporated, its concentration of sugar stronger, and its consistency thicker. Great care must be taken that syrups do not boil over, and that the boiling is not carried to such an extent as to burn the sugar.

THE FRUITS that are most suitable for preservation in syrup are apricots, peaches, nectarines, apples, greengages, plums of all kinds, and pears, the first object being to soften the fruit by blanching or boiling it in water, in order that the syrup by which it is preserved may penetrate through its substance. Any fruits that have been preserved in syrup may be converted into dry or candied preserves by first draining them from the syrup, and then drying them in a cool oven, with a quantity of sugar sifted over them.

MARMALADES AND JAMS differ little from each other; they are preserves of a half-liquid consistency, made by boiling the pulp of fruits, and sometimes part of the rind, with sugar. The appellation of marmalade is applied to those confitures which are composed of the firmer fruits, such as pineapples or the rinds of oranges, whereas jams are made of the more juicy berries, such as strawberries, raspberries, currants, mulberries, etc. Jams require the same care and attention in

UNDER THE HEAD OF CONFECTIONERY come all the various fruits, flowers, herbs, roots, and juices which, when boiled with sugar, were formerly employed in pharmacy as well as for sweetmeats and called confections, from the Latin word *conficere*, "to make up". The term embraces a very large class indeed of sweet food, many kinds of which should not be attempted in the ordinary cuisine. The thousand and one ornamental dishes that adorn the tables of the wealthy should be purchased from the confectioner, for they cannot profitably be made at home.

ALTHOUGH SUGAR is the only substance capable of undergoing fermentation, yet it will not ferment at all if the quantity be sufficient to constitute a very strong syrup. Hence, syrups are used to preserve fruits and other vegetable substances from the changes they would undergo if left to themselves. Before sugar was in use, honey was employed to preserve many vegetable productions, though this substance has now given way to the juice of sugarcane.

the boiling as marmalades; the slightest degree of burning communicates a disagreeable taste, but if they are not boiled sufficiently, they will not keep. That they may keep, it is necessary not to be sparing of sugar.

FRUIT PASTES OR CHEESES are of a thicker consistency than jams or marmalades, and may be put into moulds or spread on trays and subsequently dried in the oven; from a sheet of paste so prepared, strips may be cut and formed into any shape that may be desired, as knots, rings, etc.

FRUIT JELLIES are the juices of fruits combined with sugar, concentrated by boiling to such a consistency that the liquid, upon cooling, assumes the form of a tremulous jelly, as redcurrant, apple, gooseberry, quince jelly, etc.

COMPOTES are confitures made at the moment of need, and with much less sugar than would be ordinarily put to preserves. They are most wholesome, and suitable to most stomachs which cannot accommodate themselves to raw fruit or a large portion of sugar; they are a happy medium, and far better than ordinary stewed fruit.

ICES ARE COMPOSED, it is scarcely necessary to say, of congealed cream or water, combined sometimes with liqueurs or other flavouring ingredients, and more generally with the juices of fruits or with fruit pulp. At desserts, or at some evening parties, ices are scarcely to be dispensed with. The principal art in making ice creams and water ices is to keep the preparation smooth, which may be achieved by stirring occasionally until congelation takes place.

— A p p l e   J e l l y —

Ingredients.—To 6 lbs. of apples allow 3 pints of water; to every pint of juice allow 1 lb. of sugar, the juice of ½ lemon.

Mode.—Peel, core, and cut the apples into slices, and put them into a large jar, with water in the above proportion; cover and place in a cool oven overnight; by morning the juice will be thoroughly drawn and the apples quite soft; strain them through a jelly bag; then to every pint of juice add 1 lb. of sugar; put into a preserving pan and boil for rather more than ½ hour, removing the scum as it rises; add the lemon juice just before it is done, put into pots, and cover. This preparation is useful for garnishing sweet dishes, and may be turned out for dessert.

Time.—The apples to be put in the oven overnight; rather more than ½ hour to boil the jelly. **Sufficient** for 5 or 6 pots of jelly.

— B l a c k c u r r a n t   J a m —

Ingredients.—To every lb. of fruit, weighed before being stripped from the stalks, allow ¾ lb. of sugar, ¼ pint of water.

Mode.—Let the fruit be very ripe, and gathered on a dry day. Strip it from the stalks, and put it into a preserving pan, with ¼ pint of water to each lb. of fruit; boil together for 10 minutes, then add the sugar, allow it to dissolve, and boil again for ½ hour, reckoning from the time when the jam simmers equally all over, or longer should it not

DAMSONS.— Whether for jam, jelly, pie, pudding, water ice, wine, dried fruit or preserves, the damson or damascene (for it was originally brought from Damascus) is invaluable. It combines sugary and acid qualities in happy proportions when fully ripe. It is a fruit easily cultivated, and if budded 9 inches from the ground on vigorous stocks will grow several feet high in the first year, and make fine standards the year following. Amongst the list of the best sorts of baking plums the damson stands first, not only on account of the abundance of its juice, but also on account of its soon softening. Because of the roughness of its flavour, it requires a large quantity of sugar.

appear to set nicely when a little is poured onto a plate. Keep stirring it to prevent it from burning, carefully remove all the scum and, when done, pour it into pots. Let it cool, cover with circles of oiled paper, and seal. Great attention must be paid to the stirring of this jam, as it is very liable to burn on account of the thickness of the juice.

Time.–10 minutes to boil the fruit and water; ½ hour or longer, once the sugar is added. **Sufficient**, if 6 lbs. of fruit are used, to make 8 or 9 pots of jam.

— A p r i c o t   J a m —

Ingredients.–To every lb. of ripe apricots, weighed after being skinned and stoned, allow 1 lb. of sugar.

Mode.–Peel the apricots as thinly as possible, break them in half, and remove the stones. Weigh the fruit, and to every lb. allow the same proportion of sugar; strew the sugar over the apricots, which should be placed on trays, and let them steep for 12 hours. Break the stones, blanch the kernels, and put them with the sugar and fruit into a preserving pan; simmer very gently until the pieces of apricot are clear, and take them out as they become so; as fast as the scum rises, carefully remove it. Put the apricots into jars, pour over them the syrup and kernels, cover with circles of oiled paper, and seal.

Time.–12 hours to steep the apricots in the sugar; about ¾ hour to boil the jam. **Sufficient**, if 10 lbs. of fruit are used, for about 12 pots of jam.

— E x c e l l e n t   M i n c e m e a t —

Ingredients.–3 large lemons, 3 large apples, 1 lb. of raisins, 1 lb. of currants, 1 lb. of finely chopped suet, 2 lbs. of moist brown sugar, 1 oz. each of sliced candied citron, sliced candied orange peel, and sliced candied lemon peel, 1 teacupful of brandy, 2 tablespoonfuls of orange marmalade.

Mode.–Grate the rinds of the lemons; squeeze out the juice, strain it, and boil the remainder of the lemons until tender enough to pulp or chop very finely; add to this pulp the apples, which should be baked, and their skins and cores removed; put in the remaining ingredients one by one and, as they are added, mix everything very thoroughly together. Put the mincemeat into jars with tightly fitting lids, and in a fortnight it will be ready for use. This preserve should be made in the first or second week in December.

Sufficient for 7 or 8 jars of mincemeat.

— L e m o n   M i n c e m e a t —

Ingredients.–2 large lemons, 6 large apples, ½ lb. of finely chopped suet, 1 lb. of currants, ½ lb. of sugar, 2 oz. of candied lemon peel, 1 oz. of candied citron peel, mixed spice to taste.

Mode.–Peel the lemons, squeeze them, and boil the peel until tender enough to mash. Add to the mashed lemon peel the apples, which should be peeled, cored, and minced, the chopped suet, currants, sugar, sliced peel, and spice. Strain the lemon juice and add it to these ingredients, stir the mixture well, and put into pots with closely fitting lids. In 10 days the mincemeat will be ready for use.

Sufficient for 4 or 5 pots.

ORANGES AND CLOVES.–It appears to have been the custom formerly, in England, to make New Year's presents with oranges stuck full with cloves. We read in one of Ben Jonson's pieces, *Christmas Masque*: "He has an orange and rosemary, but not a clove to stick in it."

— Orange Marmalade —

Ingredients.–Equal weights of Seville oranges and sugar; to every lb. of sugar allow ½ pint of water.

Mode.–Weigh the sugar and oranges; score the skins of the oranges, and take them off in quarters; boil these quarters in a muslin bag in water until they are quite soft and can be pierced easily with a pin; then cut them into chips about 1 inch long, and as thin as possible; should there be a great deal of white stringy pith, remove it before cutting the rind into chips. Split open the oranges, scrape out the best part of the pulp, with the juice, rejecting the white pith and pips. Make a syrup with the sugar and water, boil it until clear, then put in the chips, pulp, and juice, and boil for 20 minutes to ½ hour, removing all the scum as it rises.

Time.–2 hours to boil the rinds, 10 minutes the syrup, 20 minutes to ½ hour the marmalade. **Seasonable** in winter, when Seville oranges are in perfection.

Orange Marmalade made with Honey

Orange Marmalade made — with Honey —

Ingredients.–To each pint of the juice and pulp of Seville oranges allow 1 lb. of honey, 1 lb. of the rinds.

Mode.–Peel the oranges, boil the rinds in water until tender, and

PLUMS.- The best sorts of plums are agreeable at the dessert and, when perfectly ripe, are wholesome, but some are too astringent. They lose much of their bad qualities by baking, and are extensively used, when in full season, in tarts and preserves. The damson takes its name from Damascus, where it grows in great quantities, and whence it was brought into Italy about 114 B.C. The Orleans plum is from France; the greengage is called after the Gage family, who first brought it into England from the monastery of the Chartreuse, at Paris, where it still bears the name of *reine-claude*; the Magnum-bonum is our largest plum, and greatly esteemed for preserves and culinary purposes.

cut them into strips. Take out the pips from the juice and pulp, and put it with the honey and rinds into a preserving pan; boil all together for about ½ hour, or until the marmalade is of a suitable consistency; put it into pots, allow to cool, then cover tightly.

Time.–2 hours to boil the rinds, ½ hour the marmalade.
Seasonable in winter, when Seville oranges are available.

— *P l u m   J a m* —

Ingredients.–To every lb. of plums, weighed before being stoned, allow ¾ lb. of sugar.

Mode.–In making plum jam, the quantity of sugar for each lb. of fruit must be regulated by the quality and size of the fruit, some plums requiring much more sugar than others. Halve the plums, take out the stones, and put them on to trays with sugar sprinkled over them in the above proportion, and let them steep for one day; then put them into a preserving pan, simmer gently for about ½ hour, then boil them rapidly for another 15 minutes. The scum must be carefully removed as it rises, and the jam must be well stirred all the time, or it will burn at the bottom of the pan and spoil the colour and flavour of the preserve. Some of the stones may be cracked and a few kernels added to the jam just before it is done; these impart a very delicious flavour.

Time.– ½ hour to simmer gently, ¼ hour to boil rapidly.

— *R e d c u r r a n t   J e l l y* —

Ingredients.–Redcurrants; to every pint of juice allow ¾ lb. of sugar.

Mode.–Clean the fruit; pick it from the stalks, put it into a jar, cover the jar and place it in a saucepan of boiling water, and let it simmer gently until the juice is well drawn from the currants; then strain them through a jelly-bag or fine muslin and, if the jelly is wished very clear, do not squeeze them too much, as the skin and pulp from the fruit will be pressed through with the juice and so make the jelly muddy. Measure the juice, and to each pint allow ¾ lb. of sugar; put juice and fruit into a preserving pan, set it over the fire, and keep stirring the jelly until it is done, carefully removing every particle of scum as it rises, using a wooden spoon for the purpose so as not to spoil the colour of the jelly. When it has boiled for 20 minutes to ½ hour, put a little of the jelly on a plate, and if firm when cool, it is done. Take it off the heat, pour it into small pots and cover tightly. Label the pots, adding the year when the jelly was made, and store away in a dry place. A jam may be made with the currants, if they are not squeezed too dry, by adding a few fresh raspberries and boiling all together with sufficient sugar to sweeten it nicely. As this preserve is not worth storing away, but is only for immediate eating, a smaller proportion of sugar than usual will be found enough; it answers very well for children's puddings or for a nursery preserve.

Time.–¾ to 1 hour to extract the juice; 20 minutes to ½ hour to boil the jelly. **Sufficient**, if 16 lbs. of currants are used, to make 10 to 12 pots of jelly.

Note.–Should the above proportion of sugar not be found sufficient for some tastes, add an extra ¼ lb. to every pint of juice.

A pot of strawberries as a table decoration

— Strawberry Jam —

Ingredients.–To every lb. of small strawberries allow ½ pint of redcurrant juice, 1¼ lbs. of sugar.

Mode.–Strip the currants from the stalks, put them into a jar, cover the jar and place it in a saucepan of boiling water, and simmer until the juice is well drawn from the fruit; strain the currants, measure the juice, and put it into a preserving pan. Select well-ripened but sound strawberries, pick them from the stalks, weigh them, and add them to the currant juice, with sugar in the above proportion; dissolve the sugar, then simmer for ½ to ¾ hour, carefully removing the scum as it rises. Stir the jam only enough to prevent it from burning at the bottom of the pan, as the strawberries should be preserved as whole as possible. Put the jam into jars and, when cold, cover down.

Time.–¾ to 1 hour to extract the juice from the currants; ½ to ¾ hour to simmer the jam. **Sufficient**, if 6 lbs. of strawberries are used, for 6 pots of jam.

— Compote of Green Figs —

Ingredients.–½ lb. of sugar, ¾ pint of water, 2 lbs. of fresh green figs, the rind of ½ lemon.

Mode.–Make a syrup by boiling together the sugar, water, and lemon rind. Put in the figs, and simmer them very slowly until tender; drain them and put them on a glass dish; reduce the syrup by boiling it quickly for 5 minutes; take out the lemon peel, pour the syrup over the figs, and the compote, when cold, will be ready for table. A little port or lemon juice, added just before the figs are done, will be found an improvement.

Time.–2 to 3 hours to stew the figs. **Sufficient** for 6 people.

— To Bottle Fresh Fruit —
(VERY USEFUL IN WINTER)

Ingredients.–Fresh fruit, such as currants, raspberries, cherries, gooseberries, plums, greengages, damsons, etc; wide-mouthed glass bottles, new corks or glass lids to fit them tightly.

Mode.–Let the fruit be full grown, but not too ripe, and gathered in dry weather (if gathered in the damp, or if the skins broken or split, the fruit will mould). Remove the stalks without bruising or breaking the skin, and reject any that are blemished. Have ready some *perfectly dry* glass bottles; burn a match in each bottle to exhaust the air, and quickly put in the fruit in to be preserved; gently cork the bottles, or put the lids on, and put into a *very cool* oven, where let them remain until the fruit has shrunk away by about a quarter. Take the bottles out, *do not open them*, but immediately push the corks in tight and seal them with melted resin, or clamp down the lids. If kept in a dry place, the fruit will remain good for many months; if stored away in a place that is in the least damp, the fruit will soon spoil.

Time.–From 5 to 6 hours in a very slow oven.

*Redcurrant Jelly
and Lemon
Mincemeat*

— Greengages in Syrup —

Ingredients.–To every lb. of fruit allow 1 lb. of sugar, ¼ pint of water.

Mode.–Boil the sugar and water together for about 10 minutes; divide the greengages, take out the stones, put the fruit into the syrup, and let it simmer gently until nearly tender. Take it off the heat, put it into a large pan, and the next day boil it up again for about 10 minutes with the kernels from the stones, which should be blanched. Put the fruit carefully into dry jars, pour over it the syrup and the kernels, and, when cold, cover down to exclude the air.

Time.–10 minutes to boil the syrup; 15 minutes to simmer the fruit the first day, 10 minutes the second day.

— Preserved Mulberries —

Ingredients.–To every 2 lbs. of fruit and 1 pint of juice allow 2½ lbs. of sugar.

Mode.–Put some of the mulberries into a preserving pan, and simmer them with a very little water until the juice is well drawn. Strain the juice, measure it, and to every pint allow the above proportion of sugar and fruit. Put the sugar into the preserving pan, moisten it with the juice, boil it up, skim well, and then add the mulberries, which should be ripe, but not soft enough to break to a pulp. Let them stand in the syrup till warm through, then simmer; when half done, turn them into a bowl, and let them remain till the next day; boil them up again, and when the syrup is thick, and becomes firm when allowed to cool on a plate, put into pots.

Time.–¾ hour to extract the juice; 15 minutes to boil the mulberries the first time, 15 minutes the second time.

MULBERRIES are esteemed for their highly aromatic flavour, and their sub-acid nature. They are considered as cooling, laxative, and generally wholesome. This fruit was very highly esteemed by the Romans, who appear to have preferred it to every other. The mulberry tree is stated to have been introduced into this country in 1548, being first planted at Sion House, where the original trees still thrive. The planting of them was much encouraged by King James I about 1605, and considerable attempts were made at that time to rear silkworms on a large scale for the purpose of making silk; but these endeavours have always failed, the climate being scarcely warm enough.

THE PEACH AND NECTARINE are among the most delicious of our fruits, and are considered as varieties of the same species, produced by cultivation. The former is characterized by a very delicate down, while the latter is smooth; as a proof of their identity as to species, trees have borne peaches on one part and nectarines on another, and even a single fruit has had down on one side and on the other none. Pliny states that the peach was originally brought from Persia, where it grows naturally. The young leaves of the peach are sometimes used in cookery, from their agreeable flavour, and a liqueur may be made by steeping them in brandy sweetened with sugar and fined with milk; gin may also be flavoured in the same manner.

— Preserved Nectarines —

Ingredients.–To every lb. of sugar allow ¼ pint of water; nectarines.

Mode.–Divide the nectarines in two, take out the stones, and make a strong syrup with sugar and water in the above proportion. Put in the nectarines, and simmer them until they have thoroughly imbibed the sugar, skimming off any scum and keeping the fruit as whole as possible. The next day boil again for a few minutes, take out the nectarines, put them into jars, boil the syrup quickly for 5 more minutes, pour it over the fruit, allow it to cool, and cover tightly.

Time.–10 minutes to boil the sugar and water; 20 minutes to boil the fruit the first time, 10 minutes the second time; 5 minutes to give the syrup a last boil.

Bottled Fruit

— Peaches in Brandy —

Ingredients.–To every lb. of fruit weighed before being stoned allow ¼ lb. of caster sugar, brandy.

Mode.–Wipe and weigh the peaches, and remove the stones as carefully as possible, without injuring the peaches much. Put them into large jars, sprinkle them with sugar in the above proportion, and pour enough brandy over to cover them. Cover the jars tightly, place in a saucepan of boiling water, and bring to simmering point, but do not allow to boil. Take the fruit out carefully, without breaking it; put it into smaller jars, pour over the brandy, and cover tightly. Apricots done in the same manner will be found delicious.

Time.–From 10 to 20 minutes to simmer the brandy.

FRESH FRUIT SALADS are made by stripping the fruit from the stalks, piling it on a dish, and sprinkling over it finely pounded sugar. They may be made of strawberries, raspberries, currants, or any of these fruits mixed; peaches also make a very good salad. After the sugar is sprinkled over, about 6 large tablespoonfuls of wine or brandy, or 3 tablespoonfuls of liqueur, should be poured in the middle of the fruit; when the flavour is liked, a little pounded cinnamon may be added. In helping the fruit, it should be lightly stirred, that the wine and sugar may be equally distributed.

— To Preserve Plums Dry —

Ingredients.–Fresh plums; to every lb. of sugar allow ¼ pint of water.

Mode.–Gather the plums when they are full-grown and just turning colour; prick them, put them into a saucepan of cold water, and set them on the heat until the water is on the point of boiling. Then take them out, drain them, and boil them gently in syrup made with the above proportion of sugar and water; if the plums shrink, and will not absorb the syrup, prick them as they lie in the pan; give them another boil, skim, and allow to cool. The next day add some more sugar to the fruit and syrup; put all together into a wide-mouthed jar, and place them in a very cool oven for 2 nights; then drain the plums from the syrup, put them on a tray, sprinkle a little powdered sugar over, and dry them in a very cool oven; store in boxes in a very dry place.

Time.–15 to 20 minutes to boil the plums in the syrup.

Almond Paste for — Sweetmeats —

Ingredients.–1 lb. of ground almonds, a few drops of almond essence, 1 lb. of caster sugar and icing sugar mixed, the whites of 2 eggs.

Mode.–Stir the egg whites into the almonds, adding almond essence to taste; put the mixture into a small preserving pan, add the sugar, and place the pan on a low heat; keep stirring until the paste is dry, then take it out of the pan, put it between two dishes and, when cold, make it into any shape that fancy may dictate.

Time.–½ hour.

— To make Barley Sugar —

Ingredients.–To every lb. of sugar allow ½ pint of water, ½ the white of an egg, lemon juice, essence of lemon.

Mode.–Put the sugar into a saucepan with the water and, when the former is dissolved, set it over a moderate heat, adding the egg white, well beaten, before the mixture gets warm; stir well. When the syrup boils, remove the scum as it rises, and keep it boiling until no more scum appears and the syrup looks perfectly clear; then strain it through a fine sieve or muslin, and put it back into the saucepan. Boil it again until a little dropped into a basin of cold water sets in brittle strands like caramel; it is then sufficiently boiled. Add a little lemon juice and a few drops of essence of lemon, and let it stand for a minute or two. Have ready a marble slab or tray, rubbed over with oil; pour on it the sugar, and cut it into strips with a pair of scissors; these strips should then be twisted, and stored away in a very dry place. Barley sugar may be formed into lozenges or drops by dropping it in a very small quantity at a time on to an oiled slab or tray.

Time.–15 minutes. **Sufficient**, if 1 lb. of sugar and ½ pint of water are used, for 5 or 6 sticks.

TO BOIL SUGAR TO CARAMEL.– To every pound of sugar allow ¼ pint of water; boil the sugar and water together very quickly until they start to colour of a pale brown; squeeze in a little lemon juice, and it is ready for use. The insides of oiled moulds are often ornamented with this sugar; a dish of light pastry, tastefully arranged, also looks very pretty with this sugar spun lightly over it.

Do LADIES KNOW to whom they are indebted for the introduction of ices, which all the fair sex are passionately fond of? To Catherine de' Medici. Will not this fact cover a multitude of sins committed by the instigator of St. Bartholomew?

— To make Everton Toffee —

Ingredients.–1 lbs. of sugar, 1 teacupful of water, ¼ lb. of butter, 6 drops of essence of lemon.

Mode.–Put the water and sugar into a pan over a very low heat, and beat the butter to a cream. When the sugar is dissolved, add the butter, and keep stirring the mixture over the fire until it sets when a little is poured on to a buttered dish; just before the toffee is done, add the essence of lemon. Butter a tin or tray, and pour in the mixture; when cool, the toffee will easily separate from it. Butterscotch, an excellent thing for coughs, is made in the same manner, but with brown instead of white sugar, omitting the water, and flavoured with ½ oz. of powdered ginger.

Time.–18 to 35 minutes. **Sufficient** to make 1 lb. of toffee.

— To make Fruit Ice Creams —

Ingredients.–To every pint of fruit juice or pulp allow 1 pint of cream, caster sugar to taste.

Mode.–Let the fruit be well ripened; if necessary, stew it gently with a little water to soften it; rub it through a sieve and sweeten it nicely with sugar; whip the cream until it is stiff, add it to the fruit, and whisk the whole for 5 minutes. Freeze the mixture for ½ hour, then whisk well again, and refreeze, turning it into an oiled mould if desired; this second mixing prevents ice crystals forming and giving the mixture a gritty consistency. If wanted less rich, custard may be substituted for half the cream. Raspberry, strawberry, currant, and all fruit ice creams are made in the above manner. A little sugar sprinkled over the fruit before it is pulped generally helps to extract the juice.

Time.–½ hour to freeze the mixture the first time; 1 to 1½ hours to freeze again.

— To make Fruit Water Ices —

Ingredients.–To every pint of fruit juice or purée allow 1 pint of syrup made from 1½ lbs. of sugar and ¾ pint of water.

Mode.–Select nice ripe fruit, pick off the stalks, and put it into a large pan with a very little water and a little sugar strewed over it; stir it about over a low heat with a wooden spoon until it is well broken, then rub it through a sieve. Make the syrup by dissolving the sugar in the water and then boiling it, but do not allow the syrup to caramelize; let it cool, add the fruit juice or purée, mix well together, turn into a bowl, and freeze for ½ hour, or until just firm; mash the mixture smooth with a fork to prevent ice crystals forming, then refreeze. Put it into small glasses to serve. Raspberry, strawberry, currant, and other fresh fruit water ices are made in the same manner.

Time.–½ hour to freeze the mixture the first time; 1½ to 2 hours to refreeze.

RASPBERRIES.– There are two sorts of raspberries, the red and the white. Both the scent and flavour of this fruit are very refreshing, and the berry itself is exceedingly wholesome and invaluable to people of a nervous or bilious temperament. We are not aware, however, of its being cultivated with the same amount of care which is bestowed upon some others of the berry tribe; neither, as an eating fruit, is it so universally esteemed as the strawberry, with whose lusciousness and peculiarly agreeable flavour it can bear no comparison. In Scotland, it is found in large quantities growing wild, and is eagerly sought after, in the woods, by children. Its juice is rich and abundant, and to many extremely agreeable.

ICES FOR DESSERT are usually moulded; when this is not the case, they are handed round in glasses with wafers to accompany them. Preserved ginger is frequently handed round after ices, to prepare the palate for the delicious dessert wines. A basin of finely sifted sugar must never be omitted at a dessert, as also a jug of fresh cold water (iced, if possible), and two goblets by its side.

ORIGIN OF THE PLUM.–The wild sloe is the parent of the plum and is a shrub common in our hedgerows; the fruit is about the size of a large pea, of a black colour, and covered with a bloom of a bright blue. The juice is extremely sharp and astringent, and was formerly employed as a medicine, where astringents were necessary. It now assists in the manufacture of a red wine made to imitate port, and also for adulteration. The leaves have been used to adulterate tea; the fruit, when ripe, makes a good preserve.

— Stewed Plums —

Ingredients.–2 lbs. of large plums, ¾ pint of syrup made with ¾ pint of water and ½ lb. of sugar, 1 glass of port, the rind and juice of 1 lemon.

Mode.–Halve and stone the plums, and stew them gently in a little water for 1 hour; strain the juice, and use it to make the syrup, adding water to make it up to the above proportions; put in the plums with the port, and the lemon juice and rind, and simmer very gently for 1½ hours. Put the plums into a dish, take out the lemon peel, pour the syrup over them, and allow them to cool. A little allspice stewed with the fruit is by many persons considered an improvement.

Time.–1 hour to stew the plums in water, 1½ hours in the syrup.
Sufficient for 5 or 6 persons.

Stewed Plums

— Whipped Syllabubs —

Ingredients.–½ pint of cream, ¼ pint of sherry, 3 tablespoonfuls of brandy, the juice of ½ lemon, a little grated nutmeg, 3 oz. of caster sugar, WHIPPED CREAM.

Mode.–Mix all the ingredients together, put the syllabub into glasses, and over the top heap a little whipped cream. Solid syllabub is made by whisking or milling the mixture to a stiff froth, and putting it in the glasses without the whipped cream on top.

Sufficient to fill 8 or 9 glasses.

TO FROST HOLLY LEAVES for garnishing and decorating dessert and supper dishes, procure some nice sprigs of holly, pick the leaves from the stalks, and wipe them dry with a clean cloth; place them in a warm place to get thoroughly dry, but not shrivelled; dip them into melted butter, sprinkle over them some powdered sugar, and dry them in a very cool oven for about 10 minutes. They should be kept in a dry place, as the least damp would spoil their appearance.

CHAPTER 12

Milk

Butter, Cheese, and
— Eggs —

MILK is one of the most complete of all articles of food. From no other substance, solid or fluid, can so great a number of distinct kinds of aliment be prepared as from milk, some forming food, others drink, some of them delicious, and deserving the name of luxuries, all of them wholesome, and some medicinal.

Milk, when drawn from the cow, is of a yellowish-white colour, and is the most yellow at the beginning of the period of lactation. In cold and wet weather, milk is not so rich as it is in summer and warm weather, and the morning's milk is always richer than the evening's. The last-drawn milk of each milking, at all times and seasons, is richer than the first-drawn, and on that account should be set apart for cream.

FRESH BUTTER should be kept in a dark, cool place, and in as large a mass as possible. Mould only as much as is required, as the more surface is exposed, the more liability there will be to spoil. Never, under any exigency whatever, be tempted into allowing butter with even a *soupçon* of "turning" to enter into the composition of any dish that appears on your table. In general, the more you can do without the employment of butter that has been subjected to the influence of heat the better.

CHEESE is the curd formed from milk by artificial coagulation, pressed and dried for use. Casein, or the basis of cheese, exists in the milk but not in the cream, and requires only to be separated by coagulation. The principal varieties of cheese used in England are the following: Cheshire cheese, single and double Gloucester cheese, Stilton cheese, sage cheese, Cheddar cheese, brickbat cheese, Dunlop cheese, skimmed milk cheese, Parmesan cheese, Dutch cheese, Gruyère and other Swiss cheeses, and cream cheese, which is not properly cheese but cream dried sufficiently to be cut with a knife.

EGGS contain, for their volume, a greater quantity of nutriment than any other article of food. Those of the common hen are most esteemed as food, particularly when new-laid, but their quality depends much upon the food given to the hen.

DEVONSHIRE CREAM.–The milk is set to stand 24 hours in the winter, half that time when the weather is warm. The milkpan is then set on a stove, where it remains until the milk is quite hot, but it must not boil. When it is sufficiently done, the undulations on the surface look thick, and small rings appear. When the cream is sufficiently scalded, the pan is placed in the dairy, and skimmed the following day. This cream is so much esteemed that it is sent to the London markets in small square tins.

Butter dish

EPPING BUTTER is the kind most esteemed in London. Fresh butter comes to London from Buckinghamshire, Suffolk, Oxfordshire, Yorkshire, Devonshire, etc. Cambridge butter is esteemed next to fresh; Devonshire butter is nearly similar in quality to the latter; Irish butter sold in London is all salted, but is generally good. Dutch butter is in good repute all over Europe, America, and even India; and no country in the world is so successful in the manufacture of this article, Holland supplying more butter to the rest of the world than any country whatever.

— Devonshire Junket —

Ingredients.–To every pint of milk allow 2 dessertspoonfuls of brandy, 1 dessertspoonful of caster sugar, and 1½ dessertspoonfuls of prepared rennet; clotted cream, pounded cinnamon or grated nutmeg.

Mode.–Make the milk blood-warm; put it into a deep dish with the brandy, sugar, and rennet; stir all together, cover over, and put in a warm place until it is set. Then spread some clotted or Devonshire cream over the top, grate some nutmeg or cinnamon, and strew some sugar over, and the dish will be ready to serve.

Time.–About 2 hours to set the milk. **Sufficient**, if 1 pint of milk is used, for 4 persons.

Devonshire Junket and Clotted Cream

— Clarified Butter —

Put the butter in a basin over the heat, and when it melts, stir it round once or twice, and let it settle. Pour it gently off into a clean dry jar, carefully leaving all sediment behind. Seal when cool.

— Cayenne Cheeses —

Ingredients.– ½ lb. of butter, ½ lb. of flour, ½ lb. of grated cheese, ⅓ teaspoonful of cayenne, ⅓ teaspoonful of salt, water.

Mode.–Rub the butter into the flour, add the grated cheese, cayenne, and salt, and mix these ingredients well together. Moisten with sufficient water to make the whole into a paste; roll out, and cut into fingers about 4 inches in length. Bake them in a moderate oven until a very light colour, and serve very hot.

Time.–15 to 20 minutes. **Sufficient** for 6 or 7 persons.

BUTTER COOLERS of red brick are now very much used for keeping butter fresh in warm weather. These coolers are made with a large bell-shaped cover, into the top of which a little cold water is poured, and in summertime very frequently changed.

STILTON CHEESE, or British Parmesan, as it is sometimes called, is generally preferred to all other cheeses by those whose authority few will dispute. Those made in May or June are usually served at Christmas, but to be in prime order they should be kept from 10 to 12 months, or even longer. An artificial ripeness in Stilton cheese is sometimes produced by inserting a small piece of decayed Cheshire into an aperture at the top. An additional flavour may also be obtained by scooping out a piece from the top, and pouring therein port, sherry, Madeira, or old ale, and letting the cheese absorb these for 2 or 3 weeks.

In serving a Stilton cheese, the top should be cut off to form a lid, and a napkin or piece of white paper, with a frill at the top, pinned round. When the cheese goes from table, the lid should be replaced.

— To make Fondue —

Ingredients.—4 eggs, the weight of 2 in Parmesan or good Cheshire cheese, the weight of 2 in butter, pepper and salt to taste.

Mode.—Separate the yolks from the whites of the eggs; beat the former in a basin, and grate the cheese, or cut it into very thin flakes. Parmesan or Cheshire cheese may be used, whichever is the most convenient, although the former is considered more suitable for this dish, or an equal quantity of each may be used. Break the butter into small pieces, add it to the other ingredients, with sufficient pepper and salt to season them nicely, and beat the mixture thoroughly. Well whisk the whites of the eggs, stir them lightly in, and either bake the fondue in a soufflé dish or small round cake tin. Fill the dish only half full, as the fondue should rise very much. Pin a napkin round the tin or dish, and serve very hot and very quickly. If allowed to stand after it is withdrawn from the oven, the beauty and lightness of this preparation will be entirely spoiled.

Time.—From 15 to 20 minutes. **Sufficient** for 4 or 5 persons.

— Macaroni —

(AS USUALLY SERVED WITH THE CHEESE COURSE)

Ingredients.— ½ lb. of pipe macaroni, ¼ lb. of butter, 6 oz. of Parmesan or Cheshire cheese, pepper and salt to taste, 1 pint of milk, 2 pints of water, breadcrumbs.

Mode.—Put the milk and water into a saucepan with sufficient salt to flavour it; place it on the heat, and when it boils drop in the macaroni; keep the water boiling until it is quite tender, then drain the macaroni and put it into a deep dish. Have ready the cheese, grated; sprinkle it amongst the macaroni, with some of the butter cut into small pieces, reserving some of the cheese for the top layer. Season with a little pepper, and cover the top layer of cheese with some very fine breadcrumbs. Warm, without oiling, the remainder of the butter, and pour it gently over the breadcrumbs. Place the dish under the grill to brown the crumbs; turn it once or twice, that it may be equally coloured, and serve very hot. In boiling the macaroni, let it be perfectly tender but firm, no part beginning to melt, and the form entirely preserved.

Time.—1 ½ to 1 ¾ hours to boil the macaroni; 5 minutes to brown it under the grill. **Sufficient** for 6 or 7 persons.

— Pounded Cheese —

Ingredients.—To every lb. of cheese allow 3 oz. of butter.

Mode.—To pound cheese is an economical way of using it if it has become dry; it is exceedingly good spread on bread, and is recommended for those whose digestion is weak. Cut up the cheese into small pieces and pound it smoothly in a mortar, adding butter in the above proportion. Press it down into a jar, cover with CLARIFIED BUTTER, and it will keep for several days. The flavour may be very much increased by adding mixed mustard (about a teaspoonful to every lb. of cheese) or cayenne, or pounded mace. Curry powder is also not unfrequently mixed with it.

Cheese glass

MODE OF SERVING CHEESE.—The usual mode of serving cheese at good tables is to cut a small quantity of it into neat square pieces, and to put them into a glass cheese dish, this dish being handed round. Should the cheese crumble much, of course this method is rather wasteful, and it may then be put on the table in the piece, and the guests may cut from it. When served thus, the cheese must always be carefully scraped, and laid on a white doyley or napkin, neatly folded. Cream cheese is often served in a cheese course, and sometimes grated Parmesan; the latter should be put into a covered glass dish. Rusks, cheese biscuits, pats or slices of butter, and salad, cucumber, or watercress, should always form part of a cheese course.

— Ramekins —

(TO SERVE WITH THE CHEESE COURSE)

Ingredients.– ¼ lb. of Cheshire cheese, ¼ lb. of Parmesan cheese,
¼ lb. of butter, 4 eggs, a teacupful of white breadcrumbs, pepper,
salt, pounded mace to taste, milk.

Mode.–Boil the breadcrumbs in milk for 5 minutes; strain them
and put them into a mortar; add the cheese, which should be finely
grated, the butter, the yolks of the eggs, and seasoning, and pound
these ingredients well together. Whisk the whites of the eggs, mix
them with the paste, and put the mixture into small buttered dishes,
which should not be more than half filled. Bake in a hot oven from
10 to 12 minutes, and serve very hot and very quickly.

Time.–10 to 12 minutes. **Sufficient** for 7 or 8 persons.

— Scotch Rarebit —

Ingredients.–A few slices of rich cheese, toast, mustard, pepper.

Mode.–Cut some nice rich sound cheese into rather thin slices;
melt it in a thick-bottomed saucepan and add a small quantity of
mixed mustard and a seasoning of pepper; stir the cheese until it is
completely melted, then pour it into a shallow serving dish and
brown it under the grill. Place the dish in another filled with hot
water, and serve with dry or buttered toasts, whichever may be
preferred. A small quantity of port is sometimes mixed with the
cheese; if it be not very rich, a few pieces of butter may also be
mixed with it to great advantage. Sometimes the melted cheese is
spread on the toasts, and then laid in a heated cheese dish. Whichever
way it is served, it is highly necessary that the mixture be very hot.

Time.–About 5 minutes to melt the cheese.

— Welsh Rarebit —

Ingredients.–Slices of bread, butter, Cheshire or Gloucester
cheese, mustard, pepper.

Mode.–Cut the bread into slices about ½ inch in thickness; pare
off the crust, toast the bread slightly without hardening or burning it,
and spread it with butter. Cut some slices, not quite so large as the
bread, from a good rich fat cheese; lay them on the toasted bread and
place under the grill; be careful that the cheese does not burn, and let
it be equally melted. Spread over the top a little made mustard and a
seasoning of pepper, and serve very hot, with very hot plates.

Time.–About 5 minutes to melt the cheese.

— Cheese Sandwiches —

Ingredients.–Slices of brown bread-and-butter, slices of cheese.

Mode.–Cut from a nice fat Cheshire, or any good rich cheese,
some slices about ½ inch thick, and place them between some slices
of brown bread-and-butter with the crusts cut off, like sandwiches.
Place them on a baking sheet in a very hot oven, and, when the bread
is toasted, serve on a napkin very hot and very quickly.

Time.–10 minutes in a brisk oven.

Hot-water cheese dish

OUR ENGRAVING
illustrates a cheese
toaster with a hot
water reservoir; the
cheese is melted in the
upper tin, which is
placed in another
vessel of boiling water,
so keeping the
preparation beautifully
hot.

— Scotch Woodcock —

Ingredients.–A few slices of hot buttered toast; allow 1 anchovy to each slice; for the sauce, ¼ pint of cream, the yolks of 3 eggs.

Mode.–Separate the yolks from the whites of the eggs; beat the former, stir them into the cream, and bring to the boiling point, but do not allow it to boil, or it will curdle. Have ready some hot buttered toast, spread with anchovies pounded to a paste; pour a little of the hot sauce on the top, and serve very hot and very quickly.

Time.–5 minutes to make the sauce hot.

Cayenne Cheeses and Cheese Ramekins

Egg stand for the breakfast table

EGGS.–When fresh eggs are dropped into a vessel *full* of boiling water, they crack, because the eggs being well filled, the shells give way to the efforts of the interior fluids, dilated by heat. If the volume of hot water be small, the shells do not crack, because its temperature is reduced by the eggs before the interior dilation can take place. Stale eggs do not crack, because the air inside is easily compressed.

To Boil Eggs for — Breakfast, Salads, etc. —

Eggs for boiling cannot be too fresh, or boiled too soon after they are laid; but a rather longer time should be allowed for boiling a new-laid egg than for one that is three or four days old. Have ready a saucepan half full of boiling water; put the eggs into it gently with a spoon, letting the spoon touch the bottom of the saucepan before it is withdrawn, that the egg may not fall and consequently crack. For those who like eggs lightly boiled, 3 minutes will be found sufficient; 3¾ to 4 minutes will be ample time to set the white nicely; and, if liked hard, 6 to 7 minutes will not be found too long. Should the eggs be unusually large, allow an extra ½ minute for them. Eggs for salads should be boiled from 10 minutes to ¼ hour, and should be placed in a basin of cold water for a few minutes; they should then be rolled on the table with the hand, and the shell will peel off easily.

EGGS.—The quality of eggs is said to be very much affected by the food of the fowls who lay them. Herbs and grain together make a better food than grain only. When the hens eat too many insects, the eggs have a disagreeable flavour.

— Eggs à la Maître d'Hôtel —

Ingredients.– ¼ lb. of butter, 1 tablespoonful of flour, ½ pint of milk, pepper and salt to taste, 1 tablespoonful of minced parsley, the juice of ½ lemon, 6 eggs.

Mode.–Put the flour and half the butter into a saucepan; stir them over the heat until the mixture thickens; pour in the milk, which should be boiling; add a seasoning of pepper and salt, and simmer the whole for 5 minutes. Put the remainder of the butter into the sauce, and add the minced parsley; then boil the eggs hard, strip off the shells, cut the eggs into quarters, and put them on a dish. Bring the sauce to the boiling point, add the lemon juice, pour over the eggs, and serve.

Time.–5 minutes to boil the sauce; 10 to 15 minutes to boil the eggs. **Sufficient** for 3 or 4 persons.

— Poached Eggs with Cream —

Ingredients.–1 pint of water, 1 teaspoonful of salt, 4 teaspoonfuls of vinegar, 4 fresh eggs, 3 tablespoonfuls of cream, salt, pepper, and sugar to taste, 1 oz. of butter.

Mode.–Eggs for poaching should be perfectly fresh, but not quite new-laid; those that are about 36 hours old are the best for the purpose. If quite new-laid, the white is so milky it is almost impossible to set it; on the other hand, if the egg be at all stale, it is equally difficult to poach it nicely. Put the water, vinegar, and salt into a deep frying-pan, and break each egg into a separate cup; bring the liquid to boil, and slip the eggs gently into it without breaking the yolks. Simmer them from 3 to 4 minutes, but not longer, then, with a slice, lift them out onto a hot dish, and trim the edges. Empty the pan of its contents, put in the cream, add a seasoning to taste of pepper, salt, and a little sugar, if liked; bring the whole to the boiling point, then add the butter broken into small pieces; shake the pan round and round till the butter is melted; pour the cream over the eggs, and serve. To ensure the eggs not being spoiled whilst the cream is preparing, it is a good plan to warm the cream with the butter, etc., before the eggs are poached, so that it may be poured over them immediately after they are dished.

Time.–3 to 4 minutes to poach the eggs; 5 minutes to heat the cream. **Sufficient** for 2 persons.

— Fried Eggs —

Ingredients.–4 eggs, ¼ lb. of lard, butter, or clarified dripping, a few slices of ham or bacon.

Mode.–Place a frying-pan over a gentle heat; put in the fat and allow it to bubble. Break the eggs into cups, slip them into the boiling fat, and let them remain until the whites are delicately set; and, whilst they are frying, ladle a little of the fat over them. Take them up with a slice, drain them for a minute from their greasy moisture, trim them neatly, and serve on slices of fried bacon or ham; or the eggs may be placed in the middle of the dish, with the bacon put round as a garnish.

Time.–2 to 3 minutes. **Sufficient** for 2 person.

Tin egg poacher

DUCKS' EGGS are usually so strongly flavoured that, plainly boiled, they are not good for eating; they answer, however, very well for various culinary preparations where eggs are required, such as puddings and custards. Being so large and highly flavoured, 1 duck's egg will go as far as 2 small hen's eggs, besides making whatever they are mixed with exceedingly rich. They are also admirable when used in puddings.

PLOVERS' EGGS are usually served boiled hard, and sent to table in a napkin, either hot or cold. They may also be shelled, and served the same as eggs à la tripe, with a good béchamel sauce poured over them. They are also used for decorating salads, the beautiful colour of the white being generally so much admired.

Eggs à la Tripe, and Fried Eggs and Ham

THE EGGS OF DIFFERENT BIRDS vary much in size and colour. Those of the ostrich are the largest: one laid in the menagerie in Paris weighed 2 pounds 14 ounces, held 1 pint, and was 6 inches deep; this is about the usual size of those brought from Africa. Travellers describe ostrich eggs as of an agreeable taste; they keep longer than hen's eggs. Drinking cups are often made of the shell, which is very strong.

— Scotch Eggs —

Ingredients.–6 eggs, 6 tablespoonfuls of FORCEMEAT, hot oil or lard, ½ pint of good brown gravy.

Mode.–Boil the eggs for 10 minutes, strip the shells from them, and cover them with forcemeat (pounded anchovies may be substituted for the ham). Fry the eggs a nice brown in boiling oil or lard, drain them in a hot oven, dish them, and pour round ¼ to ½ pint of good brown gravy. To enhance the appearance of the eggs, they may be rolled in beaten egg and sprinkled with breadcrumbs before frying, but this is scarcely necessary if they are carefully fried. The flavour of the ham or anchovy in the forcemeat must preponderate, as it should be very relishing.

Time.–10 minutes to boil the eggs; 5 to 7 minutes to fry them. **Sufficient** for 3 or 4 persons.

Spinach and poached eggs

PLAIN POACHED EGGS may be served either on toasted bread, or on slices of ham or bacon, or on spinach, etc. A poached egg should not be overdone, as its appearance and taste will be quite spoiled if the yolk be allowed to harden. When the egg is slipped into the water, the white should be gathered together to keep it a little in form, or the cup should be turned over it for ½ minute.

— Eggs à la Tripe —

Ingredients.–8 eggs, ¾ pint of BECHAMEL, 1 dessertspoonful of finely minced parsley.

Mode.–Boil the eggs hard; put them into cold water, shell them, take out the yolks whole, and shred the whites. Heat the béchamel and add the parsley. Put the yolks of the eggs into the middle of a dish, and the shredded whites round them; pour over the sauce, and garnish with leaves of puff paste or fried croûtons. There is no necessity for putting the eggs into the saucepan with the béchamel; the sauce, being quite hot, will warm the eggs sufficiently.

Time.–10 minutes to boil the eggs. **Sufficient** for 5 or 6 persons.

PRIMITIVE METHOD OF COOKING EGGS.– The shepherds of Egypt had a singular manner of cooking eggs without the aid of fire. They placed them in a sling, which they turned so rapidly that the friction of the air heated them to the exact point required for use.

CHAPTER 13

Bread
—Biscuits, and Cakes—

BREAD-MAKING is a very ancient art indeed. The Assyrians, Egyptians, and Greeks used to make bread in which oil, with aniseed and other spices, was an element, but this was unleavened, or made without yeast. In our own times, and among civilized peoples, bread has become an article of food of the first necessity, and properly so, for it constitutes of itself a complete life-sustainer.

The finest, wholesomest, and most savoury bread is made from wheaten flour. Rye bread is not so rich in gluten, but is said to keep fresh longer, and to have some laxative qualities. Bread made from barley, maize, oats, rice, potatoes, etc. "rises" badly, because the grains in question contain but little gluten, which makes the bread heavy and close in texture.

The first thing required for making wholesome bread is the utmost cleanliness; the next is the soundness and sweetness of all the ingredients used for it; and, in addition to these, there must be attention and care through the whole process. An almost certain way of spoiling dough is to leave it half-made, and to allow it to become cold before it is finished. The other most common causes of failure are using yeast which is no longer sweet, or which has been frozen, or which has had hot liquid poured over it. The fresher the yeast the smaller the quantity will be required to raise the dough.

IN MAKING AND BAKING CAKES, eggs should always be broken singly into a cup, the whites and yolks separated and strained, and both very thoroughly beaten if they are to be used to raise and lighten the mixture; sugar should be fine and sieved; currants and other dried fruits should be nicely washed and thoroughly dried as, if added damp to the other ingredients, they will produce a heavy result; good butter should always be used, and warmed a little to make it easier to beat to a cream. The heat of the oven is of great importance in baking cakes, especially large cakes. If the heat be not tolerably fierce, the batter will not rise. If the oven is too quick, and there is any danger of the cake burning or catching, put a sheet of paper over the top. To know when a cake is sufficiently baked, plunge a clean knife into the middle of it; draw it quickly out, and if it looks

ALL KINDS OF LEAVENING MATTER besides yeast from malt and hops have been used in different parts of the world in bread-making: in the East Indies "toddy", which is a liquor that flows from the wounded coconut tree, and in the West Indies "dunder", or the refuse of the distillation of rum.

in the least sticky, put the cake back and close the oven door until the cake is done.

BISCUITS belong to the class of unfermented bread, and are considered lighter than bread and less liable to create acidity and flatulence. The name is derived from the French *bis cuit*, "twice baked", because originally that was the mode of entirely depriving them of all moisture to ensure their keeping; although that process is no longer employed, the name is retained. The use of this kind of bread on land is pretty general, and some varieties are luxuries, but at sea biscuits are articles of the first necessity.

To Make Good
—Home-made Bread—
(MISS ACTON'S RECIPE)

Ingredients.–4 lbs. of flour, 1 oz. of fresh yeast, 1¼ to 1½ pints of warm milk-and-water.

Mode.–Put the flour into a large earthenware bowl; hollow out the middle but do not clear the flour entirely away from the bottom of the bowl. Next take 1 oz. of fresh yeast, put it into a basin, and mix it as smooth as cream with ¾ pint of warm milk-and-water. Pour the yeast into the hole made in the flour, and stir into it as much of the flour which lies round it as will make a thick batter, in which there must be no lumps. Strew plenty of flour on the top, throw a thick clean cloth over, and set it where the air is warm, but not where it will become too much heated. Look at it from time to time; when it has been laid for near 1 hour, and when the yeast has risen and broken through the flour, so that bubbles appear in it, you will know that it is ready to be made up into dough. Place the bowl on a table of convenient height, pour into the yeast mixture the remainder of the just warm milk-and-water, stir into it as much of the flour as you can with a spoon, then wipe the bowl out clean with your fingers and lay the dough on the table, previously sprinkled with a little flour. Next take the remaining flour, throw it on top of the dough, and begin, with the knuckles of both hands, to knead it well. When the flour is nearly all kneaded in, begin to draw the edges of the dough towards the middle, in order to mix the whole thoroughly; when it is free from flour and lumps and crumbs, and does not stick to the hands, it will be done, and may be returned to the bowl, covered again with the cloth, and left to rise a second time, again in a warm place. In ¾ hour look at it, and should it have swollen very much and have begun to crack, it will be light enough to bake; if not, leave it to rise a little longer. Turn out the dough, and with a large sharp knife divide it in two; make it up quickly into two loaves, and dispatch it to a hot hoven for the first ½ hour, then reduce the heat somewhat; one or two incisions across the tops of the loaves will help the bread to rise more easily. If baked in tins or pans, rub them with butter to prevent the dough from sticking to them. All bread should be turned upside down, or on its side, as soon as it is drawn from the oven; if this be neglected, the underpart of the loaves will become wet and blistered from the steam which cannot escape.

Time.–1 hour to rise the first time, ¾ hour the second time; 1 to 1¼ hours to bake, if made up into two loaves; 1½ to 2 hours if made up as one loaf. **Sufficient** for 2 large loaves.

THE UNWHOLE-SOMENESS OF NEW BREAD AND HOT ROLLS.–Bread should always be at least a day old before it is eaten. Hot rolls, swimming in melted butter, and new bread, ought to be carefully shunned by everybody who has the slightest respect for that much-injured individual, the Stomach.

Tin bread

Cottage loaf

ERATED BREAD. –Dr. Dauglish, of Malvern, has recently patented a process for making bread "light" without the use of leaven. The ordinary process of bread-making by fermentation is tedious, and much labour of human hands is requisite in the kneading, in order that the dough may be thoroughly interpenetrated with the leaven. The new process impregnates the bread, by the application of machinery, with carbonic acid gas, or fixed air. As corn is now reaped by machinery, and dough is baked by machinery, the whole process of bread-making is probably in the course of undergoing changes which will emancipate both the housewife and the professional baker from a large amount of labour.

— S o d a   B r e a d —

Ingredients.–To every 2 lbs. of flour allow 1 teaspoonful of cream of tartar, 1 teaspoonful of salt, 1 teaspoonful of bicarbonate of soda, 1 pint of cold milk.

Mode.–Mix the salt and cream of tartar well with the flour. Thoroughly dissolve the soda in the milk and add it to the flour. Work the whole quickly into a light dough, divide it into two loaves, and put them into a hot oven immediately, and bake for ¾ hour or rather longer. Sour milk or buttermilk may be used instead of plain milk, but then a little less cream of tartar will be needed.

Time.–¾ to 1 hour. **Sufficient** for 1 large or 2 small loaves.

— L i g h t   B u n s —

Ingredients.– ½ teaspoonful of cream of tartar, ½ teaspoonful of bicarbonate of soda, 1 lb. of flour, 2 oz. of butter, 2 oz. of caster sugar, ¼ lb. of currants or raisins, a few caraway seeds if liked, ½ pint of milk, 1 egg.

Mode.–Rub the cream of tartar, soda, and flour all together through a sieve; work the butter into the flour; add the sugar, currants, and caraway seeds, if the latter are liked. Mix all these ingredients well together; make a hole in the middle of them and pour in the milk, mixed with the egg, which should be well beaten; mix quickly, and set forkfuls of the dough on oiled baking tins, and bake for about 20 minutes. This mixture also makes a very good fruit loaf, which, if put into a tin, should be baked for 1½ hours. The same quantity of flour, soda, and cream of tartar, with ½ pint of milk and a little salt, will make either bread or teacakes, if wanted quickly.

Time.–20 minutes for the buns; if made into a cake, 1½ hours. **Sufficient** to make about 12 buns.

Crumpets and Light Buns

IN ORDER TO RENDER IT WHITE, flour undergoes a process called ''bolting''. It is passed through a series of fine sieves, which separate the coarser parts, leaving behind fine white flour, but the process tends to deprive flour of its gluten. Bran contains a large proportion of gluten, hence it will be seen why brown bread is so much more nutritious than white; in fact, we may lay it down as a general rule, that the whiter the bread the less nourishment it contains. Majendie proved this by feeding a dog for 40 days with white wheaten bread, at the end of which time he died; while another dog, fed on brown bread made with flour mixed with bran, lived without any disturbance of his health.

— Plain Buns —

Ingredients.–To every 2 lbs. of flour allow 6 oz. of caster sugar, 1 oz. of fresh yeast, ½ pint of milk, ½ lb. of butter, a little warm milk.

Mode.–Put the flour into a basin, mix the sugar well with it, make a hole in the centre, and pour in the yeast, creamed with the milk, which should be lukewarm; stir in enough of the flour to make it the thickness of batter. Cover the basin over with a cloth, and let the yeast mixture rise in a warm place, which will be accomplished in about 1½ hours. Melt the butter, but do not allow it to oil; stir it into the other ingredients, with enough warm milk to make the whole into a soft dough; then mould it into buns about the size of an egg; lay them on an oiled baking sheet in rows 3 inches apart; set them again in a warm place until they have risen to double their size; then put them into a moderately hot oven, and just before they are done, brush them over with a little milk to glaze them. From 15 to 20 minutes will be required to bake them nicely. These buns may be varied by adding a few currants, candied peel, or caraway seeds. The above mixture also answers for hot cross buns, with the addition of a little ground allspice and the form of a cross pressed in the centre of each bun.

Time.–15 to 20 minutes. **Sufficient** to make about 18 buns.

— Crumpets —

Ingredients.–1 lb. of flour, ½ oz. of fresh yeast, rather more than ¾ pint of milk, 1 teaspoonful of salt, 1 teaspoonful of sugar if liked.

Mode.–Crumpets are made in the same manner as MUFFINS, only in making the mixture more milk is used, so that it is more like batter than dough. Let it rise for about ½ hour, then pour it into crumpet rings, which should be ready on an oiled hotplate heated to a moderate degree; cook them till the underside is brown and done, and holes appear in the top, then turn them quickly on the other side. To toast them, have ready a very hot grill; put the crumpets under for no more than ½ minute on each side, spread them with good butter, cut in half, and when all are done pile them on a hot dish and send quickly to table. Muffins and crumpets should always be served on separate dishes, and toasted and sent to table as expeditiously as possible.

Time.–From 10 to 15 minutes to cook on the hotplate; 1 minute to toast. **Sufficient** for about 16 crumpets.

— Muffins —

Ingredients.–1 lb. of flour, ½ oz. of fresh yeast, ½ pint of warm milk, 1 teaspoonful of sugar if liked, 1 teaspoonful of salt.

Mode.–Dissolve the yeast in the milk, which should be only just warm, and stir it into the flour, mixed with the salt, and with the sugar if liked; work the whole into a dough of rather a soft consistency, cover with a cloth, and put in a warm place to rise; when light and nicely risen, divide the dough into 12 pieces, and round them to the proper shape with the hands; place them, in a layer of flour about 2 inches thick, on baking trays, and let them rise for a further 30 minutes; when this is effected, they will be a semi-globular shape. Then bake them in a very hot oven for 5 minutes until they are slightly browned, then turn them to do for 5 minutes on the other side. They should be sent to the tea table still warm, with a dish of butter; or they may be split open, toasted, spread with butter, and sent to table piled on a very hot dish.

Time.–About 10 minutes to bake in the oven. **Sufficient** for 12 muffins.

*Toasted
Teacakes*

— Teacakes —

Ingredients.–2 lbs. of flour, ½ teaspoonful of salt, ¼ lb. of butter or lard, 1 egg, 1 oz. of fresh yeast, warm milk.

Mode.–Put the flour into a basin, mix with it the salt, and rub in the butter or lard; then beat the egg well, stir in the yeast, and add these to the flour with as much warm milk as will make the whole into a smooth paste, and knead it well. Cover the basin with a cloth and let the dough rise in a warm place; when well risen, form it into 8 cakes; place them on oiled tins, let them rise again for a few minutes before putting them into the oven, and bake for ¼ to ½ hour in a moderate oven. These are very nice with a few currants and a little sugar added to the other ingredients; they should be put in after the butter is rubbed in. These cakes should be buttered and eaten hot as soon as baked; when stale, they are very nice split and toasted.

Time.– ¼ to ½ hour. **Sufficient** to make 8 teacakes.

Ratafias,
Macaroons,
Coconut
Biscuits, and
Rich
Gingerbread
Nuts

— Coconut Biscuits —

Ingredients.–10 oz. of caster sugar, 2 eggs, 6 oz. of grated coconut.

Mode.–Whisk the eggs until they are very light, add the sugar gradually, then stir in the coconut. Roll a tablespoonful of the paste at a time in your hands in the form of a pyramid; place the pyramids on buttered paper, put the paper on baking tins, and bake in a cool oven until they are just coloured a light brown.

Time.–About ¼ hour. **Sufficient** for about 12 biscuits.

— Rich Gingerbread Nuts —

SINCE the establishment of the large modern biscuit manufactories, biscuits have been produced both cheap and wholesome, and in endless variety. Their actual component parts are, perhaps, known only to the various makers; but there are several kinds of biscuits which have long been in use, that may here be advantageously described.

Ingredients.–1 lb. of treacle, ¼ lb. of CLARIFIED BUTTER, 1 lb. of coarse brown sugar, 2 oz. of ground ginger, 1 oz. of candied orange peel, 1 oz. of candied angelica, ½ oz. of candied lemon peel, ½ oz. of coriander seeds, ½ oz. of caraway seeds, 1 egg, flour.

Mode.–Put the treacle into a basin, and pour over it the butter, melted but not turned to oil, the sugar, and the ginger. Stir these ingredients well together, and whilst mixing, add the candied peel, which should be cut into very small pieces, and the caraway and coriander seeds, which should be pounded. Having mixed all thoroughly together, break in the egg and work the whole up with as much flour as may be necessary to form a fairly stiff paste. Roll out on a floured board and cut them to any shape or size, put them on an oiled baking sheet, and bake in a slow oven for ¼ to ½ hour.

Time.–¼ to ½ hour. **Sufficient** for 20 to 30 nuts, depending on their size.

PRESERVED GINGER comes to us from the West Indies. It is made by scalding the roots when they are green and full of sap, then peeling them and putting them into jars with a rich syrup, in which state we receive them. It should be chosen of a bright yellow colour, with a little transparency; if dark-coloured, fibrous, and stringy, it is not good. Ginger roots fit for preserving, and in size equal to West Indian, have been produced in the Royal Agricultural Garden in Edinburgh.

— Macaroons —

Ingredients.– ½ lb. of ground almonds, ½ lb. of caster sugar, the whites of 3 eggs, rice paper, orange-flower water.

Mode.–Whisk the whites of the eggs to a stiff froth, and add to them the ground almonds, the sugar, and a few drops of orange-flower water; mix all the ingredients well together. When the paste is of a soft dropping consistency, spoon it into a piping bag and pipe it on to the rice paper in rounds about 1½ inches across; put a strip of almond on the top of each, strew some sugar over, and bake in a slow oven till a light brown colour. If very light macaroons are desired, add a little more white of egg.

Time.–20 to 30 minutes. **Sufficient** for about 40 macaroons.

— Ratafias —

Ingredients.– ¾ lb. of ground almonds, ¾ lb. of caster sugar, the whites of 4 eggs, almond essence, rice-paper.

Mode.–Ratafias are made in the same manner as MACAROONS, but should be piped on to the rice-paper in very small drops, as, when baked, they should be about the size of a large button; they should be done in a slightly hotter oven than for macaroons.

Time.–10 to 12 minutes. **Sufficient** for about 100 ratafias.

— Savoy Biscuits —

Ingredients.–4 eggs, 6 oz. of caster sugar, the rind of 1 lemon, 6 oz. of flour.

Mode.–Break the eggs into a basin, separating the whites from the yolks; beat the yolks well, mix with them the sugar and grated lemon rind, and beat these ingredients together for ¼ hour. Then dredge in the flour gradually, and when the whites of the eggs have been whisked to a solid froth, stir them into the flour, etc. Beat the mixture well for another 5 minutes, then draw it along in strips upon an oiled baking tray, and bake in a moderate oven; but let them be carefully watched, as they are soon done, and a few seconds over the proper time will scorch and spoil them. These biscuits are used for making CHARLOTTE RUSSE, and for a variety of fancy sweet dishes.

Time.–5 to 8 minutes. **Sufficient** for about 20 biscuits.

— Scotch Shortbread —

Ingredients.–2 lbs. of flour, 1 lb. of butter, ¼ lb. of caster sugar, ½ oz. of caraway seeds, 1 oz. of whole almonds, a few strips of candied orange peel.

Mode.–Beat the butter to a cream, gradually dredge in the flour, and add the sugar, caraway seeds, and almonds, which should be blanched and cut into small pieces. Work the paste until it is quite smooth, and divide it into six pieces; roll each piece out square to the thickness of about 1 inch, and pinch it upon all sides; prick it well with a fork, and ornament with one or two strips of candied orange peel; put into a moderate oven, and bake for 25 to 30 minutes.

Time.–25 to 30 minutes.

Shortbread

— Almond Cake —

Ingredients.– ½ lb. of ground almonds, a few drops of almond essence, 6 eggs, 8 tablespoonfuls of caster sugar, 6 tablespoonfuls of fine flour, the grated rind of 1 lemon, 3 oz. of butter.

Mode.–Separate the whites from the yolks of the eggs; beat the latter, and add them to the almonds; stir in the sugar, flour, and grated lemon rind, and add the butter, which should be beaten to a cream; when all these ingredients are well mixed, put in the whites of the eggs, which should be whisked to a stiff froth. Butter a cake tin or mould, put in the mixture, and bake in a moderate oven for 1 ¼ to 1 ¾ hours.

Time.–1 ¼ to 1 ¾ hours.

Rich Bride or — Christening Cake —

Ingredients.–5 lbs. of flour, 3 lbs. of butter, 5 lbs. of currants, 2 lbs. of caster sugar, 2 nutmegs, ¼ oz. of mace, ½ teaspoonful of ground cloves, 16 eggs, 1 lb. of ground almonds, orange-flower water, ½ lb. of candied citron peel, ½ lb. each of candied orange and lemon peel, ¼ pint of wine, ¼ pint of brandy.

Mode.–Let the flour be well sifted, the currants washed and dried, the nutmegs grated, the spices pounded, the eggs thoroughly whisked, whites and yolks separately, the almonds mixed with a little orange-flower water, and the candied peel cut in small neat slices. When all these ingredients are prepared, mix them in the following manner: work the butter till it becomes of a cream-like consistency; stir in the sugar and the whites of the eggs, whisked to a solid froth; next, beat up the yolks for 10 minutes, add them to the flour, nutmegs, mace, and cloves, and continue stirring the whole together for ½ hour or longer, till wanted for the oven; then mix in lightly the currants, almonds, candied peel, wine, and brandy. Having lined a large cake tin with buttered paper, fill it with the mixture, and bake in a cool oven for 4 hours, then reduce the heat to very cool and bake for another 1 ½ to 2 hours, taking care not to burn the top; to prevent this, the top may be covered with a sheet of paper. To ascertain whether the cake is done, plunge a clean knife into the middle of it, withdraw it directly, and, if the blade is not sticky and looks bright, the cake is sufficiently baked. These cakes are usually spread with a thick layer of ALMOND ICING, and over that a layer of SUGAR ICING, and afterwards ornamented.

Time.–5 to 6 hours.

RAISINS.–Raisins are grapes prepared by suffering them to remain on the vine until they are perfectly ripe, and then drying them in the sun or by the heat of an oven. The sun-dried grapes are sweet, the oven-dried of an acid flavour.

— Christmas Cake —

Ingredients.–5 teacupfuls of flour, 1 teacupful of melted butter, 1 teacupful of cream, 1 teacupful of treacle, 1 teacupful of moist brown sugar, 2 eggs, ½ oz. of powdered ginger, ½ lb. of raisins, 1 teaspoonful of bicarbonate of soda, 1 teaspoonful of vinegar.

Mode.–Make the butter sufficiently warm to melt it, but do not allow it to oil; put the flour into a basin; add to it the sugar, ginger, and raisins, which should be stoned and cut into small pieces. When these dry ingredients are thoroughly mixed, stir in the butter, cream, treacle, and well whisked eggs, and beat the mixture for a few minutes. Dissolve the soda in the vinegar, add it to the dough, and be particular that these latter ingredients are well incorporated with the others; put the cake into a buttered mould or tin, place it in a moderate oven immediately, and bake it from 1¾ to 2¼ hours.

Time.–1¾ to 2¼ hours.

— Common Cake —
(SUITABLE FOR SENDING TO CHILDREN AT SCHOOL)

Ingredients.–2 lbs. of flour, ¼ lb. of butter or clarified dripping, ½ oz. of caraway seeds, ¼ oz. of ground allspice, ½ lb. of caster sugar, 1 lb. of currants, 1 pint of milk, 1 oz. of fresh yeast.

Mode.–Rub the butter lightly into the flour, add all the dry ingredients, and mix all well together. Make the milk warm, but not hot, stir in the yeast, and with this liquid make the whole into a light dough; knead it well and divide it into two; line two cake tins with strips of buttered paper (this paper should be about 6 inches higher than the top of the tins); put in the dough, and stand in a warm place to rise for rather more than 1 hour; then bake the cakes in a moderate oven.

Time.–1¾ to 2¼ hours. **Sufficient** for 2 moderate-sized cakes.

Mixture for Rich Bride or Christening Cake, with Almond and Sugar Icing

Cake mould

— Honey Cake —

Ingredients.– ½ breakfast-cupful of sugar, 1 breakfast-cupful of rich sour cream, 2 breakfast-cupfuls of flour, ½ teaspoonful of bicarbonate of soda, honey to taste.

Mode.–Mix the sugar and cream together; dredge in the flour, with as much honey as will flavour the mixture nicely; stir well, so that all the ingredients may be thoroughly mixed; add the bicarbonate of soda, and beat the cake well for another 5 minutes; put it into a buttered tin, bake it in a moderate oven for ½ to ¾ hour, and let it be eaten warm.

Time.– ½ to ¾ hour.

— Thick Gingerbread —

Ingredients.–1 lb. of treacle, ¼ lb. of butter, ¼ lb. of soft brown sugar, 1 ½ lbs. of flour, 1 oz. of ground ginger, ½ oz. of ground allspice, 2 teaspoonfuls of bicarbonate of soda, ¼ pint of warm milk, 3 eggs.

Mode.–Put the flour into a basin with the sugar, ginger, and allspice, and mix together; warm the butter and add it, with the treacle, to the other ingredients; stir well; make the milk just warm, dissolve the bicarbonate of soda in it, and mix the whole into a nice smooth dough with the eggs, which should be previously well whisked; pour the mixture into a buttered tin, and bake in a moderate oven for 1 to 1 ¼ hours, or longer should the gingerbread be very thick. Just before it is done, brush the top over with the yolk of an egg beaten up with a little milk, and put it back in the oven to finish baking.

Time.–1 to 1 ¼ hours.

A Very Good Seed Cake

Ingredients.–1 lb. of butter, 6 eggs, ¾ lb. of caster sugar, pounded mace and grated nutmeg to taste, 1 lb. of flour, ¾ oz. of caraway seeds, 1 wineglassful of brandy.

Mode.–Beat the butter to a cream, dredge in the flour, add the sugar, mace, nutmeg, and caraway seeds, and mix all well together. Whisk the eggs, stir the brandy into them, and add to the other ingredients; beat the mixture again for 10 minutes. Put it into a tin lined with buttered paper, and bake it in a moderate oven for 1 ½ to 2 hours. This cake would be equally nice made with currants, omitting the caraway seeds.

Time.–1 ½ to 2 hours.

— Sponge Cake —

Ingredients.–The weight of 8 eggs in caster sugar, the weight of 5 in flour, the rind of 1 lemon, 1 tablespoonful of brandy.

Mode.–Put the eggs into one side of the scale, and take the weight of 8 in caster sugar, and the weight of 5 in flour. Separate the yolks from the whites of the eggs; beat the former, put them into a saucepan with the sugar, and let them remain over the heat until blood-warm, keeping them well stirred. Then put them into a basin,

Sponge cake

add the grated lemon rind mixed with the brandy, and stir these well together, dredging in the flour very gradually. Whisk the whites of the eggs to a very stiff froth, stir them into the flour, etc., and beat the mixture well for ¼ hour. Put it into a buttered mould strewn with a little caster sugar, and bake in a moderate oven for 1½ hours. Care must be taken that it is put into the oven immediately, or it will not be light. The flavouring of this cake may be varied by adding a few drops of essence of almonds instead of the grated lemon rind.

Time.–1½ hours.

— A Nice Plum Cake —

Ingredients.–1 lb. of flour, ¼ lb. of butter, ½ lb. of sugar, ½ lb. of currants, 2 oz. of candied lemon peel, ½ pint of milk, 1 teaspoonful of bicarbonate of soda; 2 tablespoonfuls of milk.

Mode.–Put the flour into a basin with the sugar, currants, and sliced candied peel; beat the butter to a cream, and mix all these ingredients together with the milk. Stir the bicarbonate of soda into the 2 tablespoonfuls of milk, add it to the dough, and beat the whole well until everything is thoroughly mixed. Put the dough into a buttered tin, and bake in a moderate oven for 1½ to 2 hours.

Time.–1½ to 2 hours.

— Almond Icing for Cakes —

Ingredients.–To every lb. of caster and icing sugar mixed allow 1 lb. of ground almonds, the whites of 4 eggs, a little rosewater.

Mode.–Whisk the whites of the eggs to a strong froth; mix them with the ground almonds and rosewater, stir in the sugar, and beat all together. Before laying this preparation on the cake, great care must be taken that it is nice and smooth, which is easily accomplished by beating the mixture well. The top and sides of the cake must be brushed with a little jam to ensure that the paste attaches to them. To have the paste of an even thickness, roll it out on a sugared board, and cut a circle for the top of the cake and a strip for the sides.

— Sugar Icing for Cakes —

Ingredients.–To every lb. of icing sugar allow the whites of 2 eggs and 2 teaspoonfuls of lemon juice.

Mode.–Beat the eggs to a strong froth, and gradually add the sugar and lemon juice. Beat the mixture well until the sugar is smooth; then with a spoon or broad knife lay the icing equally over the cakes. These should then be placed in a *very* cool oven, and the icing allowed to dry and harden, but not to colour. The icing may be coloured with strawberry or currant juice, or with cochineal. On very rich cakes, such as wedding, christening cakes, etc., a layer of ALMOND ICING is usually spread over the top, and over that the white icing as described. All iced cakes should be kept in a very dry place.

CHAPTER 14

Beverages

BEVERAGES are innumerable in their variety, but the ordinary beverages drunk in the British Isles may be divided into three classes: 1. Beverages of the simplest kind not fermented, such as toast-and-water, barley water, *eau sucrée, lait sucré*, cheese and milk whey, milk-and-water, lemonade, orangeade, sherbet, apple and pear juice, capillaire, vinegar-and-water, raspberry vinegar and water. 2. Beverages, consisting of water, containing a considerable quantity of carbonic acid, such as soda water, single and double, ordinary effervescing draughts, and ginger beer. 3. Beverages composed partly of fermented liquors, such as hot spiced wines, bishop, egg flip, ale posset, sack posset, punch, and spirits-and-water.

WE WILL, HOWEVER, FORTHWITH TREAT ON TEA, the most popular of our beverages, the one which makes "the cup that cheers but not inebriates". The beverage called tea has now become almost a necessary of life. Previous to the middle of the 17th century it was not used in England.

The cultivation of the tea plant requires great care. It is raised chiefly on the sides of hills, and in order to increase the quantity and improve the quality of the leaves the shrub is pruned. They pluck the leaves, selecting them according to the kinds of tea required. Teas of the finest flavour consist of the youngest leaves; the younger the leaves the higher flavoured the tea, and the scarcer, and consequently the dearer.

FOR MAKING COFFEE, so many modes of making it are adopted in different countries that it would be impossible, in the space at our command, to enumerate them; but the following facts connected with coffee will be found highly interesting. Of the various kinds of coffee, the Arabian is considered the best. It is grown chiefly in the districts of Aden and Mocha. Mocha coffee has a smaller and rounder bean than any other, and a more agreeable smell and taste. The next in reputation and quality is the Java and Ceylon coffee, and then the coffees of Bourbon and Martinique, and that of British Guiana. The Jamaica and St. Domingo coffees are less esteemed.

DR. CHRISTISON says that everyone "will be struck with the readiness with which certain classes of patients will often take diluted meat juice or beef tea when they refuse all other kinds of food". This is particularly remarkable in cases of gastric fever, in which, he says, little or nothing else besides beef tea has been taken for weeks, or even months; and yet a pint of beef tea contains scarcely ¼ ounce of anything but water. The result is so striking that he asks: "What is its mode of action? Not simple nutriment; ¼ oz. of the most nutritive material cannot nearly replace the daily wear and tear of the tissue in any circumstances." Possibly, he says, it belongs to a new denomination of remedies.

— To make Barley Water —

Ingredients.–2 oz. of pearl barley, 4 pints of boiling water, 1 pint of cold water, sugar, lemon peel and lemon juice to taste.

Mode.–Wash the barley in cold water, put it into a saucepan with the above proportion of cold water, and when it has boiled for about ¼ hour, strain off the water, and add the 4 pints of fresh boiling water. Boil until the liquid is reduced by half, strain it, and it will be ready for use. It may be flavoured with lemon peel or a little lemon juice, after being sweetened, or a small piece may be simmered with the barley.

Time.–20 to 30 minutes to reduce the liquid by half. **Sufficient** to make 2 pints.

— Savoury Beef Tea —
(SOYER'S RECIPE)

Ingredients.–1 lb. of lean beef, 1 oz. of butter, 1 clove, 2 button onions or ½ large one, 1 saltspoonful of salt, 2 pints water.

Mode.–Cut the beef into very small dice; put it into a stewpan with the butter, clove, onion, and salt; stir the meat round over the heat for a few minutes, until it produces a thin gravy; then add the water, and let it simmer gently from ½ to ¾ hour, skimming off every particle of fat. When done, strain it through a sieve, and put it by in a cool place until required. If wanted quite plain, the vegetables, salt, and clove may be omitted; the butter cannot be objectionable, as it is taken out in skimming.

Time.– ½ to ¾ hour. **Sufficient** to make 1 pint of good beef tea.

TEA.–The tea tree or shrub commonly grows to the height of 3 to 6 feet, but in its wild or native state it reaches 20 feet or more. In its general appearance it resembles the myrtle. The blossoms are white and fragrant, not unlike those of the wild rose, but smaller.

THE COFFEE PLANT grows to the height of about 12 or 15 feet, with leaves not unlike those of the common laurel, although more pointed, and not so dry and thick. The blossoms are white, much like those of jasmine, and issue from the angles of the leaf stalks. When the flowers fade, they are succeeded by the coffee bean, or seed, which is enclosed in a berry of a red colour when ripe. The beans are then dried for about three weeks, and put into a mill to separate the husk from the seed.

Hot Chocolate

CHOCOLATE AND COCOA.–Both these preparations are made from the seeds or beans of the cacao tree, which grows in the West Indies and South America. The Spanish and the proper name is cacao, not cocoa, as it is generally spelt. From this mistake, the tree from which the beverage is procured has been often confounded with the palm that produces the edible coconuts, which are the produce of the tree known to science as *Cocos nucifera*. Chocolate was considered here as a great luxury when first introduced, after the discovery of America; but the high duties laid upon it confined it long almost entirely to the wealthier classes.

OUR GREAT NURSE Miss Nightingale remarks that "a great deal too much against tea is said by wise people, and a great deal too much of tea is given to the sick by foolish people. When you see the natural and almost universal craving in English sick for their 'tea', you cannot but feel that Nature knows what she is about. But a little tea or coffee restores them quite as much as a great deal; and a great deal of tea, and especially of coffee, impairs the little power of digestion they have. There is nothing yet discovered which is a substitute to the English patient for his cup of tea; he can take it when he can take nothing else, and he often can't take anything else if he has it not."

— To make Hot Chocolate —

Ingredients.–Allow ½ oz. of block chocolate to each person; to every oz. allow ½ pint of water, ½ pint of milk.

Mode.–Make the milk and water hot; grate the chocolate into it, and stir the mixture constantly and quickly until the chocolate is dissolved; bring it to boiling point, whisk it well, and serve directly with white sugar.

— To make Coffee —

Ingredients.–Allow ½ oz. or 1 tablespoonful of ground coffee to each person; to every oz. of coffee allow ⅓ pint of water.

Mode.–To make coffee good, *it should never be boiled*, but the boiling water merely poured on it. The coffee should always be purchased in the berry, if possible freshly roasted, and it should never be ground long before it is wanted. Many persons may think that the proportion of water we have given for each oz. of coffee is rather small; it is so, and the coffee produced from it will be very strong; ⅓ of a cup will be found quite sufficient, which should be filled with nice hot milk, or milk and cream mixed. This is the *café au lait* for which our neighbours over the Channel are so justly celebrated.

— To make Essence of Coffee —

Ingredients.–To every ¼ lb. of ground coffee allow 1 small teaspoonful of powdered chicory, and 3 small teacupfuls or 1 pint of water.

Mode.–Let the coffee be freshly ground and, if possible, freshly roasted; put it into a percolater, or filter, with the chicory, and pour slowly over it the above proportion of boiling water. When it has all filtered through, warm the coffee sufficiently to bring it to the simmering point, but do not allow it to boil; then filter it a second time, put it into a clean and dry bottle, cork it well, and it will remain good for several days. Two tablespoonfuls of this essence are quite sufficient for a breakfast-cupful of hot milk.

— To make Tea —

Mode.–There is very little art in making good tea. If the water is boiling, and there is no sparing of the fragrant leaf, the beverage will almost invariably be good. The old-fashioned plan of allowing a teaspoonful to each person, and one over, is still practised. Warm the teapot with boiling water, let it remain for 2 or 3 minutes for the vessel to become thoroughly hot, then pour it away. Put in the tea, pour in from ½ to ¾ pint of *boiling* water, close the lid, and let it stand for the tea to draw from 5 to 10 minutes; then fill up the pot with water. The tea will be quite spoiled unless made with water that is actually boiling, as the leaves will not open, and the flavour not be extracted from them.

Cocoa bean

CAFE NOIR is usually handed round after dinner, and should be drunk well sweetened, with the addition of a little brandy or liqueurs, which may be added or not at pleasure. The coffee should be made very strong and served in very small cups, but never mixed with milk or cream. *Café noir* may be made of the essence of coffee, by pouring a tablespoonful into each cup, and filling it up with boiling water. This is a very expeditious manner of preparing coffee for a large party, but the essence must be very good and kept well corked.

CAFE AU LAIT is merely very strong coffee added to a large proportion of good hot milk, about 6 tablespoonfuls of strong coffee or 2 of essence being quite sufficient for a breakfast-cupful of milk. This preparation is infinitely superior to the weak watery coffee so often served at English tables. A little cream mixed with the milk improves the taste of the coffee, as also the richness of the beverage.

L EMONADE.-
"There is a
current opinion among
women," says Brillat-
Savarin, "which every
year causes the death
of many young women:
that acids, especially
vinegar, are
preventives of obesity.
Beyond all doubt, acids
have the effect of
destroying obesity; but
they also destroy health
and freshness.
Lemonade is, of all
acids, the most
harmless; but few
stomachs can resist it
long. I knew, in 1776,
at Dijon, a young lady
of great beauty, to
whom I was attached
by bonds of friendship
almost as great as those
of love. One day, when
she had for some time
gradually grown pale
and thin, she told me
in confidence that as
her young friends had
ridiculed her for being
fat, she had been in the
habit every day of
drinking a large glass
of *vinaigre*. She died at
eighteen years of age,
from the effect of these
potions."

— *G i n g e r   B e e r* —

Ingredients.-2 ½ lbs. of sugar, 1 ½ oz. of fresh bruised ginger,
1 oz. of cream of tartar, the rind and juice of 2 lemons, 3 gallons of
boiling water, ½ oz. of fresh yeast.

Mode.-Peel the lemons, squeeze the juice, strain it, and put the
peel and juice into a large crock, with the bruised ginger, cream of
tartar, and sugar. Pour over these ingredients 3 gallons of *boiling*
water; let it stand until just warm, when add the yeast, thickly
creamed with a little warm water. Stir the contents of the crock well,
and let them remain in a warm place all night, covered with a cloth.
The next day, skim off the yeast, and pour the liquor carefully into
another vessel, leaving the sediment; then pour into bottles and cork
immediately. In 3 days the ginger beer will be fit for use. For some
tastes, the above proportion of sugar may be diminished, but the beer
will not keep so long.

Sufficient to fill 4 dozen ginger beer bottles, or 18 wine bottles.

— *L e m o n a d e* —

Ingredients.-The rind of 2 lemons, the juice of 3 large or 4 small
ones, ½ lb. of sugar, 2 pints of boiling water.

Mode.-Pound the lemon rind with the sugar so that the latter
imbibes the fragrance of the lemon oil; add the lemon juice (but no
pips), and pour over the whole 2 pints of boiling water. When the
sugar is dissolved, strain the lemonade through a fine sieve or piece of
muslin; when cool, it will be ready for use. The lemonade will be
much improved by having the white of an egg beaten up in it; a little
sherry mixed with it also makes it nicer.

Elderberries

— C o w s l i p   W i n e —

Ingredients.—To every gallon of water allow 3 lbs. of sugar, the rind of 2 lemons and the juice of 1, the rind and juice of 1 Seville orange, 1 gallon of cowslip flowers, ¼ oz. of fresh brewer's yeast; to every gallon of wine allow ¼ pint of brandy.

Mode.—Boil the sugar and water together for ½ hour, carefully removing any scum as it rises. Pour this boiling liquor on to the orange and lemon juice, which should be strained, and the rinds; when lukewarm, add the cowslips, picked from the stalks; add the yeast, creamed with a little water, cover, and let the wine ferment for 3 or 4 days; then strain into jars with brandy added in the above proportion, and let stand for 2 months, when bottle off for use.

Seasonable in April or May. **Sufficient,** if 3 gallons are made, for about 18 bottles.

— E l d e r b e r r y   W i n e —

Ingredients.—To every 3 gallons of water allow 2 gallons of elderberries; to every gallon of juice allow 3 lbs. of sugar, ½ oz. of ground ginger, 6 cloves, 1 lb. of good Turkey raisins; to every gallon of wine allow ¼ pint of brandy; to every 3 gallons of wine allow 1 oz. of fresh brewer's yeast.

Mode.—Pour the water, quite boiling, on the elderberries, which should be picked from the stalks, and let these stand, covered, for 24 hours; then strain the whole through a sieve or jelly bag, breaking the fruit to express all the juice from it. Measure the liquor, and to every gallon allow the above proportion of sugar. Boil the juice and sugar with the ginger, cloves, and raisins for 1 hour, skimming the liquor the whole time; let it stand until lukewarm, then put it into a clean dry cask or into jars, with the yeast, creamed with a little water. Let it ferment for about a fortnight; then add the brandy, bung up the cask or jars, and let the wine stand some months before it is bottled, when it will be found excellent. Elder wine is usually mulled and served with sippets of toasted bread and a little grated nutmeg.

Seasonable in September. **Sufficient,** if 3 gallons are made, for about 18 bottles.

— G i n g e r   W i n e —

Ingredients.—To 3 gallons of water allow 9 lbs. of sugar, 3 lemons, 3 oz. of fresh bruised ginger, 1 oz. of fresh brewer's yeast, ¾ lb. of raisins stoned and chopped, ⅓ pint of brandy.

Mode.—Boil together for 1 hour the water, the sugar, the rinds of the 3 lemons, and the bruised ginger; remove every particle of scum as it rises, and when the liquor is sufficiently boiled, put it into a large pan to cool. When nearly cold, add the yeast, which must be thickly creamed with a little water; the next day put all in a dry cask or fermenting jars, with the strained juice of the lemon and the chopped raisins. Stir the wine every day for a fortnight, then add the brandy, stop the containers down by degrees, and in a few weeks the wine will be fit to take off and bottle.

Sufficient for about 18 bottles.

ELDERBERRY WINE.—The elderberry is well adapted for the production of wine; its juice contains a considerable portion of the principle necessary for a vigorous fermentation, and its beautiful colour communicates a rich tint to the wine made from it. It is, however, deficient in sweetness, and therefore demands an addition of sugar. It is one of the very best of the genuine old English wines, and a cup of it mulled, just previous to retiring to bed on a winter night, is a thing to be "run for", as Cobbett would say.

Effervescing Gooseberry — Wine —

Ingredients.–To every gallon of water allow 6 lbs. of green gooseberries, 3 lbs. of sugar.

Mode.–This wine should be prepared from unripe gooseberries in order to avoid the flavour which the fruit would give to the wine when in a mature state. Its effervescence depends more upon the time of bottling than upon the unripe state of the fruit, for brisk wine can be made from fruit that is ripe as well as that which is unripe. The fruit should be selected before it shows any tendency to ripen, and any bruised or decayed berries, and those that are very small, should be rejected. The blossom and stalk ends should be removed, and the fruit well bruised in a tub, ensuring that each berry is broken without crushing the seeds. Pour the water (which should be warm) on the fruit, and squeeze and stir it with the hand until all the pulp is removed from the skin and seeds; cover the whole closely for 24 hours, then strain it through a coarse cloth, pressing it with as much force as can be conveniently applied to extract the whole of the juice and liquor. The juice should be put into a tub or pan of sufficient size to contain all of it, and the sugar added to it. Let it be well stirred until the sugar is dissolved; place the pan in a warm place, and keep it closely covered; let it ferment for a day or two. It must then be drawn off into a clean cask or jars, placed so that the scum that rises may be thrown out, and the same kept filled with the remaining "must", or fermenting liquor, a little of which should be reserved for the purpose. When the active fermentation has ceased, the containers should be loosely bunged, and again filled if necessary; after a few days, when the fermentation is a little more languid (which may be known by the hissing noise ceasing), the bungs should be driven in tight and a spike hole made, to give vent if necessary. About November or December, on a clear fine day, the wine should be racked from its lees into a clean cask or jars, which may be rinsed with brandy. After a month, it should be examined to see if it is sufficiently clear for bottling; if not, it must be fined with isinglass, which may be dissolved in some of the wine, ¼ oz. being sufficient for 3 gallons. In March or April, or when the gooseberry bushes begin to blossom, the wine should be bottled.

Seasonable at the end of May or beginning of June, before the berries ripen. **Sufficient**, if 2 gallons are made, for about 12 bottles.

— Very Superior Orange Wine —
(A VERY SIMPLE AND EASY METHOD)

Ingredients.–30 Seville oranges, 10 lbs. of sugar, water.

Mode.–Have ready two bowls, into one of which put the peel of the oranges, pared quite thin, and into the other the pulp after the juice has been squeezed from it. Strain the juice through a double thickness of muslin, and put it into a large earthenware crock with the sugar. Pour about 2 pints of cold water onto the peels and the same onto the pulp; let these stand for 24 hours, then strain the liquor into the crock; add more water to the peels and pulp, and repeat the process every day for another 6 days, being careful to stir the contents of the crock each day. On the *third* day after the crock is full–that is the *tenth* day after the commencement of making–the

GOOSEBERRIES.– The red and the white are the two principal varieties of gooseberries. The red are rather the more acid, but when covered with white sugar are most wholesome, because the sugar neutralizes their acidity. Red gooseberries make an excellent jelly, which is light and refreshing, but not very nourishing. It is good for bilious and plethoric persons, and for invalids generally, who need light and digestible food. It is a fruit from which many dishes might be made. All sorts of gooseberries are agreeable when stewed and, in this country especially, there is no fruit so universally in favour. In Scotland, there is scarcely a cottage garden without its gooseberry bush.

liquor may be poured off into jars and securely bunged down. This is a very simple and easy method, and the wine made according to it will be pronounced to be most excellent. There is no troublesome boiling, and all fermentation takes place in the crock, which should at all times be kept covered. The wine may be racked off and bottled in 8 or 9 months, and will be fit for use in a further 3 months. Ginger wine may be made in precisely the same manner, using ¾ lb. of the best whole ginger, bruised with a mallet.

Sufficient to make about 3 gallons of wine, or about 18 bottles.

— R h u b a r b   W i n e —

Ingredients.–To every 5 lbs. of rhubarb pulp allow 1 gallon of water; to every gallon of liquor allow 3 lbs. of sugar, ½ oz. of isinglass, the rind of 1 lemon.

Mode.–Wipe the rhubarb with a wet cloth and, with a mallet, bruise it in a large wooden tub or other convenient vessel. When reduced to a pulp, weigh it, and to every 5 lbs. of pulp add 1 gallon of cold water; let this stand for 3 days, stirring three or four times a day; on the fourth day, press the pulp through a sieve, put the liquor into a large vessel, and to every gallon add 3 lbs. of sugar; stir in the sugar until it is quite dissolved, then add the lemon rind; let the liquor stand, and in 4 to 6 days the fermentation will begin to subside, and a crust or head will be formed, which should be skimmed off; alternatively the liquor may be drawn off when the crust begins to crack or separate. Put the wine into a cask or jar; if, after that, it ferments, rack it off into another cask or jar, adding the isinglass, dissolved in a little warm water; in a fortnight, stop it down. If the wine should have lost any of its original sweetness, add a little more sugar, taking care that the cask or jar remains full. Bottle off 6 or 7 months later, and in another 3 it should be fit to drink. This wine improves greatly by keeping; should a very brilliant colour be desired, add a little currant juice.

Sufficient, if 3 gallons are made, for about 18 bottles.

— C h a m p a g n e   C u p —

Ingredients.–1 bottle of champagne, 1 pint of soda water, 1 liqueur glass of brandy or Curaçao, 2 tablespoonfuls of sugar, 1 lb. of pounded ice, a sprig of green borage.

Mode.–Put all the ingredients into a silver bowl; stir them together, and serve in the same manner as CLARET CUP . Should the above proportion of sugar not be found sufficient to suit some tastes, increase the quantity. When borage is not easily obtainable, substitute for it a few slices of cucumber rind.

— C l a r e t   C u p —

Ingredients.–1 bottle of claret, 1 bottle of soda water, about ½ lb. of crushed ice, 4 tablespoonfuls of caster sugar, ¼ teaspoonful of grated nutmeg, 1 liqueur glass of Maraschino, a sprig of green borage.

Mode.–Put all the ingredients into a large handsome bowl, regulating the proportion of ice by the state of the weather; if very warm, a larger quantity would be necessary.

CHAMPAGNE.– This, the most celebrated of French wines, is the produce chiefly of the province of that name, and is generally understood in England to be a brisk, effervescing, or sparkling white wine of a very fine flavour; but this is only one of the varieties of this class. There is both red and white champagne, and each of these may be either still or brisk. The brisk are, in general, the most highly esteemed, or at least are the most popular in this country, on account of their delicate flavour and the agreeable pungency which they derive from the carbonic acid they contain, and to which they owe their briskness.

CLARETS.–All those wines called in England clarets are the produce of the country round Bordeaux, or the Bordelais; but it is remarkable that there is no pure wine in France known by the name of claret, which is a corruption of *clairet*, a term that is applied there to any red or rose-coloured wine. Round Bordeaux are produced a number of wines of the first quality, which pass under the name simply of *vins de Bordeaux*, or have the designation of the particular district where they are made, as Lafite, Latour, etc. The clarets brought to the English market are frequently prepared for it by the wine-growers by mixing together several Bordeaux wines, or by adding to them a portion of some other wines, but in France the pure wines are carefully preserved distinct.

CLARET CUP may also be served in a silver flagon, with a clean napkin passed through one of the handles, that the edge of the flagon may be wiped after each guest has partaken of the contents.

LEMON RIND OR PEEL.–This contains an essential oil of a very high flavour and fragrance, and is esteemed both a wholesome and agreeable stomachic. It is used, as will be seen by many recipes in this book, as an ingredient for flavouring a number of various dishes. Under the name of candied lemon peel, it is cleared of the pulp and preserved by sugar, when it becomes an excellent sweetmeat. By the ancient medical philosopher Galen, and others, dried lemon peel was considered as one of the best digestives and recommended to weak and delicate persons.

— Lemon Brandy —

Ingredients.–1 pint of brandy, the rind of 2 small lemons, 2 oz. of sugar, ¼ pint of water.

Mode.–Peel the lemons rather thin, taking care to have none of the white pith. Put the rinds into a bottle with the brandy, and let them infuse for 24 hours, when they should be strained. Now boil the sugar with the water for a few minutes and skim it; when cold, add it to the brandy. A dessertspoonful of this will be found an excellent flavouring for boiled custards.

— Orange Brandy —

Ingredients.–To every ½ gallon of brandy allow ¾ pint of Seville orange juice, 1¼ lbs. of sugar.

Mode.–To bring out the full flavour of the orange peel, pound the sugar in a mortar with the rinds of several of the oranges; mix the brandy with the orange juice, strained, the rinds of the rest of the oranges, pared very thin, and the flavoured sugar. Let all stand in a closely covered jar for about 3 days, stirring three or four times a day. When clear, it should be bottled and closely corked for a year; it will then be ready for use, but will keep any length of time. This is a most excellent stomachic when taken pure in small quantities; as the strength of the brandy is very little deteriorated by the other ingredients, it may also be diluted with water.

— To make Negus —

Ingredients.–To every pint of port allow 2 pints of boiling water, ¼ lb. of sugar, 1 lemon, grated nutmeg to taste.

Mode.–As this beverage is more usually drunk at children's parties than at any other, the port need not be very old or expensive for the purpose. Put the port into a jug, pound the sugar with the lemon rind until all the fragrance of the skin is absorbed, then squeeze the juice, and strain it. Add the sugar and lemon juice to the port, with the grated nutmeg; pour over it the boiling water, cover the jug; when the beverage has cooled a little, it will be fit for use. Negus may also be made with sherry, or any other sweet white wine, but is more usually made of port than of any other beverage.

Sufficient for a party of 9 or 10 children.

— Home-made Noyeau —

Ingredients.–3 oz. of ground almonds, a few drops of almond essence, 1 lb. of sugar, the rind of 3 lemons, 2 pints of Irish whiskey or gin, 1 tablespoonful of clear honey, ½ pint of milk.

Mode.–Mix together the almonds and the sugar; add a few drops of almond essence to the milk and bring it to boiling point; let it stand until quite cold, then add to it all the other ingredients; put them into a bottle and cover tightly; let the mixture stand for 10 days, shaking it every day, after which strain the mixture through filter paper into smaller bottles, and cork tight. Noyeau will be found useful for flavouring many sweet dishes.

Sufficient to make about 2½ pints.

CHAPTER 15

Dinners
— and Dining —

MAN, IT HAS BEEN SAID, IS A DINING ANIMAL. Creatures of the inferior races eat and drink; man only dines. It has also been said that he is a cooking animal, but some races eat food without cooking it. It is equally true that some races of men do not dine any more than the tiger or the vulture. Dining is the privilege of civilisation. The rank which a people occupy in the grand scale may be measured by their way of taking their meals, as well as by their way of treating their women. The nation which knows how to dine has learnt the leading lesson of progress.

DINNER, BEING THE GRAND SOLID MEAL OF THE DAY, is a matter of considerable importance, and a well served table is a striking index of human ingenuity and resource. Describing a dinner party given by Lord and Lady Amundeville at Norman Abbey, Lord Byron says:

> *Their table was a board to tempt even ghosts*
> *To pass the Styx for more substantial feast.*
> *I will not dwell upon ragoûts or roasts,*
> *Albeit all human history attests*
> *That happiness for man – the hungry sinner! –*
> *Since Eve ate apples, much depends on dinner.*

There is infinite zest in the famous description of a dainty supper, given by Keats in his "Eve of Saint Agnes". Could Queen Mab herself desire to sit down to anything nicer, both as to its appointments and serving, and as to its quality, than the collation served by Porphyro in the lady's bedroom while she slept?

> *There by the bedside, where the faded moon*
> *Made a dim silver twilight, soft he set*
> *A table, and, half-anguish'd, threw thereon*
> *A cloth of woven crimson, gold, and jet.*
> *   *   *
> *While he, from forth the closet, brought a heap*
> *Of candied apple, quince, and plum, and gourd;*
> *With jellies smoother than the creamy curd,*
> *And lucent syrups tinct with cinnamon;*
> *Manna and dates, in argosy transferr'd*
> *From Fez; and spicèd dainties, every one,*
> *From silken Samarcand to cedar'd Lebanon.*

SHORT OR VERBAL INVITATIONS, except where persons are exceedingly intimate or are very near relations, are very far from proper, although of course very much always depends on the manner in which the invitation is given. True politeness, however, should be studied even amongst the nearest friends and relations, for the mechanical forms of good breeding are of great consequence, and too much familiarity may have, for its effect, the destruction of friendship.

But Tennyson has ventured beyond dates, and quinces, and syrups, which may be thought easy to be brought in by a poet. In his idyll of "Audley Court" he gives a most appetising description of a pasty at a picnic:

> There, on a slope of orchard, Francis laid
> A damask napkin wrought with horse and hound;
> Brought out a dusky loaf that smelt of home,
> And, half cut down, a pasty costly made,
> Where quail and pigeon, lark and leveret, lay
> Like fossils of the rock, with golden yolks
> Imbedded and injellied.

Leaving great men of all kinds, however, to get their own dinners, let us, who are not great, look after ours. Dine we must, and we may as well dine elegantly as well as wholesomely.

DINNER PARTIES

IN GIVING OR ACCEPTING AN INVITATION FOR DINNER, the following is the form of words generally made use of. They, however, can be varied in proportion to the intimacy or position of the hosts and guests:

> Mr. and Mrs. A_____ present their compliments to Mr. and Mrs. B_____, and request the honour [or hope to have the pleasure] of their company to dinner on Wednesday, the 6th of December next.
> A_____ STREET,
> November 13th, 1859.   R. S. V. P.

The letters in the corner imply "Répondez, s'il vous plaît", meaning "an answer will oblige". The reply, accepting the invitation, is couched in the following terms:

> Mr. and Mrs. B_____ present their compliments to Mr. and Mrs. A_____, and will do themselves the honour of [or will have much pleasure in] accepting their kind invitation to dinner on the 6th of December next.
> B_____ SQUARE,
> November 18th, 1859.

Cards or invitations for a dinner party should be issued a fortnight or three weeks (sometimes even a month) beforehand, and care should be taken by the hostess in the selection of the invited guests, that they should be suited to each other. Much also of the pleasure of a dinner party will depend on the arrangement of the guests at table, so as to form a due admixture of talkers and listeners, the grave and the gay. If an invitation to dinner is accepted, the guests should be punctual, and the mistress ready in her drawing-room to receive them. At some periods it has been considered fashionable to come late to dinner, but lately *nous avons changé tout cela*.

THE HALF-HOUR BEFORE DINNER has always been considered as the great ordeal through which the mistress, in giving a dinner

Supper table, with floral decorations, arranged for 16 persons

THE VARIETY IN THE DISHES which furnish forth a modern dinner table does not necessarily imply anything unwholesome, or anything capricious. The appetite of the overworked man of business, or statesman, or of any dweller in towns, whose occupations are exciting and exhausting, is jaded and requires stimulation. Men and women who are in rude health, and who have plenty of air and exercise, eat the simplest food with relish and digest it well, but those conditions are out of the reach of many men. They must suit their mode of dining to their mode of living, if they cannot choose the latter.

party, will either pass with flying colours or lose many of her laurels. The anxiety to receive her guests, her hope that all will be present in due time, her trust in the skill of her cook and the attention of the other domestics all tend to make these few minutes a trying time. The mistress, however, must display no kind of agitation, but show her tact in suggesting light and cheerful subjects of conversation.

DINNER BEING ANNOUNCED, the host offers his arm to, and places on his right hand at the dinner table, the lady to whom he desires to pay most respect, either on account of her age, position, or from her being the greatest stranger in the party. If this lady be married and her husband present, the latter takes the hostess to her place at table, and seats himself at her right hand. The rest of the company follow in couples, as specified by the master and mistress of the house, arranging the party according to their rank and other circumstances which may be known to them.

The guests being seated at the dinner table, the lady begins to help the soup, which is handed round, commencing with the gentlemen on her right and on her left, and continuing in the same order till all are served. It is generally established as a rule not to ask for soup or fish twice as, in so doing, part of the company may be kept waiting too long for the second course, when, perhaps, a little revenge is taken by looking at the awkward consumer of a second portion.

We have given plans for placing the various dishes of the First Course, Entrées, Second Course, and Third Course. Following these

Flower vase for dinner table

Bowl of roses

will be found bills of fare for smaller dinner parties. A menu for a dinner *à la russe* is also included in the present chapter.

Dinners *a la russe* differ from ordinary dinners in the mode of serving the various dishes. In a dinner *à la russe*, the dishes are cut up on a sideboard, and handed round to the guests, and each dish may be considered a course. The table for a dinner *à la russe* should be laid with flowers and plants in fancy flowerpots down the middle, together with some of the dessert dishes. A menu or bill of fare should be laid by the side of each guest. However, dinners *à la russe* are scarcely suitable for small establishments, a large number of servants being required to carve, and to help the guests, besides there being a necessity for more plates, dishes, knives, forks, and spoons than are usually to be found in any other than a very large establishment. Where, however, the procedure is practicable, there is, perhaps, no mode of serving a dinner so enjoyable as this.

JANUARY.

DINNER FOR 18 PERSONS.

First Course.

Mock Turtle Soup,
removed by
Cod's Head and Shoulders.

Stewed Eels.

Vase of
Flowers.

Red Mullet.

Clear Oxtail Soup,
removed by
Fried Filleted Soles.

Entrées.

Riz de Veau aux
Tomatos.

Ragoût of
Lobster.

Vase of
Flowers.

Cotelettes de Porc
à la Robert.

Poulet à la Marengo.

Second Course.

Roast Turkey.

Boiled Turkey and
Celery Sauce.

Pigeon Pie.

Vase of
Flowers.

Boiled Ham.

Tongue, garnished.

Saddle of Mutton.

Third Course.

Charlotte
à la Parisienne.

Pheasants,
removed by
Plum-pudding.

Apricot-Jam
Tartlets.

Jelly.

Cream.

Vase of
Flowers.

Cream.

Jelly.

Mince
Pies.

Snipes,
removed by
Pommes à la Condé.

Maids
of Honour.

Dessert and Ices.

DINNER FOR 12 PERSONS (January)

First Course

Carrot Soup à la Crécy   Oxtail Soup
Turbot and Lobster Sauce   Fried Smelts with Dutch Sauce

Entrées

Mutton Cutlets with Soubise Sauce   Sweetbreads
Oyster Patties   Fillets of Rabbits

Second Course

Roast Turkey   Stewed Rump of Beef à la Jardinière
Boiled Ham, garnished with Brussels Sprouts
Boiled Chickens and Celery Sauce

Third Course

Roast Hare   Teal
Eggs à la Neige   Vol-au-Vent of Preserved Fruit   1 Jelly   1 Cream
Potatoes à la Maître d'Hôtel   Grilled Mushrooms

Dessert and Ices

DINNER FOR 6 PERSONS (January)

First Course

Pea Soup
Baked Haddocks   Soles à la Crème

Entrées

Mutton Cutlets and Tomato Sauce   Fricasséed Rabbit

Second Course

Roast Pork and Apple Sauce   Breast of Veal, rolled and stuffed
Vegetables

Third Course

Jugged Hare
Whipped Cream   Blancmange
Mince Pies   Cabinet Pudding

Dessert and Ices

PLACING GUESTS AT THE DINNER TABLE.–It will be found of great assistance to have the names of the guests neatly (and correctly) written on small cards, and placed at that part of the table where it is desired they should sit. With respect to the number of guests, it has often been said that a private dinner party should consist of not less than the number of the Graces, or more than that of the Muses. A party of ten or twelve is perhaps, in a general way, sufficient for the guests to enjoy themselves and be enjoyed. White kid gloves are worn by ladies at dinner parties, but should be taken off before the business of dining commences.

JULY.

DINNER FOR 18 PERSONS.

First Course.

Whitebait.	Green-Pea Soup, removed by Salmon and dressed Cucumber. Vase of Flowers. Soup à la Reine, removed by Mackerel à la Maître d'Hôtel.	**Stewed Trout.**

Entrées.

Lobster Curry en Casserole.	Lamb Cutlets and Peas. Vase of Flowers. Chicken Patties.	**Scollops of Chickens.**

Second Course.

Boiled Capons.	Haunch of Venison. Pigeon Pie. Vase of Flowers. Braised Ham. Saddle of Lamb.	**Spring Chickens.**

Third Course.

Prawns. / **Creams.**	**Cherry Tart.**	Roast Ducks, removed by Vanilla Soufflé. Raspberry Cream. Vase of Flowers. Strawberry Cream. Green Goose, removed by Iced Pudding.	**Raspberry-and-Currant Tart.**	**Custards.** / **Tartlets.**

Dessert and Ices.

WINE.—It is not usual, where taking wine is *en règle*, for a gentleman to ask a lady to take wine until the fish or soup is finished, and then the gentleman honoured by sitting on the right of the hostess may politely inquire if she will do him the honour of taking wine with him. This will act as a signal to the rest of the company, the gentleman of the house most probably requesting the same pleasure of the ladies at his right and left. At many tables, however, the custom or fashion of drinking wine in this manner is abolished, and the servant fills the glasses of the guests with the various wines suited to the course which is in progress.

WHEN DINNER IS FINISHED, THE DESSERT is placed on the table, accompanied with finger-glasses. It is the custom of some gentlemen to wet a corner of the napkin, but the hostess, whose behaviour will set the tone to all the ladies present, will merely wet the tips of her fingers, which will serve all the purposes required. The French and other continentals have a habit of gargling the mouth, but it is a custom which no English gentlewoman should, in the slightest degree, imitate.

When fruit has been taken, and a glass or two of wine passed round, the time will have arrived when the hostess will rise, and thus give the signal for the ladies to leave the gentlemen and retire to the drawing-room. The gentlemen of the party will rise at the same time, and he who is nearest the door will open it for the ladies, all remaining courteously standing until the last lady has withdrawn.

In former times, when the bottle circulated freely amongst the guests, it was necessary for the ladies to retire earlier than they do at present, for the gentlemen of the company soon became unfit to conduct themselves with that decorum which is essential in the presence of ladies. Thanks, however, to the improvements in modern society, and the high example shown to the nation by its most illustrious personages, temperance is, in these happy days, a striking feature in the character of a gentleman.

DINNER FOR 12 PERSONS (July)

First Course

Soupe à la Jardinière   Chicken Soup
Crimped Salmon and Parsley-and-Butter
Trout aux fines herbes, in cases

———

Entrées

Tendrons de Veau and Peas   Lamb Cutlets and Cucumbers

———

Second Course

Loin of Veal à la Béchamel   Roast Fore-quarter of Lamb
Salad   Braised Ham, garnished with Broad Beans
Vegetables

———

Third Course

Roast Ducks   Turkey Poult
Stewed Peas à la Française   Lobster Salad   Cherry Tart
Raspberry and Currant Tart   Custards, in glasses
Lemon Creams   Nesselrode Pudding   Marrow Pudding

———

Dessert and Ices

DINNER FOR 6 PERSONS (July)

First Course

Soupe à la Jardinière
Salmon Trout and Parsley-and-Butter
Fillets of Mackerel à la Maître d'Hôtel

———

Entrées

Lobster Cutlets   Beef Palates à l'Italienne

———

Second Course

Roast Lamb   Boiled Capon and White Sauce
Boiled Tongue, garnished with small Vegetable Marrows
Bacon and Beans

———

Third Course

Goslings
Whipped Strawberry Cream   Raspberry and Currant Tart
Meringues   Cherry Tartlets   Iced Pudding

———

Dessert and Ices

T HE ELEGANCE WITH WHICH A DINNER IS SERVED is a matter which depends, of course, partly upon the means, but still more upon the taste of the master and mistress of the house. It may be observed, in general, that there should always be flowers on the table, and as they form no item of expense, there is no reason why they should not be employed every day.

Sugar basket for dessert

— MENU —

SERVICE A LA RUSSE (November)

Oxtail Soup   **Soupe à la Jardinière**

Turbot and Lobster Sauce   **Crimped Cod and Oyster Sauce**

Stewed Eels   **Soles à la Normande**

Pike and Cream Sauce   **Fried Filleted Soles**

Filets de Bœuf à la Jardinière   **Croquettes of Game aux Champignons**

Chicken Cutlets   **Mutton Cutlets and Tomato Sauce**

Lobster Rissoles   **Oyster Patties**

Partridges aux Fines Herbes   **Larded Sweetbreads**

Roast Beef   **Poulets aux Cressons**
Haunch of Mutton   **Roast Turkey**
Boiled Turkey and Celery Sauce   **Ham**

Grouse   **Pheasants**   **Hare**

Salad   **Artichokes**   **Stewed Celery**

Italian Cream   **Charlotte aux Pommes**   **Compote of Pears**

Croûtes macérées aux Fruits   **Pastry**   **Punch Jelly**

Iced Pudding

Dessert and Ices

AFTER-DINNER INVITATIONS MAY BE GIVEN, by which we wish to be understood invitations for the evening. The time of the arrival of these visitors will vary according to their engagements, or sometimes will be varied in obedience to the caprices of fashion. Guests invited for the evening are, however, generally considered at liberty to arrive whenever it will best suit themselves, usually between nine and twelve, unless earlier hours are specifically named. By this arrangement, many fashionable people and others, who have numerous engagements to fulfil, often contrive to make their appearance at two or three parties in the course of one evening.

Entrée dish

BILL OF FARE FOR A GAME DINNER FOR
30 PERSONS (November).

First Course.

Purée of Grouse.	Hare Soup. Vase of Flowers. Soup à la Reine.	Pheasant Soup.

Entrées.

Salmi of Widgeon. Lark Pudding. Salmi of Woodcock.	Fillets of Hare en Chevreuil. Perdrix aux Choux. Vase of Flowers. Curried Rabbit. Fillet of Pheasant and Truffles.	Salmi of Woodcock. Game Patties. Salmi of Widgeon.

Second Course.

Cold Pheasant Pie à la Périgord.	Larded Pheasants. Leveret, larded and stuffed. Vase of Flowers. Grouse. Larded Partridges.	Hot raised Pie of mixed Game.

Third Course.

Snipes. Golden Plovers. Wild Duck.	Pintails. Quails. Vase of Flowers. Teal. Woodcocks.	Snipes. Widgeon. Ortolans.

Entremets and Removes.

Apricot Tart. Vol-au-Vent of Pears. Maids of Honour.	Boudin à la Nesselrode. Dantzic Jelly. Vase of Flowers. Charlotte Russe. Plum-pudding.	Maids of Honour. Gâteau Génoise glacé. Compôte of Apples.

Dessert.

Olives. Preserved Cherries. Ginger-Ice Cream.	Strawberry-Ice Cream. Pineapples. Grapes. Pears. Vase of Flowers. Apples. Grapes. Pears. Lemon-Water Ice.	Dried Fruit. Figs. Filberts. Wafers. Orange-Water Ice. Walnuts. Biscuits. Dried Fruit. Preserved Cherries. Olives. Figs.

DR. JOHNSON has a curious paragraph on the effects of a dinner on men. "Before dinner," he says, "men meet with great inequality of understanding; and those who are conscious of their inferiority have all the modesty not to talk. When they have drunk wine, every man feels himself happy, and loses that modesty, and grows impudent and vociferous; but he is not improved, he is only not sensible of his defects." This is rather severe, but there may be truth in it.

EVENING PARTIES AND SUPPERS

THE ETIQUETTE OF THE DINNER PARTY TABLE being disposed of, let us now enter slightly into that of an evening party or ball. The invitations issued and accepted for either of these will be written in the same style as those already described for a dinner party. They should be sent out *at least* three weeks before the day fixed for the event, and should be replied to within a week of their receipt. If the entertainment is to be simply an evening party, this must be specified on the card or note of invitation.

As the ladies and gentlemen arrive, each should be shown to a room exclusively provided for their reception, and in that set apart for the ladies, attendants should be in waiting to assist in uncloaking, and helping to arrange the hair and toilet of those who require it. It will be found convenient, in those cases where the number of guests is large, to provide numbered tickets, so that they can be attached to the cloaks and shawls of each lady, a duplicate of which should be handed to the guest. Coffee is sometimes provided in this or an ante-room for those who would like to partake of it.

As the visitors are announced by the servant, it is not necessary for the lady of the house to advance each time towards the door, but merely to rise from her seat to receive their courtesies and congratulations. If, indeed, the hostess wishes to show particular favour to some peculiarly honoured guests, she may introduce them to others whose acquaintance she may imagine will be especially suitable and agreeable. It is very often the practice of the master of the house to introduce one gentleman to another, but occasionally the lady performs this office.

The custom of non-introduction is very much in vogue in many houses, and guests are thus left to discover for themselves the position and qualities of the people around them. The servant, indeed, calls out the names of all the visitors as they arrive but, in many instances, mispronounces them. In our opinion, it is a cheerless and depressing custom, although, in thus speaking, we do not allude to the large assemblies of the aristocracy, but to the smaller parties of the middle classes.

A SEPARATE ROOM OR CONVENIENT BUFFET should be appropriated for refreshments, and to which the dancers may retire, and cakes and biscuits, with wine, negus, lemonade, and ices handed round. At the evening parties of the middle classes a supper is also usually provided, and this requires, on the part of the hostess, a great deal of attention and supervision. It usually takes place between the first and second parts of the programme of the dances, of which there should be several prettily written or printed copies distributed about the ballroom.

IN THE ARRANGEMENT OF A SUPPER TABLE, much may be done at a very small expense, provided taste and ingenuity are exercised. The colours and flavours of the various dishes should contrast nicely, there should be plenty of fruit and flowers on the table, and the room should be well lighted. We have endeavoured to show how the various dishes may be placed, but of course these little matters entirely depend on the length and width of the table used, on individual taste, whether the tables are arranged round the room, whether down the centre, with a cross one at the top, or whether the

DURING THE PROGRESS OF A BALL, the hostess or host will courteously accost and chat with their friends, and take care that the ladies are furnished with seats, and that those who wish to dance are provided with partners. A gentle hint from the hostess, conveyed in a quiet ladylike manner, that certain ladies have remained unengaged during several dances, is sure not to be neglected by any gentleman. Thus will be studied the comfort and enjoyment of the guests, and no lady, in leaving the house, will feel the chagrin and disappointment of not having been invited to "stand up" in a dance during the whole of the evening.

Jelly of 2 Colours.

Macedoine of Fruits with Jelly

Lemon Cream

Victoria Sandwiches.

Meringues.

Grape Jelly.

Chocolate Cream.

Trifle.

Iced Oranges.

Stewed Pears.

Tipsy Cake

Rout Cakes.

Crystalized Fruits

Apples à la Parisienne

Nougat Almond Cake.

Blanc-Mange à la Vanille

JELLIES, CREAMS and SWEET DISHES.

supper is laid in two separate rooms, etc. The garnishing of the dishes has also much to do with the appearance of a supper table. Hams and tongues should be ornamented with cut vegetable flowers, raised pies with aspic jelly cut in dice, and all the dishes garnished sufficiently to be in good taste without looking absurd. The eye, in fact, should be as much gratified as the palate. Hot soup is now often served at suppers, but is not placed on the table. The servants fill the plates from a tureen on the buffet, and then hand them to the guests; when these are removed, the business of supper commences.

Where small rooms and large parties necessitate having a standing supper, many things enumerated in the following bill of fare may be placed on the buffet. Dishes for these suppers should be selected which may be eaten standing without any trouble.

The constituents of a pleasing supper may include: beef, ham, and tongue sandwiches, lobster and oyster patties, sausage rolls, meat rolls, lobster salad, dishes of fowls, the latter all cut up; dishes of sliced tongue, sliced beef, and galantine of veal; various jellies, blancmanges, and creams; custards in glasses, compotes of fruit, tartlets of jam, and dishes of small fancy pastry; dishes of fresh fruit, bonbons, sweetmeats, sponge cakes, and biscuits; and besides the articles just enumerated, ices, wafers, tea, coffee, soda water, ginger beer, lemonade, wines, and liqueurs will be required.

BILL OF FARE FOR A BALL SUPPER,

Or a Cold Collation for a Summer Entertainment, or Wedding or Christening Breakfast for 70 or 80 Persons (July).

```
Left vertical column (outer):          Center column:                      Right vertical column (outer):
3 Compôtes of Fruit.          Dish of         Tongue.          Veal-and-Ham    20 Small Dishes of various Summer Fruits.
3 Dishes of Small Pastry.     Lobster,        Ribs of Lamb.    Pie.            3 Fruit Tarts.
4 Blancmanges, to be          cut up.         Two Roast Fowls.                 4 Blancmanges, to be placed down the table.
placed down the table.                        Mayonnaise of Salmon.
3 English Pines.              Charlotte    [Lobster Salad]                 [Lobster Salad]   Savoy Cake.    3 Cheesecakes.
                             Russe à la       | Epergne, with Flowers. |                   3 English Pines.
                             Vanille.         Mayonnaise of Trout.
                                              Tongue, garnished.            Dish of
                             Pigeon Pie.      Boiled Fowls and Béchamel     Lobster,
                                              Sauce.                        cut up.
                                              Collared Eel.
                                              Ham.
                                              Raised Pie.
                             [Lobster Salad]  Two Roast Fowls.             [Lobster Salad]
                                              Shoulder of Lamb, stuffed.
                             Dish of          Mayonnaise of Salmon.
3 Fruit Tarts.               Lobster,   [Larded Capon]              [Boar's Head]  Pigeon Pie.  3 Dishes of Small Pastry.
4 Jellies, to be placed      cut up.          | Epergne, with Flowers. |
down the table.              [Lobster Salad]  Mayonnaise of Trout.
3 Cheesecakes.                                Tongue.                      [Lobster Salad]
20 Small Dishes of                            Boiled Fowls and Béchamel
various Summer Fruits.                        Sauce.                        Dish of
                             Pigeon Pie.      Raised Pie.                   Lobster,
                                              Ham, decorated.               cut up.
                                              Shoulder of Lamb, stuffed.
                             Dish of   Savoy  Two Roast Fowls.      Char-    Veal
                             Lobster,  Cake.  Mayonnaise of Salmon. lotte    and    4 Jellies, to be placed down the table.
                             cut up.      [Lobster Salad]           Russe    Ham    3 Compôtes of Fruit.
                                              | Epergne, with Flowers. | à la  Pie.
                                              Mayonnaise of Trout.    Vanille.
                                              Tongue, garnished.
                                              Boiled Fowls and Béchamel     Dish of
                                              Sauce.                        Lobster,
                                              Collared Eel.                 cut up.
```

The length of the page will not admit of our giving the dishes as they should be placed on the table; they should be arranged with the large and high dishes down the centre, and the spaces filled up with the smaller dishes, fruit, and flowers, taking care that the flavours and colours contrast nicely, and that no two dishes of a sort come together. A few dishes of fowls, lobster salads, etc., should be kept in reserve to replenish those that are most likely to be eaten first. A joint of cold roast or boiled beef should be placed on the buffet, as something substantial for the gentlemen of the party to partake of.

BILL OF FARE FOR A BALL SUPPER FOR 60 PERSONS (for Winter).

Lobster Salad.		BOAR'S HEAD, garnished with Aspic Jelly.		Lobster Salad.
	Fruited Jelly.	Mayonnaise of Fowl.	Charlotte Russe.	
	Small Pastry.	Small Ham, garnished.	Biscuits.	
		Iced Savoy Cake.		
Two Roast Fowls, cut up.	Vanilla Cream.	Epergne, with Fruit.	Fruited Jelly.	Two Roast Fowls, cut up.
	Prawns.	Two Boiled Fowls, with Béchamel Sauce.	Prawns.	
	Biscuits.	Tongue, ornamented.	Small Pastry.	
	Custards, in glasses.	Trifle, ornamented.	Custards, in glasses.	
		Raised Chicken Pie.		
Lobster Salad.	Fruited Jelly.	Tipsy Cake.	Swiss Cream.	Lobster Salad.
		Roast Pheasant.		
	Meringues.	Epergne, with Fruit.	Meringues.	
	Raspberry Cream.	Galantine of Veal.	Fruited Jelly.	
		Tipsy Cake.		
Two Roast Fowls, cut up.	Small Pastry.	Raised Game Pie.	Biscuits.	Two Roast Fowls, cut up.
	Custards, in glasses.	Trifle, ornamented.	Custards, in glasses.	
	Prawns.	Tongue, ornamented.	Prawns.	
	Biscuits.	Two Boiled Fowls, with Béchamel Sauce.	Small Pastry.	
		EPERGNE, WITH FRUIT.		
Lobster Salad.	Fruited Jelly.	Iced Savoy Cake.	Blancmange.	Lobster Salad.
		Small Ham, garnished.		
		Mayonnaise of Fowl.		
	Charlotte Russe.	Larded Capon.	Fruited Jelly.	

*Supper tables
and buffet*

THE DANCING IS GENERALLY OPENED, that is the first place
in the first quadrille is occupied, by the lady of the house. When
anything prevents this, the host will usually lead off the dance with
the lady who is either the highest in rank, or the greatest stranger.
It will be well for the hostess, even if she be very partial to the
amusement and a graceful dancer, not to participate in the ball to any
great extent, lest her lady guests should have occasion to complain of
her monopoly of the gentlemen and other causes of neglect. A few
dances will suffice to show her interest in the entertainment, without
unduly trenching on the attention due to her guests.

In private parties, a lady is not to refuse the invitation of a
gentleman to dance, unless she be previously engaged. The hostess
must be supposed to have asked to her house only those persons
whom she knows to be perfectly respectable and of unblemished
character, as well as pretty equal in position; thus, to decline the offer
of any gentleman present would be a tacit reflection on the master
and mistress of the house. It may be mentioned here, more especially
for the young who will read this book, that introductions at balls or
evening parties cease with the occasion that calls them forth, no
introductions at these times giving a gentleman a right to address,
afterwards, a lady. She is, consequently, free next morning to pass
her partner at a ball of the previous evening without the slightest
recognition.

FAMILY DINNERS

A FAMILY DINNER AT HOME, compared with either giving or going to a dinner or evening party, is of course of much more frequent occurrence and, many will say, of much greater importance. Both, however, have to be considered with a view to their nicety and enjoyment, and the latter more particularly with reference to economy. For both mistress and servants, in large as well as small households, it will be found by far the better plan to cook and serve the dinner, and to lay the tablecloth and the sideboard, with the same cleanliness, neatness, and scrupulous exactness whether it be for the mistress herself alone, a small family, or for "company". If this rule be strictly adhered to, all will find themselves increasing in managing skill.

Plain Family Dinners for May

Sunday.–1. Vegetable soup. 2. Saddle of mutton, asparagus, potatoes. 3. Gooseberry tart, custards.

Monday.–1. Fried whitings, anchovy sauce. 2. Cold mutton, mashed potatoes, stewed veal. 3. Fig pudding.

Tuesday.–1. Haricot mutton, made from remains of cold mutton, rumpsteak pie. 2. Macaroni.

Wednesday.–1. Roast loin of veal and spinach, boiled bacon, mutton cutlets and tomato sauce. 2. Gooseberry pudding and cream.

Thursday.–1. Spring soup. 2. Roast leg of lamb, mint sauce, spinach, curried veal and rice. 3. Lemon pudding.

Friday.–1. Boiled mackerel and parsley-and-butter. 2. Stewed rumpsteak, cold lamb and salad. 3. Baked gooseberry pudding.

Saturday.–1. Vermicelli. 2. Rump steak pudding, lamb cutlets and cucumbers. 3. Macaroni.

Plain Family Dinners for August

Sunday.–1. Salmon pudding. 2. Roast fillet of veal, boiled bacon cheek garnished with tufts of cauliflowers, French beans, potatoes. 3. Plum tart, boiled custard pudding.

Monday.–1. Baked soles. 2. Cold veal and bacon, salad, mutton cutlets and tomato sauce. 3. Boiled currant pudding.

Tuesday.–1. Rice soup. 2. Roast fowls and watercress, boiled knuckle of ham, minced veal garnished with croûtons, vegetables. 3. College puddings.

Wednesday.–1. Curried fowl with remains of cold fowl, dish of rice, stewed rump steak, vegetables. 2. Plum tart.

Thursday.–1. Boiled brisket of beef, carrots, turnips, suet dumplings, potatoes. 2. Baked bread pudding.

Friday.–1. Vegetable soup, made from liquor that beef was boiled in. 2. Cold beef and dressed cucumber, veal cutlets and tomato sauce. 3. Fondue.

Saturday.–1. Bubble-and-squeak, made from remains of cold beef; cold veal and ham pie, salad. 2. Baked raspberry pudding.

OF THE MANNER OF PASSING EVENINGS AT HOME, there is none pleasanter than in such recreative enjoyments as those which relax the mind from its severer duties, whilst they stimulate it with a gentle delight. Where there are young people, interesting and agreeable pastimes should especially be promoted, for if they do not find pleasure at home, they will seek it elsewhere. It ought, therefore, to enter into the domestic policy of every parent to make her children feel that home is the happiest place in the world; to imbue them with this delicious home feeling is one of the choicest gifts a parent can bestow.

BREAKFASTS

It will not be necessary to give here a long bill of fare of cold joints, etc. which may be placed on the buffet or sideboard, and do duty at the breakfast table. Any cold meat the larder may furnish should be nicely garnished and be placed on the buffet. Collared and potted meats or fish, cold game or poultry, veal and ham pies, and game and rump steak pies are all suitable dishes for the breakfast table, as also cold ham, tongue, etc.

The following list of hot dishes may perhaps assist our readers in knowing what to provide for the comfortable meal called breakfast: broiled fish, such as mackerel, whiting, herrings, dried haddocks; mutton chops and rump steaks, broiled sheep's kidneys, kidneys à la maître d'hôtel, sausages, plain rashers of bacon, bacon and poached eggs, ham and poached eggs, omelettes, plain boiled eggs, œufs-au-plat, poached eggs on toast, muffins, toast, marmalade, butter, etc.

In the summer, and when they are obtainable, always have a vase of freshly gathered flowers on the breakfast table and, when convenient, a nicely arranged dish of fruit; when strawberries are in season, these are particularly refreshing, as also grapes, or even currants.

Fruit for a fête champêtre

LUNCHEONS, SUPPERS, AND PICNICS

The remains of cold joints, nicely garnished, a few sweets, or a little hashed meat, poultry or game, are the usual articles placed on the table for luncheon, with bread and cheese, biscuits, butter, etc. If a substantial meal is desired, rump steaks or mutton chops may be served, as also veal cutlets, kidneys, or any dish of that kind. In families where there is a nursery, the mistress of the house often partakes of the meal with the children, and makes it her luncheon. In the summer, a few dishes of fresh fruit should be added to the luncheon, or a compote of fruit, or a fruit tart, or a pudding.

Of suppers we have little to say, as we have already given two bills of fare for a large party, which will answer very well for a smaller number by reducing the quantity of dishes and by omitting a few. Hot suppers are now very little in request, as people now generally dine at an hour which precludes the possibility of requiring supper, at all events not one of a substantial kind. Should, however, a bill of fare be required, one of those under the head of DINNERS, with slight alterations, will be found to answer for a hot supper.

Bill of Fare for a Picnic for 40 Persons

Meat and salads.–A joint of cold roast beef, a joint of cold boiled beef, 2 ribs of lamb, 2 shoulders of lamb, 4 roast fowls, 2 roast ducks, 1 ham, 1 tongue, 2 veal and ham pies, 2 pigeon pies, 6 medium-sized lobsters, 1 piece of collared calf's head, 18 lettuces, 6 baskets of salad, 6 cucumbers.

Fruit, cakes, bread, and biscuits.–Stewed fruit well sweetened, and put into glass bottles well corked, 3 or 4 dozen plain pastry biscuits to eat with the stewed fruit, 2 dozen fruit turnovers, 4 dozen cheesecakes, 2 cold cabinet puddings in moulds, 2 blancmanges in moulds, a few jam puffs, 1 large cold plum pudding (this must be good), a few baskets of fresh fruit, 3 dozen plain biscuits, a piece of cheese, 6 lbs. of butter (this, of course, includes the butter for tea), several 4-lb. loaves of household bread, 3 dozen rolls, 6 loaves of tin or pan bread (for tea), 2 plain plum cakes, 2 pound cakes, 2 sponge cakes, a tin of mixed biscuits, ½ lb. of tea.

Things not to be forgotten.–A stick of horseradish, a bottle of mint sauce well corked, a bottle of salad dressing, a bottle of vinegar, made mustard, pepper, salt, good oil, and sugar. If it can be managed, take a little ice. It is scarcely necessary to say that plates, tumblers, wine glasses, knives, forks, and spoons, must not be forgotten, as also teacups and saucers, 3 or 4 teapots, some lump sugar, and milk, if this last-named article cannot be obtained in the neighbourhood. Take 3 corkscrews.

Beverages.–½ lb. of tea (coffee is not suitable for a picnic, being difficult to make), 3 dozen quart bottles of ale, packed in hampers; ginger beer, soda water, and lemonade, of each 2 dozen bottles; 6 bottles of sherry, 6 bottles of claret, champagne *à discrétion*, any other light wine that may be preferred, and 2 bottles of brandy. Water can usually be obtained so it is useless to take it.

Wicker sauce basket

Mahogany folding luncheon tray

CHAPTER 16

Household Management

OF ALL THOSE ACQUIREMENTS which more particularly belong to the feminine character, there are none which take a higher rank, in our estimation, than such as enter into a knowledge of household duties, for on these are perpetually dependent the happiness, comfort, and well-being of a family. We may add that to be a good housewife does not necessarily imply an abandonment of proper pleasures or amusing recreation; and we think it the more necessary to express this as the performance of the duties of a mistress may, to some minds, perhaps seem to be incompatible with the enjoyment of life.

GOOD TEMPER should be cultivated by every mistress, as upon it the welfare of the household may be said to turn. Gentleness, not partial and temporary, but universal and regular, should pervade her conduct, for where such a spirit is habitually manifested, it not only delights her children, but makes her domestics attentive and respectful; her visitors are also pleased by it, and their happiness is increased.

EARLY RISING is one of the most essential qualities which enter into good household management, as it is not only the parent of health, but of innumerable other advantages. Indeed, when a mistress is an early riser, it is almost certain that her house will be orderly and well managed. On the contrary, if she remain in bed till a late hour, then the domestics will surely become sluggards. It is well to remember that early rising is almost impossible if late going to bed be the order, or rather disorder, of the house. The younger members of a family should go early and at regular hours to their beds, and the domestics as soon as possible after a reasonably appointed hour. Either the master or the mistress of a house should, after all have gone to their separate rooms, see that all is right with respect to the lights and fires below; and no servants should, on any account, be allowed to remain up after the heads of the house have retired.

THE CHOICE OF ACQUAINTANCES is very important to the happiness of a mistress and her family. A gossiping acquaintance, who indulges in the scandal and ridicule of her neighbours, should be

TO SELF-INDULGENCE all are more or less disposed, and it is not to be expected that servants are freer from this fault than the heads of houses. The great Lord Chatham thus gave his advice in reference to this subject: "I would have inscribed on the curtains of your bed, and the walls of your chamber, 'If you do not rise early, you can make progress in nothing'."

IN MAKING A FIRST CALL, either upon a newly married couple, or persons newly arrived in the neighbourhood, a lady should leave her husband's card together with her own, at the same time stating that the profession or business in which he is engaged has prevented him from having the pleasure of paying the visit with her. It is also a custom with many ladies, when on the eve of an absence from their neighbourhood, to leave or send their own and husband's cards, with the letters P. P. C. in the right-hand corner. These letters are the initials of the French words "*Pour prendre congé*", meaning "To take leave".

IT IS NOT ADVISABLE, at any time, to take favourite dogs into another lady's drawing-room, for many persons have an absolute dislike to such animals; and besides this, there is always a chance of a breakage of some article occurring through their leaping and bounding here and there. Children, unless they are particularly well-trained and orderly, should not accompany a lady in making morning calls. Where a lady, however, pays her visits in a carriage, the children can be taken in the vehicle and remain in it until the visit is over.

avoided as a pestilence. Friendships should not be hastily formed, nor the heart given at once to every newcomer. There are ladies who uniformly smile at and approve everything and everybody, and who possess neither the courage to reprehend vice, nor the generous warmth to defend virtue. The friendship of such persons is without attachment, and their love without affection or even preference.

MORNING CALLS AND VISITS, made and received after luncheon, may be divided under three heads: those of ceremony, friendship, and congratulation or condolence. Visits of ceremony, or courtesy, which occasionally merge into those of friendship, are to be paid under various circumstances. Thus, they are uniformly required after dining at a friend's house, or after a ball, picnic, or any other party. These visits should be short, a stay of from fifteen to twenty minutes being quite sufficient. A lady paying a visit may remove her boa or neckerchief, but neither her shawl nor bonnet.

IN CONVERSATION, trifling occurrences such as small disappointments, petty annoyances, and other everyday incidents, should never be mentioned to your friends. The extreme injudiciousness of repeating these will be at once apparent, when we reflect on the unsatisfactory discussions which they too frequently occasion, and on the load of advice which they cause to be tendered, which is often of a kind neither to be useful nor agreeable. Greater events, whether of joy or sorrow, should be communicated to friends, and on such occasions their sympathy gratifies and comforts. If the mistress be a wife, never let an account of her husband's failings pass her lips; and in cultivating the power of conversation, she should keep the advice of Cowper continually in her memory, that it

> Should flow like water after summer showers,
> Not as if raised by mere mechanic powers.

THE DRESS OF THE MISTRESS should always be adapted to her circumstances, and be varied with different occasions. Thus, at breakfast she should be attired in a very neat and simple manner, wearing no ornaments. If this dress should decidedly pertain only to the breakfast hour, then it would be well to exchange it before the time for making or receiving morning calls. Jewellery and ornaments are not to be worn until the full dress for dinner is assumed.

In purchasing articles of wearing apparel, whether it be a silk dress, a bonnet, shawl, or riband, it is well for the buyer to consider three things: that it be not too expensive for her purse; that its colour harmonize with her complexion, and its size and pattern with her figure; that its tint allow of its being worn with the other garments she possesses. Our good wife sets up a sail according to the keel of her husband's estate; if of high parentage, she doth not so remember what she was by birth that she forgets what she is by match.

CHARITY AND BENEVOLENCE ARE DUTIES which a mistress owes to herself as well as to her fellow creatures, and there is scarcely any income so small but something may be spared from it. Visiting the houses of the poor is the only practical way really to understand the actual state of each family; although there may be difficulties in following out this plan in the metropolis and other large cities, yet in country towns and rural districts these objections do not obtain.

TO BRUNETTES, or those ladies having dark complexions, silks of a grave hue are adapted. For blondes, or those having fair complexions, lighter colours are preferable, as the richer, deeper hues are too overpowering. The colours which go best together are green with violet; gold-colour with dark crimson or lilac; pale blue with scarlet; pink with black or white; and grey with scarlet or pink. A cold colour generally requires a warm tint to give life to it. Grey and pale blue, for instance, do not combine well, both being cold colours.

Great advantages may result from visits paid to the poor, there being, unfortunately, much ignorance amongst them with respect to all household knowledge, there will be opportunities for advising and instructing them, in a pleasant and unobtrusive manner, in cleanliness, industry, cookery, and good management.

ENGAGING DOMESTICS is one of those duties in which the judgment of the mistress must be keenly exercised. There are some respectable registry offices, where good servants may sometimes be hired, but the plan rather to be recommended is for the mistress to make inquiry amongst her circle of friends and acquaintances, and her tradespeople. In obtaining a servant's character, it is better not to be guided by a written one from some unknown quarter, but to have an interview, if at all possible, with the former mistress.

It is the custom of "Society" to abuse its servants, a *façon de parler* such as leads matronly ladies, and ladies just entering on their probation in that honoured and honourable state, to talk of servants as if they were the greatest plague in life. It is another conviction of "Society" that the race of good servants has died out, at least in

	When not found in Livery.	When found in Livery.
The House Steward....................	From £40 to £80	—
The Valet	,, 25 to 50	From £20 to £30
The Butler.............................	,, 25 to 50	—
The Cook	,, 20 to 40	—
The Gardener	,, 20 to 40	—
The Footman..........................	,, 20 to 40	,, 15 to 25
The Under Butler	,, 15 to 30	,, 15 to 25
The Coachman	—	,, 20 to 35
The Groom.............................	,, 15 to 30	,, 12 to 20
The Under Footman	—	,, 12 to 20
The Page or Footboy	,, 8 to 18	,, 6 to 14
The Stableboy	,, 6 to 12	—

	When no extra allowance is made for Tea, Sugar, and Beer.	When an extra allowance is made for Tea, Sugar, and Beer.
The Housekeeper......................	From £20 to £45	From £18 to £40
The Lady's-maid	,, 12 to 25	,, 10 to 20
The Head Nurse	,, 15 to 30	,, 13 to 26
The Cook	,, 14 to 30	,, 12 to 26
The Upper Housemaid	,, 12 to 20	,, 10 to 17
The Upper Laundry-maid	,, 12 to 18	,, 10 to 15
The Maid-of-all-work	,, 9 to 14	,, 7½ to 11
The Under Housemaid	,, 8 to 12	,, 6½ to 10
The Still-room Maid	,, 9 to 14	,, 8 to 12
The Nursemaid........................	,, 8 to 12	,, 5 to 10
The Under Laundry-maid	,, 9 to 14	,, 8 to 12
The Kitchen-maid	,, 9 to 14	,, 8 to 12
The Scullery-maid	,, 5 to 9	,, 4 to 8

THIS TABLE OF THE AVERAGE YEARLY WAGES paid to domestics, with the various members of the household placed in the order in which they are usually ranked, will serve as a guide to regulate the expenditure of an establishment. All the domestics mentioned in it would enter into the establishment of a wealthy nobleman. The number of servants, of course, would become smaller in proportion to the lesser size and income of the establishment. We enumerate also a scale of servants suited to various incomes.

About £1,000 a year—A cook, upper housemaid, nursemaid, under housemaid, and a man servant.

About £750 a year—A cook, housemaid, nursemaid, and footboy.

About £500 a year—A cook, housemaid, and nursemaid.

About £300 a year—A maid-of-all-work and nursemaid.

About £200 or £150 a year—A maid-of-all-work (and girl occasionally).

WHEN ENGAGING A SERVANT, the mistress should expressly tell her all the duties which she will be expected to perform. Every portion of work which she will have to do should be plainly stated by the mistress, and understood by the servant. If this plan is not carefully adhered to, domestic contention is almost certain to ensue, and this may not be easily settled.

England, although they do order these things better in France; that there is neither honesty, conscientiousness, nor the careful and industrious habits which distinguished the servants of our grandmothers and great-grandmothers; that domestics no longer know their place; that the introduction of cheap silks and cottons, and still more recently those ambiguous "materials" and tweeds, have removed the landmarks between the mistress and her maid, between the master and his man.

When the distinction really depends on things so insignificant, this is very probably the case; when the lady of fashion chooses her footman without any other consideration than his height, shape, and *tournure* of his calf, it is not surprising that she should find a domestic who has no attachment for the family, who considers the figure he cuts behind her carriage, and the late hours he is compelled to keep, a full compensation for the wages he exacts, for the food he wastes, and for the perquisites he can lay his hands on. But such cases are the exceptions which prove the existence of a better state of things. The great masses among us are not thus deserted; there are few families of respectability, from the shopkeeper in the next street to the nobleman whose mansion dignifies the next square, which do not contain among their dependents attached and useful servants. The sensible master and the kind mistress know that with a proper amount of care in choosing servants, and treating them like reasonable beings, and making slight excuses for the shortcomings of human nature, they will, save in some exceptional case, be tolerably well served.

THE HOUSEKEEPER

AS SECOND IN COMMAND IN THE HOUSE, except in large establishments where there is a house steward, the housekeeper must consider herself as the immediate representative of her mistress, and bring to the management of the household all those qualities of honesty, industry, and vigilance in the same degree as if she were at the head of *her own* family. Cleanliness, punctuality, order, and method are essentials in the character of a good housekeeper, and a further necessary qualification is that she should thoroughly understand accounts.

Although in the department of the cook the housekeeper does not generally much interfere, yet it is necessary that she should possess a good knowledge of the culinary art, as it may be requisite for her to take the superintendence of the kitchen. As a rule, the housekeeper, in those establishments where there is no house steward or man cook, undertakes the preparation of the confectionery, attends to the preserving and pickling of fruits and vegetables, and to the more difficult branches of the art of cookery. Much of these arrangements will depend, however, on the qualifications of the cook.

THE DAILY DUTIES OF A HOUSEKEEPER are regulated, in a great measure, by the extent of the establishment she superintends. She should, however, rise early, and see that all the domestics are duly performing their work, and that everything is progressing satisfactorily for the preparation of the breakfast for the household and family. After breakfast, she will, on various days set apart for each purpose, carefully examine the household linen, see that the furniture throughout the house is well rubbed and polished, and

WHEN A HOUSE-KEEPER IS KEPT, it will be advisable for the mistress to examine her accounts regularly. Then any increase of expenditure which may be apparent can easily be explained, and the housekeeper will have the satisfaction of knowing whether her efforts to manage her department well and economically have been successful.

THE HOUSE-KEEPER'S room is generally made use of by the lady's maid, butler, and valet, who take there their breakfast, tea, and supper. The lady's maid will also use this apartment as a sitting-room, when not engaged with her lady, or with some other duties. In different establishments, according to their size and the rank of the family, different rules of course prevail. For instance, in the mansions of those of very high rank, where there is a house steward, there are two distinct tables kept, one in the steward's room for the principal members of the household, the other in the servants' hall for the other domestics. At the steward's dinner table, the steward and housekeeper preside; and here, also, are present the lady's maid, butler, valet, and head gardener. Should any visitors be staying with the family, their servants, generally the valet and lady's maid, will be admitted to the steward's table.

attend to all the necessary details of marketing and ordering goods from the tradesmen. After dinner, the housekeeper, having seen that all the members of the establishment have regularly returned to their various duties, will have many important matters claiming her attention. She will, possibly, have to give the finishing touch to some article of confectionery, or be occupied with some of the more elaborate processes of the still-room. There may also be the dessert to arrange, ice creams to make, etc., and attention paid to the breaking of lump sugar, the stoning of raisins, the washing, cleansing, and drying of currants, etc. The evening, too, is the best time for setting right her accounts, and also for making memoranda of any articles she may require for her storeroom or other departments.

THE BEST SEASONS for various occupations connected with Household Management should be known by both the mistress and the housekeeper. Accordingly, we subjoin a few hints which we think will prove valuable.

As, in the winter months, servants have much more to do in consequence of the number of fires throughout the household, not much more than the ordinary everyday work can be attempted. In the summer, however, when the absence of fires gives the domestics more leisure, then any extra work that is required can be more easily performed.

The spring is the usual period set apart for house cleaning and removing all the dust and dirt which will, with the best of housewives, accumulate during the winter months. This season is also well adapted for washing and bleaching linen, etc., as, the weather, not being then too hot for the exertions necessary in washing counterpanes, blankets, and heavy things in general, the work is better and more easily done than in the intense heats of July. Winter curtains should be taken down and replaced by the summer white ones, and furs and woollen clothes also carefully laid by. The former should be well shaken and brushed, and then pinned upon paper or linen, with camphor to preserve them from the moths. Furs, etc., will be preserved in the same way. Included under the general description of house-cleaning must be understood: turning out all the nooks and corners of drawers, cupboards, lumber rooms, lofts, etc., with a view of getting rid of all unnecessary articles, which only create dirt and attract vermin; sweeping of chimneys; taking up carpets; painting and whitewashing the kitchen and offices; papering rooms, when needed; and, generally speaking, the house putting on, with the approaching summer, a bright appearance and a new face in unison with Nature. Oranges now should be preserved, and orange wine made.

The summer will be found the best period for examining and repairing household linen, and for "putting to rights" all those articles which have received a large share of wear and tear during the dark winter days. Sheets, for example, should be turned "sides to middle" before they are allowed to get very thin.

In June and July, gooseberries, currants, raspberries, strawberries, and other summer fruits should be preserved, and jams and jellies made. In July, too, the making of walnut ketchup should be attended to, as the green walnuts will be approaching perfection for this purpose. Mixed pickles may also be made, and it will be found a good plan to have ready a jar of pickle juice into which to put occasionally some young French beans, cauliflowers, etc.

THE STILL-ROOM was formerly much more in vogue than at present, and in constant requisition for the supply of sweet-flavoured waters for the purposes of cookery, scents and aromatic substances used in the preparation of the toilet, and cordials in cases of accidents and illness. There are some establishments, however, in which distillation is still carried on.

In the early autumn, plums of various kinds are to be bottled and preserved, and jams and jellies made. A little later, tomato sauce, a most useful article to have by you, may be prepared; a supply of apples should be laid in, if you have a place to keep them, as also a few keeping pears and filberts; endeavour also to keep a large vegetable marrow – it will be found delicious in the winter.

In October and November, it will be necessary to prepare for the cold weather, and get ready the winter clothing for the various members of the family. The white summer curtains will now be carefully put away, the fireplaces, grates, and chimneys looked to, and the house put in a thorough state of repair so that no "loose tile" may, at a future day, interfere with your comfort and extract something considerable from your pocket.

In December, the principal household duty lies in preparing for the creature comforts of those near and dear to us, so as to meet old Christmas with a happy face, a contented mind, and a full larder; in stoning the plums, washing the currants, cutting the citron, beating the eggs, and mixing the pudding, a housewife is not unworthily greeting the genial season of all good things.

THE BUTLER

THE DOMESTIC DUTIES OF THE BUTLER are to bring in the eatables at breakfast, and wait upon the family at that meal, assisted by the footman, and see to the cleanliness of everything at table. On taking away, he removes the tray with the china and plate, for which he is responsible. At luncheon, he arranges the meal, and waits unassisted, the footman being now engaged in other duties. At dinner, he places the silver and plated articles on the table, sees that everything is in its place, and rectifies what is wrong. He carries in the first dish, and announces in the drawing-room that dinner is on the table, and respectfully stands by the door until the company are seated, when he takes his place behind his master's chair on the left, to remove the covers, handing them to the other attendants to carry out. After the first course of plates is supplied, his place is at the sideboard to serve the wines, but only when called on. The first course ended, he rings the cook's bell, and hands the dishes from the table to the other servants to carry away, receiving from them the second course, which he places on the table, removing the covers as before, and again taking his place at the sideboard. At dessert, the butler receives the dessert from the other servants, and arranges it on the table, with plates and glasses, and then takes his place behind his master's chair to hand the wines and ices, while the footman stands behind his mistress for the same purpose, the other attendants leaving the room. Having served everyone with their share of the dessert, put the fires in order, and seen the lights are all right, at a signal from his master, he and the footman leave the room.

He now proceeds to the drawing-room, arranges the fireplace, and sees to the lights; he then returns to his pantry, prepared to answer the bell and attend to the company, while the footman is clearing away and cleaning the plate and glasses. At bedtime he appears with the candles, locks up the plate, secures doors and windows, and sees that all the fires are safe.

In addition to these duties, the butler, where only one footman is kept, will be required to perform some of the duties of the valet, to

IN OPENING WINE, let it be done quietly, and without shaking the bottle; if crusted, let it be inclined to the crusted side, and decanted while in that position. In opening champagne, it is not necessary to discharge it with a pop; properly cooled, the cork is easily extracted without an explosion; when the cork is out, the mouth of the bottle should be wiped with the napkin.

Butler's tray and stand

THE OFFICE OF BUTLER is one of very great trust in a household. Here, as elsewhere, honesty is the best policy. The butler should make it his business to understand the proper treatment of the different wines under his charge, which he can easily do from the wine merchant, and faithfully attend to it; his own reputation will soon compensate for the absence of bribes from unprincipled wine merchants, if he serves a generous and hospitable master. Nothing spreads more rapidly in society than the reputation of a good wine cellar.

Claret Cup on the butler's sideboard

pay bills, and superintend the other servants. But the real duties of the butler are in the wine cellar; there he should be competent to advise his master as to the price and quality of the wine to be laid in, and to "fine", bottle, cork, and seal it, and place it in the bins. Brewing, racking, and bottling malt liquors belong to his office, as well as their distribution. These and other drinkables are brought from the cellar every day by his own hands.

THE FOOTMAN

THE FOOTMAN only finds himself in stockings, shoes, and washing. Where silk stockings or other extra articles of linen are worn, they are found by the family, as well as his livery and a working dress, consisting of a pair of overalls, a waistcoat, and a fustian jacket, with a white or jean one for times when he is liable to be called to answer the door or wait at breakfast; and, on quitting his service, he is expected to leave behind him any livery had within six months.

WHERE A SINGLE FOOTMAN, or odd man, is the only male servant, he is required to make himself generally useful. He has to clean the knives, the boots and shoes, the furniture, the plate, the decanters, and the lamps; answer the visitors who call, and the drawing-room and parlour bells; and do all the errands. His life is no sinecure.

The footman is expected to rise early in order to get through all his dirty work before the family are stirring; boots and shoes, and knives and forks, having been cleaned, lamps in use trimmed, his master's clothes brushed, and the furniture rubbed over, he puts aside his working dress, tidies himself, and appears in a clean jean jacket to lay the cloth and prepare the breakfast table for the family. Having set the breakfast things in order, he then proceeds to wait upon his master, if he has any of the duties of a valet to perform. He then waits at breakfast, assisted by the housemaid, when there is no butler. Breakfast over, he removes the tray and other things off the table, and sets the room in order. At luncheon nearly the same routine is observed.

For dinner, the footman lays the cloth, taking care that the table is not too near the fire. He prepares knives, forks, and glasses, with five or six plates for each person. This done, he places chairs enough for

THE BOOT-CLEANING PROCESS.–Three good brushes and good blacking must be provided; one of the brushes hard, to brush off the mud; the other soft, to lay on the blacking; the third of a medium hardness, for polishing; and each should be kept for its particular use. The blacking should kept corked up, and applied to the brush with a sponge tied to a stick. When boots come in very muddy, it is a good practice to wash off the mud and wipe them dry with a sponge, then leave them to dry very gradually on their sides, taking care they are not placed near the fire or scorched. Much delicacy of treatment is required in cleaning ladies' boots, so as to make the leather look well polished, and the upper part retain a fresh appearance, with the lining free from hand marks, which are very offensive to a lady of refined tastes.

the party, and opposite to each a napkin neatly folded, within it a piece of bread or small roll. About half an hour before dinner, he rings the dinner bell, and occupies himself with carrying up everything he is likely to require. At the expiration of the time, having communicated with the cook, he rings the real dinner bell. Having ascertained that all is in order, that his own dress is clean and presentable, and his white cotton gloves are without a stain, he announces in the drawing-room that dinner is served. When the company are seated, he places himself on the left, behind his master, who is to distribute the soup; where soup and fish are served together, his place will be at his mistress's left hand; but he must be on the alert to see that whoever is assisting him, whether male or female, is at their post, and to render such assistance to others as he can, so that every guest has what he requires. This necessitates both activity and intelligence, and should be done without bustle. While attentive to all, the footman should be obtrusive to none; he should give nothing but on a waiter, and always hand it with the left hand and on the left side of the person he serves, and hold it so that the guest may take it with case. In lifting dishes from the table, he should use both hands, and remove them with care, so that nothing is spilt on the table cloth or on the dresses of the guests.

During dinner, each person's knife, fork, plate, and spoon should be changed as soon as he has done with it, and the vegetables and sauces belonging to the different dishes presented without remark to the guests; and the footman should tread lightly in moving round, and, if possible, should bear in mind, if there is a wit or humorist of the party whose good things keep the table in a roar, that they are not expected to reach his ears.

After each meal, the footman's place in his pantry. Here perfect order should prevail – a place for everything and everything in its place. A sink, with hot and cold water laid on, is very desirable. All plate and plated articles which are greasy are to be washed in hot water, and wiped before cleaning with the brush.

When required to go out with the carriage, it is the footman's duty to see that it has come to the door perfectly clean. When the house he is to call at is reached, he should knock, and return to the carriage for orders. In closing the door upon the family, he should see that the handle is securely turned, and that no part of the ladies' dress is shut in.

It is the footman's duty to carry messages or letters for his master or mistress to their friends, to the post, or to the tradespeople; nothing is more important than dispatch and exactness in doing so, although writing even the simplest message is now the ordinary and very proper practice.

THE COACHMAN, GROOM, AND STABLE BOY

THE ESTABLISHMENT WE HAVE IN VIEW will consist of coachman, groom, and stable boy, who are capable of keeping in perfect order four horses, and perhaps a pony. Of this establishment the coachman is chief. Besides skill in driving, he should possess a good general knowledge of horses; he has usually to purchase provender, see that the horses are regularly fed and properly groomed, watch over their condition, apply simple remedies to trifling ailments, and report the symptoms of more serious ones. He has either to clean the carriage himself, or see that the stable boy

A FRESH YOUNG HORSE can bruise its own oats, but aged horses, after a time, lose the power of masticating and bruising their oats, and bolt them whole, thus much impeding the work of digestion. Oats should be bright and dry, and not too new. Where they are new, sprinkle them with salt and water; otherwise, they overload the horse's stomach. Chopped straw mixed with oats, in the proportion of a third of straw or hay, is a good food for horses in full work. Carrots, of which horses are remarkably fond, have a perceptible effect in a short time on the gloss of the coat.

CARRIAGES in an endless variety of shapes and names are continually making their appearance, but the hackney cab or clarence seems most in request for light carriages, the family carriage of the day being a modified form of the clarence adapted for family use. The carriage is a valuable piece of furniture, requiring all the care of the most delicate upholstery, with the additional disadvantage of continual exposure to the weather and to the muddy streets.

does it properly. These duties, however, are incidental to his office, which is to drive, and much of the enjoyment of those in the carriage depends on his proficiency in his art, much also of the wear of the carriage and horses. He should have sufficient knowledge of the construction of the carriage to know when it is out of order, to know also the pace at which he can go over the road he has under him, without risking the springs and without shaking those he is driving too much.

The groom's first duties are to keep his horses in condition, but he is sometimes expected to perform the duties of a valet, to ride out with his master, to wait at table, and otherwise assist in the house; in these cases, he should have the means of dressing himself, and keeping his clothes entirely away from the stables. In the morning, about six o'clock, or rather before, the stables should be opened and the horses fed, dressed, and watered. While this is going on, the stable boy removes the stable dung, and sweeps and washes out the stables, both of which should be done every day. Where the horses are not taken out for early exercise, the work of grooming immediately commences. All horses not in work require at least two hours' exercise daily; and in exercising them a good groom will put them through the paces to which they have been trained. In the case of saddle horses, he will walk, trot, canter, and gallop them in order to keep them up to their work. With draught horses, they ought to be kept up to a smart walk and trot. Feeding must depend on their work, but they require feeding three times a day.

THE VALET

"NO MAN IS A HERO TO HIS VALET" saith the proverb, and the corollary may run "No lady is a heroine to her maid". The infirmities of humanity are, perhaps, too numerous and too equally distributed to stand the severe microscopic tests which attendants on the person have opportunities of applying. The valet and lady's maid are placed near the persons of the master and mistress, receiving orders only from them, dressing them, accompanying them in all their journeys, the confidants and agents of their most unguarded moments, of their most secret habits, and of course subject to their commands, even to their caprices. Their duty leads them to wait on those who are, from sheer wealth, station, and education, more polished, and consequently more susceptible of annoyance, and any vulgar familiarity of manner is opposed to all their notions of self-respect.

POLISH FOR THE BOOTS is an important matter to the valet, which he can make for himself after the following recipe:–Take of ivory black and treacle each 4 oz., sulphuric acid 1 oz., best olive oil 2 spoonfuls, best white wine vinegar 3 half pints; mix the ivory-black and treacle well in an earthen jar; then add the sulphuric acid, continuing to stir the mixture; next pour in the oil; and, lastly, add the vinegar, stirring it in by degrees, until thoroughly incorporated.

Some of the duties of the valet we have just hinted at in treating of the duties of the footman in a small family. His day commences by seeing that his master's dressing-room is in order; that the housemaid has swept and dusted it properly; that the fire is lighted and burns cheerfully; and some time before his master is expected, he will do well to throw up the sash to admit fresh air, closing it, however, in time to recover the temperature which he knows his master prefers. It is now his duty to place the body linen on the horse before the fire, to be aired properly; to lay the trousers intended to be worn, carefully brushed and cleaned, on the back of his master's chair; while the coat and waistcoat, carefully brushed and folded, and the collar cleaned, are laid in their place ready to put on when required. Gentlemen are sometimes indifferent as to their clothes and appearance; it is the valet's duty, in this case, where his master

THE COAT COLLAR–which, where the hair is oily and worn long, is apt to get greasy–should be closely examined; a careful valet will correct this by removing the spots day by day as they appear, first by moistening the grease spots with a little rectified spirits of wine or spirits of hartshorn, and then removing them by gentle scraping.

permits it, to select from the wardrobe such things as are suitable for the occasion. All the articles of the toilet should be in their places, the razors properly set and stropped, and hot water ready for use. Gentlemen generally prefer performing the operation of shaving themselves, but a valet should be prepared to do it if required; he should, besides, be a good hairdresser.

Having seen his master dressed, if he is about to go out, the valet will hand his cane, gloves, and hat, the latter well brushed on the outside with a soft brush, and wiped inside with a clean handkerchief, respectfully attend him to the door, and open it for him, and receive his last orders for the day.

It is, perhaps, unnecessary to add that having discharged all the commissions entrusted to him by his master, such as conveying notes or messages to friends, or the tradesmen, all of which he should punctually and promptly attend to, it is his duty to be in waiting when his master returns home to dress for dinner, or for any other occasion, and to have all things prepared for this second dressing. Previous to this, he brings under his notice the cards of visitors who may have called, delivers the messages he may have received for him, and otherwise acquits himself of the morning's commissions, and receives his orders for the remainder of the day. The routine of his evening duty is to have the dressing-room and study, where there is a separate one, arranged comfortably for his master, the fires lighted, candles prepared, dressing gown and slippers in their place, and aired, and everything in order that is required for his master's comforts.

THE LADY'S MAID

THE DUTIES OF A LADY'S MAID are more numerous, and perhaps more onerous, than those of the valet, for while the latter is aided by the tailor, the hatter, the linen draper, and the perfumer, the lady's maid has to originate many parts of the mistress's dress herself; she should, indeed, be a tolerably expert milliner and dressmaker, a good hairdresser, and possess some chemical knowledge of the cosmetics with which the toilet table is supplied.

Her first duty in the morning, after having performed her own toilet, is to examine the clothes put off by her mistress the evening before, and either to put them away or to see that they are all in order to put on again. During the winter, and in wet weather, the dresses should be carefully examined, and the mud removed.

These various preliminary offices performed, the lady's maid should prepare for dressing her mistress, arranging her dressing room, toilet table, and linen according to her mistress's wishes and habits. The details of dressing we need not touch upon, but the maid should move about quietly, performing any offices about her mistress's person, as lacing stays, gently, and adjusting her linen smoothly.

Hairdressing is the most important part of the lady's maid's office. Lessons in hairdressing may be obtained, and at not an unreasonable charge. If a mistress finds her maid handy and willing to learn, she will not mind the expense of a few lessons, which are almost necessary, as the fashion and mode of dressing the hair is so continually changing. Brushes and combs should be kept scrupulously clean.

THE CHAUSSERIE, OR FOOT GEAR of a lady, is one of the few things left to mark her station, and requires special care. Satin boots or shoes should be dusted with a soft brush, or wiped with a cloth. Kid or varnished leather should have the mud wiped off with a sponge charged with milk, which preserves its softness and polish. The following is also an excellent polish for applying to ladies' boots, instead of blacking them: equal proportions of sweet oil, vinegar, and treacle, mixed with 1 oz. of lamp black.

Bedroom ewer and basin

DURING WINTER, where fires are required in the dressing-rooms, they should be lighted an hour before the usual time of retiring, placing a fire-guard before each fire. At the same time, the night things on the horse should be placed before it to be aired, with a tin can of hot water, if the mistress is in the habit of washing before going to bed. We may add that there is no greater preservative of beauty than washing the face every night in hot water.

A good Wash for the Hair

Ingredients.–1 oz. of borax, ½ pint of olive oil, 1 pint of boiling water.

Mode.–Pour the boiling water over the borax and oil, let it cool, then put the mixture into a bottle, shake it before using, and apply with a flannel. Camphor and borax, dissolved in boiling water and left to cool, also make a very good wash for the hair, as does rosemary water mixed with a little borax. After using any of these washes, when the hair is thoroughly dry, a little pomatum should be rubbed in to make it smooth and glossy.

An excellent Pomatum

Ingredients.–1 ½ lbs. of lard, ½ pint of olive oil, ½ pint of castor oil, 4 oz. of spermaceti, bergamot or any other scent; elderflower water.

Mode.–Wash the lard well in the elderflower water; drain, and beat it to a cream. Mix the olive oil and castor oil together, and heat them sufficiently to dissolve the spermaceti, which should be beaten fine in a mortar. Mix with the lard, the bergamot, or whatever kind of scent may be preferred, and whilst warm pour into glass bottles for use, keeping them well corked. The best way to liquefy the pomatum is to set the bottle in a saucepan of warm water. It will remain good for many months.

To promote the Growth of Hair

Ingredients.–Equal quantities of olive oil and rosemary water, a few drops of oil of nutmeg.

Mode.–Mix the ingredients together, rub the roots of the hair every night with a little of this liniment, and the growth of it will very soon sensibly increase.

Hand mirror

Having dressed her mistress for breakfast, and breakfasted herself, the further duties of the lady's maid will depend altogether upon the habits of the family, in which hardly two will probably agree. Where the duties are entirely confined to attendance on her mistress, it is probable that the bedroom and dressing room will be committed to her care; these the housemaid will rarely enter, except for the weekly or other periodical cleaning. Every morning, immediately after her mistress has left it, and while breakfast is on, the lady's maid should throw the bed open by taking off the clothes, open the windows (except in rainy weather), and leave the room to air for half an hour. After breakfast, if the rooms are carpeted, she should sweep them carefully, and dust every table and chair, taking care to penetrate to every corner and moving every article of furniture that is portable. This done satisfactorily, and having cleaned the dressing glass, polished up the furniture and the ornaments, and made the glass jug and basin clean and bright, emptied all slops, emptied the water jugs and filled them with fresh water, and arranged the rooms, her next care is to see what requires replacing in her department and to furnish her mistress with a list that she may use her discretion about ordering them.

The evening duties of a lady's maid are pretty nearly a repetition of

FURS, FEATHERS, AND WOOLLENS require the constant care of the lady's maid. Furs and feathers not in constant use should be wrapped up in linen washed in lye. From May to September they are subject to being made the depository of moth eggs. They should be looked to, and shaken and beaten from time to time in case some of the eggs should have been lodged in them, and laid up again, or rather folded up as before, wrapped in brown paper, which is itself a preservative.

those of the morning. She is in attendance when her mistress retires, assists her to undress if required, brushes her hair, and renders such other assistance as is demanded, removes all slops, and takes care that the fire, if any, is safe before she retires to rest herself.

Ironing is a part of the duties of a lady's maid, and she should be able to do it in the most perfect manner when it becomes necessary. A lady's maid will have a great deal of "ironing out" to do, such as light evening dresses, muslin dresses, etc. which are not dirty enough to be washed but merely require smoothing out to remove the creases.

Before sending linen to wash, the lady's maid should see that everything under her charge is properly mended; for her own sake she should take care that it is sent out in an orderly manner, each class of garments by themselves, with a proper list, of which she retains a copy. On its return, it is still more necessary to examine every piece separately, so that all missing buttons be supplied, and only the articles properly washed and in perfect repair passed into the wardrobe.

Among other duties, the lady's maid should understand the various processes for washing, and cleaning, and repairing laces and edgings of collars, and removing stains and grease spots from dresses.

JEWELS are generally wrapped up in cotton and kept in their cases, but they are subject to tarnish from exposure to the air, and require cleaning. This is done by preparing clean soap suds, using fine toilet soap. Dip any article of gold, silver, gilt, or precious stones into this lye, and dry them by brushing with a brush of soft badger's hair or a fine sponge, then with a piece of fine cloth, and lastly with a soft leather.

To restore Whiteness to scorched Linen

Ingredients.—½ pint of vinegar, 2 oz. of fuller's earth, 1 oz. of dried fowls' dung, ½ oz. of soap, the juice of 2 large onions.

Mode.—Boil all these ingredients together to the consistency of paste; spread the composition thickly over the damaged fabric, and if the threads be not actually consumed, after it has been allowed to dry on, and the place has subsequently been washed once or twice, every trace of scorching will disappear.

To clean Silk or Ribbons

Ingredients.—½ pint of gin, ½ lb. of honey, ½ lb. of soft soap, ½ pint of water.

Mode.—Mix the above ingredients together; then lay the silk upon a clean kitchen table or dresser, and scrub it well on the soiled side with the mixture. Have ready three vessels of cold water; take each piece of silk at two corners, and dip it up and down in each vessel, but do not wring it, and take care that each piece has one vessel of quite clean water for the last dip. Hang it up dripping for a minute or two, then dab it with a cloth, and iron it quickly with a very hot iron.

Preservatives against the Ravages of Moths

Place pieces of camphor, cedar wood, Russian leather, tobacco leaves, bog myrtle, or anything else strongly aromatic, in the drawers or boxes where furs or other things to be preserved from moths are kept, and they will never take harm.

Long-hair broom

THE HOUSEMAID

"CLEANLINESS IS NEXT TO GODLINESS," saith the proverb, and "order" is in the next degree; the housemaid then may be said to be the handmaiden to two of the most prominent virtues. Her duties are very numerous, and many of the comforts of the family depend on their performance, but they are simple and easy to a person naturally clean and orderly, and desirous of giving satisfaction. The housemaid who studies her own ease will certainly be at her work by six o'clock in the summer, and probably half-past six or seven in the winter months.

The first duty of the housemaid in winter is to open the shutters of all the lower rooms in the house, and take up the hearth rugs of those rooms, including the breakfast room, which she is going to "do" before breakfast. First she sweeps the dust towards the fireplace, previously removing the fender. She should then lay a cloth over the carpet in front of the fireplace, and on it place her housemaid's box, containing black lead brushes, leathers, emery paper, cloth, black lead, and all utensils necessary for cleaning the grate, with the cinder pail on the other side. Having blackened, brushed, and polished every part of the grate, and made all clean and bright, she now proceeds to lay the fire. The several fires lighted, the housemaid proceeds with her dusting, polishing, and sweeping. Before sweeping carpets, it is a good practice to sprinkle them all over with tea leaves, which not only lay all dust, but give a slightly fragrant smell.

Next follows bedmaking, at which the cook or kitchen maid, where one is kept, usually assists; before beginning, velvet chairs or other things injured by dust should be removed to another room. It is not enough in cleaning furniture just to pass lightly over the surface; the rims and legs of tables, and the backs and legs of chairs and sofas, should be rubbed vigorously daily; if there is a bookcase, every corner of every pane and ledge requires to be carefully wiped.

Rooms should be swept and thoroughly cleaned once a week, and to be methodical and regular in her work, the housemaid should have certain days for doing certain rooms thoroughly. For instance, the drawing-room on Monday, two bedrooms on Tuesday, two on Wednesday, and so on, reserving a day for thoroughly cleaning the plate, bedroom candlesticks, etc.

Furniture Paste for French-polished Furniture

Ingredients.—3 oz. of common beeswax, 1 oz. of white wax, 1 oz. of curd soap, 1 pint of turpentine, 1 pint of boiled water.
Mode.—Mix the ingredients together, adding the water when cold; shake the mixture frequently in the bottle, and do not use it for 48 hours after it is made. It should be applied with a piece of flannel, the furniture polished with a duster, and then with an old silk rubber.

To brighten Gilt Frames

Mode.—Take sufficient flowers of sulphur to give a golden tinge to about 1½ pints of water, and in this boil 4 or 5 bruised onions (or garlic, which will answer the same purpose). Strain off the liquid and allow it to cool. Apply a little to a soft brush, and with it wash any gilding which requires restoring; when dry it will come out as bright as new work.

FIRE-LIGHTING, however simple, is an operation requiring some skill; a fire is readily made by laying a few cinders at the bottom in open order; over this a few pieces of paper, and over that again eight or ten pieces of dry wood; over the wood, a course of moderate-sized pieces of coal, taking care to leave hollow spaces between for air at the centre; and taking care to lay the whole well back in the grate, so that the smoke may go up the chimney and not into the room. This done, fire the paper with a match from below, and, if properly laid, it will soon burn up, the stream of flame from the wood and paper soon communicating to the coals and cinders, provided there is plenty of air at the centre.

FOR WAITING AT TABLE, the housemaid should be neatly and cleanly dressed, and her dress made with closed sleeves, the large open ones dipping and falling into everything on the table and being very much in the way. She should not wear creaking boots, and should move about the room as noiselessly as possible, anticipating people's wants by handing them things without being asked for them, and altogether be as quiet as possible.

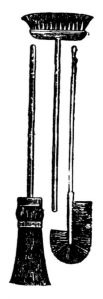

Housemaid's brushes

Scrubbing brushes

Crumb brush

THE MAID-OF-ALL-WORK

THE GENERAL SERVANT, OR MAID-OF-ALL-WORK, is perhaps the only one of her class deserving of commiseration; her life is a solitary one and, in some places, her work is never done. She is also subject to rougher treatment than either the housemaid or kitchen maid, especially in her earlier career; she starts in life, probably a girl of thirteen, with some small tradesman's wife as her mistress, just a step above her in the social scale; and although the class contains among them many excellent, kind-hearted women, it also contains some very rough specimens of the feminine gender, and to some of these it occasionally falls to give our maid-of-all-work her first lessons in her multifarious occupations. By the time she has become a tolerable servant, she is probably engaged in some respectable tradesman's house, where she has to rise with the lark, for she has to do in her own person all the work which in larger establishments is performed by cook, kitchen maid, and housemaid, and occasionally the part of a footman's duty as well.

Carpet brooms

Stove and grate brushes

THE LAUNDRY MAID

THE LAUNDRY MAID is charged with the duty of washing and getting up the family linen, a situation of great importance where the washing is all done at home, but in large towns, where there is little convenience for bleaching and drying, it is chiefly done by professional laundresses and companies. In many families, however, the fine linen, cottons, and muslins are washed and got up at home, even where the bulk of the washing is given out. The laundry establishment consists of a washing house, an ironing and drying room, and sometimes a drying closet heated by furnaces.

The laundry maid commences her labours on Monday morning by a careful examination of the articles committed to her care, separating the white linen and collars, sheets and body linen, into one heap, fine muslins into another, coloured cotton and linen fabrics into a third, woollens into a fourth, and the coarser kitchen and other greasy cloths into a fifth. Every article should be entered in the washing book, and then examined for ink or grease spots, or for fruit or wine stains, and these carefully removed.

Every article having been examined and assorted, the sheets and fine linen should be placed in tub and just covered with lukewarm water, in which a little soda has been dissolved and mixed, and left there to soak till the morning. The greasy cloths and dirtier things should be laid to soak in another tub till the morning, in a liquor composed of ½ lb. of unslaked lime to every 1½ gallons of water which has been boiled for two hours, then left to settle, and strained off when clear. Coppers and boilers should then be filled, and the fires laid ready to light.

Early on the following morning the fires should be lighted, and as soon as hot water can be procured, washing commence. Operations should be concluded by hanging everything to drain or dry, rinsing the tubs, cleaning the coppers, scrubbing the floors of the washing house, and restoring everything to order and cleanliness. Thursday and Friday, in a laundry in full employ, are usually devoted to mangling, starching, and ironing.

T O BE ABLE TO IRON properly requires much practice and experience. It is a good plan to try the heat of the iron on a coarse cloth or apron before ironing anything fine; there is then no danger of scorching. For ironing fine things, such as collars, cuffs, muslins, and laces, there is nothing so clean and nice to use as the box iron; the bottom being bright, and never placed near the fire, it is always perfectly clean. Gauffering tongs or irons must be placed in a clear fire for a minute, then withdrawn, wiped with a coarse rubber, and the heat of them tried on a piece of paper before use.

Gauffering irons

Box iron

UPPER AND UNDER NURSEMAIDS

CROUP is one of the most alarming diseases of childhood; it is accompanied with a hoarse, croaking, ringing cough, and comes on very suddenly, and most so in strong, robust children. A very hot bath should be instantly administered, followed by an emetic, either in the form of tartar emetic, croup powder, or a teaspoonful of ipecacuanha, wrapping the body warmly up in flannel after the bath. The slightest delay in administering the bath, or the emetic, may be fatal.

THE NURSERY IS OF GREAT IMPORTANCE in every family, and in families of distinction, where there are several young children, it is an establishment kept apart from the rest of the family, under the charge of an upper nurse, assisted by under nursemaids. The responsible duties of the upper nursemaid commence with the weaning of the child; it must now be separated from the mother or wet nurse, at least for a time, and the cares of the nursemaid, which have hitherto been only occasionally put in requisition, are now to be entirely devoted to the infant. She washes, dresses, and feeds it; walks out with it, and regulates all its little wants; and, even at this early age, many good qualities are required to do these things in a satisfactory manner. Patience and good temper are indispensable qualities; truthfulness, purity of manners, minute cleanliness, and docility and obedience almost equally so. She ought also to be acquainted with the art of ironing and trimming little caps, and be handy with a needle.

Where the nurse has the entire charge of the nursery, and the mother is too much occupied to do more than pay a daily visit to it, it is desirable that she be a person of observation, and possess some acquaintance with the diseases incident to childhood. Measles, thrush, scarlatina, croup, whooping cough, and other childish complaints are all preceded by well-known symptoms, which may be alleviated and rendered less virulent by simple remedies instantaneously applied. Dentition is usually the first serious trouble, bringing many other disorders in its train.

It may not be out of place if we conclude this brief notice of the duties of a nursemaid by an extract from Florence Nightingale's admirable *Notes on Nursing*. Referring to children, she says: "They are much more susceptible than grown people to all noxious influences. They are affected by the same things, but much more quickly and seriously; by want of fresh air or proper warmth; want of cleanliness in house, clothes, bedding, or body; by improper food, want of punctuality, by dullness, by want of light, by too much or too little covering in bed or when up." She then quotes a passage from a lecture on sudden deaths in infancy, to show the importance of careful nursing of children: "In the great majority of instances, when death suddenly befalls the infant or young child, it is an *accident*; it is not a necessary, inevitable result of any disease. That which is known to injure children most seriously is foul air; keeping the rooms where they sleep closely shut up is destruction to them."

Persons moving in the best society will see, after perusing Miss Nightingale's remarks that this "foul air", "want of light", "too much or too little clothing", and "improper food" is not confined to Crown Street or St. Giles's; Belgravia and the squares have their north rooms, where the rays of the sun never reach. "Don't treat your children like sick" she sums up. "Don't dose them with tea. Let them eat meat and drink milk, or half a glass of light beer. Give them fresh, light, sunny, and open rooms, cool bedrooms, plenty of outdoor exercise, facing even the cold, and wind, and weather in sufficiently warm clothes, and with sufficient exercise, plenty of amusements and play; more liberty, and less schooling, and cramming, and training; more attention to food and less to physic."

MOST CHILDREN HAVE SOME BAD HABIT of which they must be broken, but this is never accomplished by harshness without developing worse evils; kindness, perseverance, and patience in the nurse are here of the utmost importance. When finger-sucking is one of these habits, the fingers are sometimes rubbed with bitter aloes, or some equally disagreeable substance. Others have dirty habits, which are only to be changed by patience, perseverance, and above all by regularity in the nurse. She should never be permitted to inflict punishment on these occasions, or indeed on any occasion. But if punishment is to be avoided, it is still more necessary that all kinds of indulgences and flattery be equally forbidden. Yielding to all the whims of a child would be intolerable. A child should never be led to think others inferior to it, to beat a dog, or even the stone against which it falls, as some children are taught to do by silly nurses. Neither should the nurse affect or show alarm at any of the little accidents which must inevitably happen; if it falls, treat it as a trifle; otherwise she encourages a spirit of cowardice and timidity. But she will take care that such accidents are not of frequent occurrence, or the result of neglect.

ACKNOWLEDGEMENTS

As a mark of gratitude for the most generous and enthusiastic help given by so many people in preparing the recipes and providing the settings for the photography, the editors wish to name names. Here, for the benefit of all who appreciate good food and traditional comfort, is a miniature hotel, restaurant and shopping guide:

At The Sign of the Angel, 6 Church Street, Lacock, Chippenham, Wiltshire SN15 2LA. Tel. 024 973 230;

John Baily & Son, Poulterers and Game Dealers, 116 Mount Street, London W1Y 5HD. Tel. 01-499 1833;

Cliveden, Maidenhead, Buckinghamshire SL6 0JF. Tel. 06286 68561;

Dorchester Hotel, Park Lane, London W1A 2HJ. Tel. 01-629 8888;

The English House, 3 Milner Street, London SW3 2QA. Tel. 01-580 3002;

Flitwick Manor, Church Road, Flitwick, Bedfordshire MK45 1AE. Tel. 0525 712242;

Harrods Ltd., 87 Brompton Road, Knightsbridge, London SW1X 7XL. Tel. 01-730 1234;

Hobbs & Co. (Mayfair) Ltd., 29 South Audley Street, London W1Y 5DJ. Tel. 01-409 1058;

C. Lidgate, Family Butcher, 110 Holland Park Avenue, London W11 4UA. Tel. 01-727 8243;

Mark's Club (Charles Street) Ltd., 46 Charles Street, London W1X 7PB. Tel. 01-629 0650;

Neals Yard Dairy, 9 Neals Yard, Covent Garden, London WC2H 9DP. Tel. 01-379 7646;

Overton's Restaurant and Oyster Bar, 5 St. James's Street, London SW1A 1FF. Tel. 01-839 3774;

Royal Crescent Hotel, Royal Crescent, Bath BA1 2LS. Tel. 0225 319090;

Rules Restaurant, 35 Maiden Lane, London WC2E 7LB. Tel. 01-836 5314;

Sheekey's Restaurant, 28 St. Martin's Court, London WC2N 4AL. Tel. 01-240 2565;

Simpson's-in-the-Strand, 100 The Strand, London WC2R OEW. Tel. 01-836 9112;

Ston Easton Park, Ston Easton, near Bath, Avon BA3 4DF. Tel. 076 121 631.

For lending precious tableware and utensils for photography, grateful thanks go to Kate Dyson of The Dining Room Shop, 64 White Hart Lane, Barnes, London SW13 OPZ (01-878 1020), whose advice on period detail proved invaluable, and also to Angel of Tobias and the Angel, 68 White Hart Lane, SW13 OPZ, (01-878 8902), Mrs. P.N. O'Mahony, London, and Ann Norman and Diana Frost, Country Antiques (01-435 0314).

Picture Credits

With the exceptions noted below, all the engravings are reproduced from the first edition of *Beeton's Book of Household Management*. The exceptions are the black and white engravings on pages *22, 23, 203, 206, 210, 219, 220, 229, 230, 232*, and *233*, and the colour engravings on pages *20, 205*, and *213*, all reproduced from the 1898 edition, and the colour plate on page *216* reproduced from the 1907 edition. The illustrations in the Introduction are from the archives of Ward Lock Limited and of the Beeton family.

The majority of photographs in this book were specially commissioned and shot on location by Bob Komar and Nic Barlow.

The front cover illustrations and the culinary symbols decorating the chapter titles are by Jane Lydbury.

Picture sources are as follows: Title page-Jane Lydbury. *7,8,9,11,12,15,20*-Ward Lock. *26*-Bob Komar. *29*-Nic Barlow. *30*-Ward Lock. *32,34*-Nic Barlow. *36*-Alex Dufort. *38,41* Nic Barlow. *42,45* Bob Komar. *47*-Nic Barlow. *49*-Bob Komar. *50,52*-Bob Komar. *54*-Nic Barlow. *59,61*-Bob Komar. *62,65,66, 70*-Nic Barlow. *72*-Tate & Lyle. *74,75*-Nic Barlow. *76, 78*-Bob Komar. *80,84,86*-Ward Lock. *89*-Nic Barlow. *90,94*-Bob Komar. *96, 99,101,102,104*-Nic Barlow. *106*-Bob Komar. *110*-Nic Barlow. *112*-Ward Lock. *114,116,118,120,122,124,127*-Nic Barlow. *129,130,133*-Ward Lock. *134,137,138,141*-Nic Barlow. *144*-Ward Lock. *146,149,151,153,155,157,159*-Nic Barlow. *160*-Ward Lock. *162,166, 169,170*-Nic Barlow. *173*-Ward Lock. *174,176,179,181,182,185,187,188,191, 194,196,198,218,226*-Nic Barlow.

The publishers have endeavoured to observe all copyright requirements in respect of photographs and other illustrations.

Further Reading

For a detailed account of the life and times of Mrs. Beeton the reader is referred to three biographies: *Mrs. Beeton and Her Husband* by Nancy Spain (Collins, 1946), *Mr. and Mrs. Beeton* by H. Montgomery Hyde (Harrap, 1956), and *Isabella and Sam: The Story of Mrs. Beeton* by Sarah Freeman (Gollancz, 1977).

Index

Bold numerals refer to photographs, italic numerals to marginal notes.

WEIGHTS, MEASURES, AND OVEN TEMPERATURES

Because exact metric and American equivalents of imperial weights
and measures are rather awkward to work with, the converted
quantities below have been rounded up or down; very small
discrepancies will not be found to affect the success of any of the
recipes in this book.

Dry measures

IMPERIAL	METRIC
1 oz.	25g
2 oz.	50g
4 oz. or ¼ lb.	100g
½ lb.	225g
¾ lb.	350g
1 lb.	450g
1 ½ lb.	675g
2 lbs.	900g

Liquid measures

IMPERIAL (1 pint = 20 fl. oz.)	METRIC	AMERICAN (1 pint = 16 fl. oz.)
¼ pint	150 ml	⅓ pint or ⅔ cup
½ pint	300 ml	⅔ pint or 1 ¼ cups
¾ pint	450 ml	1 pint or 2 cups
1 pint	600 ml	1 ¼ pints or 2 ½ cups
1 ½ pints	900 ml	1 ¾ pints or 3 ¾ cups
2 pints	1.1 litres	2 ½ pints or 5 cups
1 gallon (8 pints)	4.5 litres	1 ¼ gallons

Spoon and cup measures

IMPERIAL	METRIC	AMERICAN
1 tablespoonful	18 ml	1 tablespoon
2 tablespoonfuls	35 ml	3 tablespoons
4 tablespoonfuls	70 ml	6 tablespoons or ⅓ cup
1 dessertspoonful	12 ml	2 teaspoons
1 teaspoonful	6 ml	1 teaspoon
1 teacupful (approx. ¼ pint)	150 ml	⅔ cup or ⅓ pint
1 breakfast-cupful (approx. ½ pint)	300 ml	1 ¼ cups or ⅔ pint

Oven temperatures

	F°	C°	GAS
Very cool/very slow	150–250	70–120	¼–½
Cool/slow	275–300	130–150	1–2
Moderate/warm	325–350	160–180	3–4
Moderately hot/fairly hot/brisk	375–400	190–210	5–6
Hot/quick	425–450	220–230	7–8
Very hot	475–500	240–250	9

Yeast.– ½ oz. of dry yeast is equivalent to 1 oz. of fresh yeast.

Sauces as flavourings.–Mushroom, tomato, and walnut ketchup, and
anchovy, soy, and Harvey's sauce are all obtainable from most good
grocery shops; a little Worcestershire Sauce may be substituted for
Harvey's if this is not available.